The Environments of the Poor
in Southeast Asia, East Asia
and the Pacific

The **Institute of Southeast Asian Studies (ISEAS)** was established as an autonomous organization in 1968. It is a regional centre dedicated to the study of socio-political, security and economic trends and developments in Southeast Asia and its wider geostrategic and economic environment. The Institute's research programmes are the Regional Economic Studies (RES, including ASEAN and APEC), Regional Strategic and Political Studies (RSPS), and Regional Social and Cultural Studies (RSCS).

ISEAS Publishing, an established academic press, has issued more than 2,000 books and journals. It is the largest scholarly publisher of research about Southeast Asia from within the region. ISEAS Publishing works with many other academic and trade publishers and distributors to disseminate important research and analyses from and about Southeast Asia to the rest of the world.

The Environments of the Poor in Southeast Asia, East Asia and the Pacific

Edited by
Aris Ananta • Armin Bauer • Myo Thant

Asian Development Bank

Asian Development Bank Institute

INSTITUTE OF SOUTHEAST ASIAN STUDIES
Singapore

First published in Singapore in 2013
by ISEAS Publishing
Institute of Southeast Asian Studies
30 Heng Mui Keng Terrace, Pasir Panjang
Singapore 119614

E-mail: publish@iseas.edu.sg
Website: http://bookshop.iseas.edu.sg

The responsibility for facts and opinions in this publication rests exclusively with the authors and their interpretations do not necessarily reflect the views or the policy of ADB, ADB Institute, ISEAS or their supporters.

ISEAS Library Cataloguing-in-Publication Data

The environments of the poor in Southeast Asia, East Asia, and the Pacific / edited by
   Aris Ananta, Armin Bauer, and Myo Thant.
1. Southeast Asia—Environmental conditions—Congresses.
2. East Asia—Environmental conditions—Japan—Congresses.
3. Poverty—Environmental aspects—Southeast Asia—Congresses.
4. Poverty—Environmental aspects—East Asia—Congresses.
5. Poverty—Environmental aspects—Islands of the Pacific—Congresses.
6. Economic development—Environmental aspects—Southeast Asia—Congresses.
7. Economic development—Environmental aspects—East Asia—Congresses.
I. Ananta, Aris, 1954-
II. Bauer, Armin.
III. Myo Thant, 1957-
IV. Conference on The Environments of the Poor (2010 : Delhi, India)
HC415 E5E531   2013

ISBN 978-981-4517-99-7 (soft cover)
ISBN 978-981-4519-00-7 (e-book, PDF)

Cover photo: Life on the river in Cambodia.
Source: ADB Photo databank.

Typeset by International Typesetters Pte Ltd
Printed in Singapore by Mainland Press Pte Ltd

CONTENTS

Part III PACIFIC ISLANDS

Part IV MAINLAND SOUTHEAST ASIA
(Cambodia, Thailand, Vietnam)

Part V ARCHIPELAGIC SOUTHEAST ASIA
(Indonesia, Malaysia, Philippines)

PREFACE

Southeast Asia and East Asia have been hailed as success stories of economic growth, but poverty, the environment, and climate change remain major challenges. Poverty reduction is often said to compete with efforts to save the environment and respond to climate change. It is also argued that policies on the environment and climate change should not be carried out at the expense of eradicating poverty or promoting economic growth. This book tries to show that it is possible to reduce poverty, protect the environment, and respond to climate change at the same time — if certain policies are followed. The book provides evidence from Southeast Asia, East Asia, and the Pacific as a basis for recommending triple-win development policies. To emphasize the relationships between the three "wins", the book introduces a spatial approach to poverty, one that focuses on the environments in which the poor live, i.e., regions where the environment — often aggravated by climate change — are major determinants of poverty. These areas are flood-prone and disaster-affected lands, uplands, coastlands, dryland, and slums.

"Environments of the Poor" was the theme of a conference which the Asian Development Bank and seventeen development partners organized on 24–26 November 2010 in New Delhi.[1] The papers on Southeast Asia, East Asia, and the Pacific at this conference were revised and edited for this publication. The papers on South Asia make up a separate volume, being jointly published by Oxford University Press of India and the Asian Development Bank. A third volume will be published that includes papers of a more general nature, including the conceptual background. The main title shared by all three volumes is *The Environments of the Poor*.

This volume is published jointly by the Asian Development Bank (ADB) and the Institute of Southeast Asian Studies (ISEAS), with co-financing from the ADB Institute. Armin Bauer of ADB is editor-in-chief for the whole project, and he also designed the book cover. Assisting Armin Bauer was Paul Bullen, who developmentally edited all the papers. Aris Ananta from ISEAS is the primary editor of the present volume. Myo Thant of ADB helped with the contents and did some copy-editing. Rahilah Yusuf of ISEAS Publishing copy-edited the final manuscipt and prepared it for publication.

We would like to thank various development partners who helped to make the original conference and this book a success, i.e. development institutions (ADB, AFD, DFID, GIZ, ILO, JICA, UNDP and UNEP); research networks in the Asia-Pacific region (ADBI, EEPSEA, NCAER, SANDEE, TEEB, TERI); and climate change and poverty related funding facilities and other initiatives (CDIA, GM-EOC, APCF).

The Editors

Note

1. For more information on the New Delhi conference, see the Environments of the Poor website at <http://www.adb.org/themes/poverty/topics/environments-of-the-poor>.

LIST OF CONTRIBUTORS

Danang ADHINATA is currently working at the KPPU (Komisi Pengawas Persaingan Usaha — Committee for Supervising Business Competition). Previously, he worked at the Indonesia's Statistical Office in South Kalimantan to conduct the population census.

Gusti Fahmi ADLIANSYAH is a lecturer at the LPEI College in Banjarmasin, South Kalimantan Indonesia.

Aris ANANTA is Senior Research Fellow at the Institute of Southeast Asian Studies (ISEAS), Singapore. He is an economist-demographer with a multi-disciplinary perspective. His research covers two broad regional areas: Southeast Asia and Indonesia. On Southeast Asia, he focuses on migration, ageing, and development (including poverty and environment). On Indonesia, he works on various social, economic, and political issues, including ethnicity, religion, and democracy.

Marife BALLESTEROS is Senior Research Fellow at the Philippine Institute for Development Studies. She holds a doctorate degree in Development Economics from the Katholieke University of Nijmegen, the Netherlands. Her research work concerns land and housing policy studies. Dr Ballesteros is concurrently a member of the Southeast Asia Urban Environment Management Network (SEA-UEM), where she serves as resource person for urban environment issues.

Armin BAUER is principal economist in ADB's Regional and Sustasinable Development Department. As poverty is his focal point, he is working particularly on inclusive growth. Among others, Dr Bauer is championing ADB's environments of the poor project and the inclusive business initiative.

Stephane BOULAKIA is a CIRAD (Centre de Cooperation Internationale en Recherche Agronomique pour le Développement) agronomist, specializing in conservation agriculture (DMC and agroforestry). He has been working within research and development programmes in contrasted agro-ecosystems of Madagascar, Gabon, and Vietnam. Since 2003, he has been acting as principal technical assistant of an R&D project of the Cambodian Minister for Agriculture granted by the French Development Agency (AFD).

Paul BULLEN has a PhD and an MA from the University of Chicago and a BA from the University of California at Berkeley, all in political science. Dr Bullen is an interdisciplinary researcher, writer, and editor based in Chicago. He can be reached at pbullen@uchicago.edu.

Stephane CHABIERSKI is a CIRAD (Centre de Cooperation Internationale en Recherche Agronomique pour le Développement) agronomist. He has been working for a decade on the development of conservation agriculture (CA) techniques and their adaptation to different agro-ecological and socio-economic contexts. During his stay in Madagascar from 2003 to 2007, he implemented several CA dissemination programmes, more specifically in the Lac Alaotra area. He is currently seconded to the Ministry of Agriculture, Forestry and Fisheries of Cambodia and analyses the CA adoption process among smallholders in the country.

Jonna P. ESTUDILLO (from the Philippines) is with the National Graduate Institute for Policy Studies in Tokyo, Japan.

Haris FADILLAH is the Vice Dean and Lecturer of the Faculty of Economics, University of Lambung Mangkurat, South Kalimantan, Indonesia. He is working on economic development, including poverty, particularly on issues related to South Kalimantan.

Kensuke FUKUSHI is Associate Professor at the Integrated Research System for Sustainability Science (IR3S), University of Tokyo, Japan.

Olivier GILARD is programme officer in the French Development Agency (AFD), and in charge of climate change related agriculture, water resources and environment programmes in Southeast Asia.

Mr Gilard has a background in water resources and related risk management and works in Asia since 2001.

Madhumita GUPTA is social development specialist in ADB's East Asia department.

Somchai JITSUCHON is Research Director at the Thailand Development Research Institute (TDRI), specializing in macroeconomic policies, macroeconomic modeling (computable general equilibrium models and econometric models), theories and empirical applications of poverty and income distribution, social protection and welfare system. Dr Jitsuchon received his PhD in Economics from the University of British Columbia, Canada. He worked as visiting researcher at the Economic Planning Agency (EPA) in Tokyo (Japan), special lecturer at the National Institute for Development and Administration (NIDA) and Thammasat University, both in Thailand.

Anjeela JOKHAN is Director of the University of South Pacific, Fiji.

Murari LAI is Research Assistant at the University of South Pacific, Fiji.

LING How Kee is Associate Professor (Social Work and Social Policy) at the Faculty of Social Sciences, Universiti Malaysia Sarawak (UNIMAS), Malaysia. Currently the Director of the Centre of Excellence for Disability Studies at UNIMAS, she has a long-standing interest in community development for marginalized groups. She has published papers and given seminars on indigenous social work practice and education, cultural competency in social work practice both in Malaysia and internationally.

Yong-Seong KIM is Research Fellow at the Korea Development Institute. His research interests are labour economics, applied econometrics and programme evaluation. He earned a PhD in economics at the University of Michigan, Ann Arbor, USA.

Tran Thi Viet NGA is a lecturer at the Institute of Environmental Science and Engineering, Hanoi University of Civil Engineering, Hanoi, Vietnam.

QI Gubo is professor for rural development at the College of Humanities and Development Studies at China Agricultural University. She obtained a PhD degree in Agricultural Economics at China Agricultural University in 1996. Her main research interests include community common resources management, rural technology and institutional innovation, and gender issues in development.

Arianto A. PATUNRU was Director of the Institute for Economic and Social Research, Department of Economics, University of Indonesia (LPEM-FEUI). He has also taught at the Department of Economics, University of Indonesia. He is now Fellow at the Arndt-Corden Department of Economics, Crawford School of Economics and Government, College of Asia and the Pacific, The Australian National University. Mr Patunru holds a PhD from University of Illinois at Urbana-Champaign, and has been working in the areas of globalization, trade, poverty, and environmental economics. Prior to being the Director of LPEM-FEUI, he was the research director at the institute, covering issues of investment climate, poverty, and macroeconomics. He has served as consultant to OECD, World Bank, ADB, and Government of Indonesia (Bappenas, MOF, MOT, and CMEA). Dr Patunru has published in the *American Journal of Agricultural Economics*, *Asian Economic Journal*, *Choices*, and *Bulletin for Indonesian Economic Studies*. He is also a co-editor of *Economics and Finance in Indonesia*.

Emma PORIO is Professor of Sociology at the Department of Sociology and Anthropology, School of Social Sciences, of the Ateneo de Manila University. Previously, she was Chairman of the Governing Council of the Philippines Social Science Council, President of the Philippines Sociological Society, President of the Institute of Development and Policy Research, and a consultant to international organizations, such as the ADB, World Bank, and the United Nations. Her research focuses on children, gender, urban poverty, urban development, and governance. She sits on the board of the Researchers Forum for Human Settlements (Rome), Water and Sanitation Council (Rome), International Cooperative Housing Foundation (Washington, D.C.) and the Huairou Commission (New York). She also sits in the editorial board of the *Journal of Southeast Asian Studies* (Singapore), *Social Movements* (London), *Inter-Cultural Studies Asia* (Sage/Taiwan) and *Contemporary Politics* (London).

Daniel ROBERTS is a consultant to ADB and works at the University of London.

Satoshi SAKAI is a specialist on Enterprise Development and Job Creation, ILO Office for China and Mongolia.

Boparath SRY is a research assistant for the Cambodia Development Resource Institute (CDRI) in Economic, Trade, and Regional Cooperation programme. She has been involved in the International Development Research Center (IDRC) project on the Global Financial Crisis and Vulnerability in Cambodia, a perspective from eleven villages in Cambodia. She obtained her bachelor degree in Economics from the Royal University of Law and Economics in Cambodia and Diploma of Commerce from Royal Melbourne Institute of Technology in Australia.

Myo THANT is a Myanmar national who received his academic degrees from the Institute of Economics, Rangoon and New York University. Prior to joining the Asian Development Bank he worked at the United Nations and taught at NYU. He is widely known for his pioneering work on the economics of HIV/AIDS and regional economic cooperation. He is well known for his path-breaking work on growth triangles and economic corridors and involvement in the GMS programme from its inception.

Kimsun TONG is a research fellow and Program Coordinator for the Cambodia Development Resource Institute's (CDRI) Economic, Trade, and Regional Cooperation. He has been heavily involved in Poverty Dynamic Study, Chinese Investment in Cambodia, the Impact of Global Financial Crisis on Cambodian Households, Land Tenure and Paddy Productivity, the Impact of Migration (internal and external remittance) on Poverty and Agricultural Productivity, and Water Resource Management Research Capacity Development Programme. Dr Tong has a PhD in Economic Development. He was educated at Kobe University, Japan.

Songporne TONGRUKSAWATTANA was Research Associate and PhD student at the Institute of Development and Agricultural Economics, School of Economics and Management at the Leibniz University of Hannover in Germany. She obtained her PhD in Economics in 2011.

Her research interests focus on economics of poverty and vulnerability of rural households in Asia, shock, coping and risks mitigation strategies, agriculture and rural development, technology adoption and economics of aquaculture.

TSUI Yenhu is a Professor at the Institute of Social Cultural Anthropology, Xinjiang Normal University, Urumqi, Xinjiang, China. He was a visiting research scholar to the Department of Social Anthropology at Cambridge University (1991–94) when he participated in an international cooperative project initiated by Professor Caroline Humphrey, "Cultural and Environmental Conservation in Inner Asia". Since then, he has conducted social anthropological studies (focusing on eco-anthropology and social development) in pastoral areas of northwest China and published papers and field reports from his field research.

Sann VATHANA is the Deputy General Secretary of the Cambodia Council for Agriculture and Rural Development.

Marc VOELKER was Research Associate and PhD student at the Institute of Development and Agricultural Economics, School of Economics and Management at the Leibniz University of Hannover in Germany. He obtained his PhD in Economics in 2010. He has worked in Vietnam in the context of the DFG-funded research unit FOR756 on vulnerability in Southeast Asia. Since late 2011 he has held a position with the Statistical Office of the State Rhineland-Palatinate, Germany.

Pen VUTH is Director General of the Ministry of Agriculture, Forestry, and Fishery in Cambodia.

Hermann WAIBEL is Professor of Agricultural Economics and the Director of the Institute of Development and Agricultural Economics, School of Economics and Management at the Leibniz University of Hannover in Germany. He is currently the Director of a Research Consortium of four German universities on "Impact of Risks and Shocks on Rural Households in Emerging Market Economies in South East Asia". His current research focus is on rural development in Asia. He has published widely on topics of natural resources management, biotechnology, agriculture and environment in developing countries. Dr Waibel obtained his PhD in Agricultural Economics and his MSc in Agricultural Economics from the University of Hohenheim, Germany.

Wendy WALKER is a Senior Social Development Specialist in the East Asia Urban and Social Sectors Division of the ADB. She is responsible for social protection and social development in the portfolio for China and Mongolia. She has worked in a wide variety of sectors, focusing on the social consequences of policy reforms, environment and adaptation and social impact assessment of infrastructure and in Africa and Asia.

WONG Swee Kiong is Senior Lecturer at the Department of Development Studies, Faculty of Social Sciences in Universiti Malaysia Sarawak (UNIMAS), Malaysia. She is a trained natural resource and environmental economist and has carried out various research projects particularly among the indigenous communities such as the Semai tribe in West Malaysia, Iban and Bidayuh communities in Sarawak. She has also published journal articles internationally.

I

Overview

1

A NEW TRIPLE-WIN OPTION FOR THE ENVIRONMENT OF THE POOR

Aris Ananta, Armin Bauer and Myo Thant

The Southeast and East Asia regions have made major progress in reducing income poverty by bringing down the level of poverty incidence from 57 per cent in 1990 to 16 per cent in 2008 for the US$1.25 international poverty line and from 81 per cent to 28 per cent for the US$2 international poverty line, over the same period. However, living standards for many poor people remain a major challenge due to worsening environmental degradation and increasing vulnerability to climate change. Southeast and East Asia's remarkable economic growth over the last twenty years was often accompanied by environmental stress such as deforestation and overfishing, transformation of green areas into commercial and industrial land, and massive pollution and congestion in mega-cities.

Although the environmental problems of the Southeast and East Asia regions are reasonably well documented, less is known on how environmental policies, climate change mitigation and adaptation measures can be used to further reduce poverty and improve the situation of the poor who frequently live in the most environmentally fragile areas. This book argues that trade-offs between poverty reduction, improvement in quality of environment, and mitigation as well as adaption to climate change, can be avoided. Policy makers can design policies which manage these three issues together to produce a triple-win outcome: raising the welfare of the population by simultaneously reducing poverty, improving the environmental quality, and mitigating and adapting to climate change.

This book presents empirical observations of this triple-win option in Southeast Asia, East Asia, and the Pacific. It describes livelihood and income generation opportunities for the poor, as well as environmental policies that directly influence the living standard of low-income people. This book, utilizing a multidisciplinary approach, argues that more triple-win outcomes would be possible for the poor, the environment, and the climate, if awareness of the environment in which the poor live were greater and consequently appropriate policies were implemented.

POVERTY, ENVIRONMENT AND CLIMATE CHANGE

Climate change has affected and will affect people through the increased frequency of hot days, heat waves, tropical cyclones, heavy precipitation, and rising sea levels. Climate change will aggravate many existing development problems, including those involving poverty and the environment. For example, the effect of the over-exploitation of forest resources on the local people will be much worse when heavy precipitation and heat waves occur more often and cyclones become more intense. The poor as a group are the least able to cope with environmental degradation. They are also likely to be least capable of adapting to climate change because of obvious constraints in terms of access to knowledge and financial resources.

The effects of changes in physical environment on poverty are illustrated by Nga and Fukushi who quantify the effects of flooding in Metro Manila, in particular health risks associated with gastrointestinal illness. The city is in the centre of the tropical monsoon climatic zone and has suffered from frequent flooding. The high rates and amount of migration to the city and inadequate flood prevention infrastructure have worsened flooding in the city. Water-borne diseases are transmitted directly by contaminated water, which is either consumed or in contact with people. The probability of infection depends on the depth of the floods. The deeper the flood level, the higher is the probability of being infected. However, the probability of infection will increase if, because of climate change, floods occur more frequently, last longer and flood depth is more than two metres. They conclude that the highest probability of getting water-borne disease is found among the young, and urban poor women as these groups are more exposed to contaminated water during floods.

The effects of climate change can be calamitous, such as wiping out an entire small island country and therefore are peace and security issues in addition to being environmental concerns. Indeed, as noted by Jokhan and Lal, the effects of climate change induced flooding will hit the Pacific Island countries the hardest. Their small size, remote geography, fragile environments and economies make them especially vulnerable to climate change and attendant sea level rise. Food security is a particularly critical issue, as the local people no longer produce and store their own food and instead rely on imported food. It is not surprising that the leaders of Nauru, Micronesia, and Kiribati have urged the United Nations to take immediate actions to offset the serious effects of climate change in the Pacific Island countries.

BEYOND GROWTH-ORIENTED DEVELOPMENT

New statistics, such as "green" GDP and "green" budgeting, should be used to measure the progress of economic development and make possible the design of triple-win polices. Green GDP would be calculated by using multi-indicator statistics to measure economic development. All evaluations of economic development should include statistics on poverty and inequality, environment, and climate change. Patunru distinguishes between "green" and "brown" GDP and budgeting in measuring economic development. Green GDP and budgeting include the losses caused by environmental degradation unlike brown GDP. Green GDP would be lower than brown GDP in cases where there has been much environmental degradation. Green budgeting would, for example, cut subsidies that harm the environment and direct deve-lopment programmes to those which are environmentally friendly. The author also proposes the publication of these statistics, to increase public awareness so that those who destroy the environment should ultimately be made to pay the costs. Using Indonesia as an illustration, he suggests cuts in gasoline and kerosene subsidies to reflect the real price of consumption of these fuels and thereby optimize the use of gasoline and kerosene.

Kim uses a mathematical model to show that even if economic development is measured with conventional economic growth, there should not necessarily be any trade-off between environment, poverty and economic development. He concludes that by implementing a well-chosen combination of welfare and tax policies, a country can promote both economic growth and fair income distribution. The government should tax environmental pollution, as it may also increase capital accumulation and economic growth. His conclusion is that it is possible to have a triple-win solution even when "brown" economic growth is primarily being pursued although there will be differences depending on underlying social, cultural, political, and economic conditions.

Tsui concludes that poverty and environmental degradation in north and northwest China's large grassland area is mostly attributable to economic policies which prioritize conventional economic and household income growth. The government needs to utilize local knowledge in its poverty reduction programmes within the context of climate change. Walker, Gupta, and Roberts also show the negative impact of economic growth oriented policies in China. In particular, they discuss the situation of the Chinese urban poor, many of who have been living in degraded environments and subjected to new forms of social exclusion. Economic growth oriented policies have successfully resulted in higher economic growth for many years, but have also brought rising social vulnerabilities, including those associated with increasing "new urban poverty". It is "new" because urban poverty has been a relatively new concept in China. Though recognizing that economic growth is important in alleviating poverty, they stress the need to create liveable and inclusive cities, which are able to respond to the rising social vulnerabilities among the urban poor.

The important role of local knowledge on adaptation to climate change is given special attention by Waibel, Tongruksawattana, and Voelker, who examine the role of the perception of the rural poor have on impact of climate change, in Thailand and Vietnam. The rural poor depend greatly on agriculture and natural resources for their livelihood. The success of programmes to help them adapt to climate change is much affected by how they perceive the dangers of climate change. If they do not feel climate change will affect them severely, or if they do but feel that there is nothing which can be done, government initiated programmes such as the use of new and environmentally friendly technology, will not work. Increasing frequency of natural disasters may lead to increased fear of climate change but they may be unable to leave their homes. This creates so-called "poverty pockets", that is climate change sustained poverty. The authors recommend that climate change related programmes should take into consideration the perception and knowledge of the people on climate change and should be locally tested and not externally developed.

CLIMATE CHANGE MITIGATION THROUGH BETTER LIVELIHOODS

Tong and Bopharath show how important quality and accessibility of natural resources are for the livelihood of the poor in Cambodia. Destruction of natural resources, including that caused by climate change, is likely to harm the poor. The authors show that poverty would increase if rural households cannot support their livelihood from forestry and hunting. The rise in poverty would also be a result of drought and flooding. Moreover, poverty has often limited the choices the poor make in many aspects of life, including choosing environmentally friendly livelihoods. They may focus more on their own immediate survival and ignore long-run environmental impacts. Therefore, one way to help the poor preserve or even improve the environment of the places of residence is to provide environmentally friendly and rewarding alternative livelihoods.

Qi examines the impact of climate change on food security and poverty in the dry land areas in northern China, particularly as related to the problem of desertification. She argues that projects on afforestation, reforestation, food security, and bio-energy should be able to make the poor survive better. The projects should at the very least compensate for whatever earnings are lost by the poor because of environmental projects, and strive to improve the livelihood of the poor. She also recommends that the government support the poor by providing capital and insurance, as farmers usually already have their own ways of adapting to climate change and ensuring food security.

Ananta et al. show how in the upland areas of South Kalimantan, Indonesia, the local people depend heavily on the environment. Lucrative livelihoods from the mining industry have made them leave agricultural work to join the mining industry although they are aware of the long-term negative impact of mining on their environment. The mining industry has also provided the community with many "gifts", such as improvement in roads as well as religious, educational, and recreational facilities. The authors conclude that the government and society must be able to provide alternative, better paying, and environmentally friendly livelihood to the community. They further recommend that global consumers not buy goods produced using inputs and processes which harm the environment. Changes in global consumption behaviour are likely to reduce demand for environmentally unfriendly goods and services and thereby, reduce incentives for business to pursue environmentally harmful activities and practices.

Sasaki discusses the policies of the Nanjing Municipal government, China, which has promoted low carbon consumption behaviour in the city — making people only consume goods and services which are processed using environmentally friendly technologies and inputs. Social media marketing was utilized to create awareness among consumers, including the poor, on the need to consume in an environmentally friendly way. Sasaki recommends the involvement of business communities in the creation of environmentally friendly livelihoods. The Green Business Options (GBO) in China is an example of such an involvement of business communities which is particularly important for small and medium enterprises. He recommends that micro-enterprises be able to tap emerging green markets and, at the same time, create labour-intensive jobs. These business opportunities are expected to help produce a low carbon economy. The government should help the growth of GBOs by providing financial and fiscal support for those who are working in green enterprises and consuming green goods and services.

The need to create better alternative livelihoods is also stressed by Wong and Ling in their study on the role of oil palm plantations in upland communities, in the district of Lundu, Sarawak, Malaysia. They find that development programmes have improved the economic status of the community but, at the same time, degraded the environment. They also find that people living relatively far from oil palm plantations suffer less from environmental degradation and yet enjoy economic benefits from the plantation. The challenge for policy makers is that what may be seen by the people as improvement in economic status at present may transform into a future economic burden if the environment continues to be degraded, particularly by government-initiated development projects. No group should be deprived from enjoying the fruits of development because of short-run, economic "success" which does not pay sufficient attention to environmentally adverse impacts.

The need to create environmentally friendly yet remunerative livelihoods is also discussed by Jitsuchon who shows that organic agriculture, which is environmentally friendly and more able to adapt to climate change, has become more profitable in Thailand because the cost of using chemical fertilizer and pesticides has exceeded the revenue from selling the product. He argues that the government should continue making organic agriculture more profitable than traditional agriculture. He also finds that climate-related poverty is seen less often among farmers practising organic agriculture. He recommends giving payments to farmers who adopt agro-ecological systems.

Boulakia et al. provide an illustration of a programme which can simultaneously solve the issues of poverty and climate change. The authors use the example of an agriculture system in Cambodia and show that it is possible to avoid the "usual" conflict between agriculture and environment, and also between reduction in poverty and mitigation/adaptation to climate change. In Cambodia, as in other Mekong countries, the agricultural sector mainly uses an irrigated rice cropping system in the lowland areas. However, as the system with its conventional tillage techniques reaches its geographic limits and degrades soil fertility, a new system needs to be used. A new system, the so-called Direct sowing (seeding) Mulch-based Cropping system (DMC), was started in Cambodia in 2008. This is a "no-tillage" system which sees the soil as the main capital in agriculture. They conclude that the project has produced a triple-win solution. The first win is that this system can better mitigate and adapt to climate change. It uses more organic matter and the soil, serves as a CO_2 sinkhole. The system is also better able to adapt to natural disasters. The second win is improved agricultural productivity because of the long-term sustainability of soil fertility and the recovery of fertility which has been damaged by previous use of chemical inputs. Higher productivity, coupled with much smaller use of relatively expensive chemicals, in turn reduces poverty, and provides the third win.

ADAPTATION TO CLIMATE CHANGE

Government help to the poor when they are hit by natural disasters is very vital because the poor often do not have the means to protect themselves. Estudillo shows how poor landless households were the hardest hit by the Milenyo storm in the Philippines which was the tenth worst storm globally in 2006. The community and the government were able to work together to respond to the storm but the response from the community, in the form of help from relatives and friends, in helping the victims was still very crucial. The government played only a complementary role. Estudillo suggests that the government should have been more active, including formulating *ex-ante* risk management policies such as disaster preparedness strategies and an early warning system. As a longer term adaptation strategy, rural households should diversify their livelihood, such as working more in non-farm activities.

Frequent floods have also resulted in people's "surrendered" attitude in the Philippines: they feel that they cannot avoid floods and that flooding is normal. Porio shows how some people in low-lying "Kamanava" areas (mostly wetlands or swamp lands) of Metro Manila have developed a "water-based lifestyle". They are always in an "evacuation mode" and consider such a lifestyle to be normal. Creation of alternative and better livelihoods in areas which are not flood-prone is therefore important to change this "water-based lifestyle" and outlook. As Porio points out, their fatalistic attitude has put them at high risk to income losses, morbidity, and social loss. In turn, the high risks from staying in water-logged areas have put them in a spiral of vulnerability and poverty. She recommends that the government make a "water-sensitive" urban design that is integrated with land use and building practices, particularly by anticipating the impact of climate change. She also stresses the importance of taking into account the issues of gender, ethnicity/

migration status, and age when designing policies for people living in flood-prone areas.

Ballesteros recommends implementing effective town and shelter planning, including the improvement of underserviced infrastructure in the case of slum settlements in Metro Manila. She notes that households in slum areas may not be very poor. They typically earn between US$2 and US$4 per day, but live in slum areas simply because they cannot afford the cost of travelling to work if they have to live in physically better settlement areas. However, this inequality in the form of shelter deprivation has not been receiving adequate attention from the government. Poverty in slum settlements cannot be simply overcome through traditional poverty reduction programmes in the Philippines, such as cash transfers. The author argues that the government should take regulatory actions that cut cross administrative boundaries, as environmental issues cannot be isolated by geographical and political boundaries.

Walker, Gupta, and Roberts suggest that settlement programmes for the urban poor in China go beyond housing improvement and should encompass many aspects of life. They show that the challenges faced by the government include the provision of services to the poor, such as the creation of welfare support and sustainable urban communities in the context of rapidly developing cities with a rising number of circulating population. They argue that the government should shift its policies from those focused on housing improvement to those on liveable cities which will enable the government to better manage the urban poor's rising social vulnerabilities. They however realize that physical and financial conditions may constrain the government from implementing these policies.

Jitsuchon examines social safety nets for poor farmers in Thailand. As society's capacity in assisting those suffering from natural disasters is limited, he recommends financial innovations such as weather insurance, which is more market-based and effective in protecting the poor. In addition to market-based insurance, the government should provide direct assistance to those, and particularly the poorest, who cannot use the market mechanism to protect themselves. A more complete, universal, welfare system should be created to complement market-based weather insurance, to ensure that the poorest will be taken care of.

CONCLUSION

This book provides many important insights on poverty, environment and climate change issues from different parts of Asia. The insights are enriched by the use of a multidisciplinary approach in examining these pressing issues. The papers in this volume clearly show that many people in Asia are threatened with an increase in poverty due to the changes in the environment and climate. Increase in the incidence and severity of poverty are likely to be particularly high in cases where the poor live in environmentally fragile areas. This book shows that it is nevertheless possible to successfully carry out programmes that simultaneously reduce poverty, improve the quality of the environment, and mitigate and adapt to climate change. Using data and case studies from East and Southeast Asia and the Pacific Islands, the book provides two major policy lessons.

First, is that trade-offs do not have to exist between poverty reduction, improving the quality of the environment, and climate change mitigation and adaptation. A triple-win approach is possible: simultaneously reducing poverty and inequality, raising the quality of environment, as well as mitigating and adapting to climate change.

However for this to be successful, the second policy lesson is that there is a need to go beyond conventional growth-oriented economic development models. This requires the creation and use of a broader set of indicators to measure economic development, which includes poverty and inequality reduction, improvement in quality of environment, as well as mitigating and adapting to climate change. Urban policies to create sustainable cities as well as specific fiscal policies and proactive disaster management programmes are needed. Above all, this requires strong and far-sighted public policy which pays adequate attention to the spatial dimensions of poverty and is able to effectively address issues which cut across the responsibilities of many different government agencies. At the same time, the private sector in both urban and rural areas should be encouraged through market incentives to invest in businesses which protect and promote the quality of environments.

II

East Asia
(People's Republic of China and Republic of Korea)

II

2

POVERTY, ENVIRONMENT, AND CLIMATE CHANGE IN THE GRASSLANDS OF CHINA

Tsui Yenhu

In north and northwest China lie vast areas of grassland. Most of which are also dryland. In the past fifty years, there have been drastic changes to the ecology and environment of this area due to ongoing drought, rising temperature, and imprudent human activities, including unsustainable development. Of the 70 million people who live in the area, 7 or 8 million are nomadic or settled herders. Poverty is a serious problem for herders.

The vast grasslands of north and northwest China are in the semi-arid and arid belts of the east part of the Eurasian grassland. Drought is always a great threat to the environment and people there. In some areas (e.g., western Inner Mongolia and southern Xinjiang), the annual rainfall is below 200mm, having the largest area of arid pastures and poor vegetation in terms of height, coverage, and number of grass species.

In the past half century, there have been drastic changes to the area's ecology and environment due to persistent drought, rising temperatures, imprudent human activities. Degradation of the pastures in the north and northwest China is a common phenomenon. The grassland of north and northwest China has been in a condition of non-self-maintenance, non-sustainable in ecology and non-sustainable in environment (Wang 2010). And deterioration of the grassland eco-environment has been happening in most of the grassland areas. The following are the most serious issues:

- of the 2.87 billion hectares grassland, about 90 per cent of the pastures are deteriorated to certain degrees;
- the pastures that are deteriorated, desertified, and salinized constitute about 53 per cent in area of the total;
- the production capacity of the grassland has decreased by 17–40 per cent, of which the arid grassland pastures is the most serious, a 40 per cent reduction is very common;
- the area of soil erosion in the north and northwest China increased from 2,870,000 km^2 in 1989 to 2,940,000 km^2 in 2000, most of which occurred in the grassland areas;
- many rivers and lakes of the areas have either dried up or reduced in the volume of water and area; and
- the composition of plant species community in the grassland areas has changed with the disappearance of more fine forage grasses and more poisonous grass species. This is especially obvious in the western part of Inner Mongolia, Gansu and Xinjiang.

The total desertified area and arid area of north and northwest China provinces amounts to about 2 million (1,968,599) km^2, which forms about half (or 45.1 per cent) of the total desertified area and arid area of the country, and most of the desertified and arid area lie in the dryland and in the grassland. In recent years there has been a decrease in the desertified arid area of north and northwest China provinces as Chinese government and local governments have taken measures such as restoration of pastures and growing trees. However, the general situation has not fundamentally changed in some areas of Inner Mongolia, Xinjiang and Qinghai partially due to climate changes (Ma and Shu 2008).

The reasons for the deterioration of the environment of China's grassland areas are complex. Extensive studies have been made. The following are the most important factors:

- reclamation of grassland to farmland (about 5 per cent of the grasslands were reclaimed);
- over-capacity and overgrazing (which are seen in all of the grassland areas);
- rapid population growth;
- mining and industry development related to exploitation of mineral resources;
- climate changes over the past fifty and more years; and
- non-sustainable management of grassland eco-environment.

CLIMATE CHANGE AND THE POVERTY OF GRASSLAND HERDERS

According to the surveys on the question of whether climate in the areas has visibly changed or not, of the 140 herder households, 91 per cent herders believe that the changes are an obvious and constant existence.[1] See Table 2.1.

No matter whether they are still practising nomadic herding or they have settled into farming, the herders who were interviewed have a common knowledge about climate change in the grassland areas in the four provinces or regions. See Table 2.2.

Many of the herders who were interviewed reported what they saw and felt about climate change and its effects on their production and life.

Case 2.1: Jinser, a Mongolian herder of Handgarte Mongolian Town, Altay Steppe, Xinjiang:

"Handgarte is a hilly pasture area in Altay Mountain and it was cool in the past years. But we are feeling that it is getting warmer and warmer now. In the past there was a lot of snow in the winter and we used sleighs as a means of transportation, but they are gone as there is no much snow on the ground. And the time for snow to stay on the ground is much shorter than before (How long has this been so?).

TABLE 2.1
Perception of Climate Changes by Local Herders

Place of Surveys	Ethnic Groups of Herders surveyed	Not settled	Settled	Very Obvious Change	Changed but not obvious[a]
Altay Steppe	Kazak herders	32	19	Non-Settled: 30	2
				Settled: 17	2
West Tianshan Mountain	Kazak and Mongolian herders	24	21	24	0
				19	2
Ordos, Inner Mongolia	Mongolian herders		18	18	0
Kezilesu, West Tianshan Mountain	Kirkiz herders	28	23	27	1
				19	4
Yushu, Qinghai	Tibetan herders	16	12	16	0
				11	
Gannan Gansu	Tibetan herders	20	20	20	1
				18	2

Notes: [a] The field survey was conducted in 2007, 2008 and 2009. Those who answered "changed but not obvious" were all young herders under 30 years old.
Source: From the author's fieldwork and the data obtained from their filed work. (Cf. the above description).

TABLE 2.2
Perception of the Impacts of Climate Changes by Herders

Place of Surveys	Number of Herders	Very Serious	Serious	Yes, but Not Serious	Do Not Know
Xinjiang	149	121	22	6	0
Inner Mongolia	18	18	0	0	0
Gansu	40	34	5	1	0
Qinghai	28	27	1	0	9

Source: From the author's fieldwork and the data obtained from their filed work. (Cf. the above description).

Well, about 15 years. What is worse is that the water in the river is less and less and the there are no fish at all now. And grass growing in the spring pastures around here is shorter and thinner and many springs from which we get drink water have dried up. In the past we were worried about too much snow but now we are worried about too little snow." (author's interview)

Case 2.2: Naranbater, a Mongolian herder of Ushen Qi, Ordos, Inner Mongolia

"In our grassland, there were many lakes, and some of them were very big and some were small. But many of them dried up and the lake basins are desertland now. In the past it was cool here but now it is very hot. I raise fine wool sheep for 35 years and they do not like to stay in a place where it is hot. In the past, we did not have any problem with this (too hot for the sheep), but now they have troubles with the summer temperature. I am worried about it because we will have to give up raising fine wool sheep if the climate goes on like this." (Author's interview).

Case 2.3: Hishankhan, a Kazak herder of Oyimok Town, Altay Steppe, Xinjiang

(Before the interview, the old man brought me around to look at the high mountain pastures which are about 3,000 metres above sea level. The grass was rather thin, yellowish and short; it would be dificult for his sheep to have enough hay on the way of migration. (mid-July 2008).)

"I am 72 years old but I have never seen this situation before. Of the four seasonal pastures, the summer pasture here was usually very abundant with high-quality grass, usually 40 cm high. But as you can see, there is no grass at all on the slopes and the top of the mountain. We have not had any rain since March and most of the streams have dried up. My sheep and other animals have had a very hard time here, and this is something I have not experienced in my life. I am worried about my animals because in two months' time, we will move them down to our autumn pastures, but there are no grass on the way down. How could they walk there without anything to eat on the way?" (Author's interview).

These ethnographic data correspond to the data collected by the author and other researchers in other areas of dryland of north and northwest China. They are supported by the research of ecologists and meterologists who studied the climate changes of the area (Zhai 2006; Han 2008). Taking Altay Steppes as an example, from 2002 to 2008, there were droughts in the summer and snowstorms in winter for almost every year. The climate change which has serious effect on the local grassland environment and the pastoral society is a "social factor" that is experienced by the local herders.

GRASSLAND DEGRADATION IN THE CONTEXT OF CLIMATE CHANGE

Poverty in the grasslands of north and northwest China has been observed by many researchers and data disclosed by the country's official sources (Li 2007; Du 2008; Wang 2010; Annual Reports of Poverty in China). The number of national-level poverty-stricken counties in the areas is more than that in other areas of the country. By the end of 2008, there were seventy-four national-level poverty-stricken counties, about 15 per cent of the total in China. The percentage of poverty-stricken households takes about 18–22 per cent of the whole number of households of the areas. For example, in Qinghe County of Altay Steppes, Xinjiang, the number of poor herder households is 35 per cent of the total herder households. The average income of each herder household of the areas is 25–40 per cent lower than the average income of rural households of the country. Due to environmental changes, the income growth of herder households of the areas is much slower than that of rural households of the country in general. According to a report of Greenpeace and Oxfam on the poverty conditions of Inner Mongolia, Gansu and Qinghai (Greenpeace and Oxfam 2009), about 60 per cent of the herder households were affected by grassland degradation and some of them lived at the edge of poverty.

The continuing grassland degradation in the areas not only makes the poor herder households poorer but also makes some average-income herder households return to poverty. For the poor households, they have to sell more sheep and other animals to make their ends meet and the degraded pastures cannot support their animals grazing.

The result is that the more they sell, the fewer they keep, and the reduction of the number of animals they keep becomes inevitable. In the year of 1984, the average-income herder households obtained both the right to use the pastures by household base and number of domestic animals at lowest value of fixed assets (including sheep, goats, cattle, horses and camels). Ten years (from 1984 to 1994) their income increased, which enabled them to obtain more animals. As a result, the rapid increase of animal population resulted in even greater pressure on the pastures than before, which, in turn, degraded the pastures. Many households cannot keep as many animals as they did due to the constant drought and worsening degradation of the pastures. Their income declined from 1996 to today by about 16–27 per cent, and an estimated 15–20 per cent of the herders have returned to the poverty condition.[2]

Case 2.4: Herders Returning Poverty in Inner Mongolia

In 1983 when the "responsibility system" was implemented in Inner Mongolian grassland areas, there were no "poor herder households" in the area (cf: Hai Shan 2009). However, the poverty happened in the following years. Take a Gacha of Xinlinguolen Prefecture, Inner Mongolia, as an example, as shown in Table 2.3.

TABLE 2.3
Poverty Increase at Yingtu Gacha of Zhengxiangbai Qi, 1983–2005

Year	Number of Poor Households	Percentage of the total Herder Households
1983	0	0%
1985	2	0.29%
1990	8	1.16%
1995	5	0.72%
2000	20	29%
2005[a]	32	46%

Notes: a. Of the poor herder households, 25 do not own any animals.
     b. The poverty line of Xilinguoleng Meng (Prefecture) in the respective year was calculated only for those households where the average number of sheep per person possessed is below 30.
Source: Wang Xiaoyi (2009); Hai Shan (2009).

A similar situation is seen in other Qis or Gachas of Inner Mongolia. For example, in Abaga Qi, each person in 70 per cent of herder households owned only twenty-eight sheep units in 2002, visibly below the poverty line of the region.

POVERTY OF THE SETTLED HERDERS

For those herder households that were settled and had turned to farming, the number of poor households has been increasing. Poverty among them is mainly due to degradation of grassland, lack of resources, lack of farming technology, natural disasters, poor management, and lack of labour.

The herder households of Qinghaojia Village, Wenquan County, Xinjiang, were settled at the end of 1990s and they were allocated with farmland and other farming resources and provided with training for farming after they were settled. Before 1998 when they were nomadic herders, there were only three poor households that needed poverty aids from the local government. In 2007, 42 per cent of settled herder households were in poverty.

Case 2.5: Jiamali, head of the village, Qinghaojia Village, Wenquan County, Xinjiang

The amount of land the villagers actually cultivate is only about 630 mu — approximately 5.4 mu of land per person. Due to the year-round low temperatures the climate is not suitable for growing cotton, so the main crops are wheat and oil-sunflower. There are two types of land in the village: near the Bortala River there is an embankment which takes up about 320 mu, and the leftover land is gobi or desert which takes up about 310 mu. These lands are poor and barren, so 5.4 mu per person is not enough, and the land is frequently contracted out. In 2010, the village had a total of forty-four households, six of which practised cultivation, three of which are Mongolian and three of which are Kazakh. In recent years, along the banks of the Bortala River in the townships a large amount of land has been opened up, but it is difficult to calculate the surface area exactly, as it stretches continuously for several kilometres, no less than 1 kilometre from the river. Most of this land is used for growing oil-sunflower, which is a water-intensive crop. Another side of Qinghaojia village is for a Herding Unit. After sedentarization, each herder family received 30 or so mu of fodder land which, according to the plan, was supposed to be used for raising alfalfa for the livestock. In reality, however, most of these alfalfa fields are contracted out to outside businessmen who use them for wheat or oil-sunflower production. The herders have preserved their nomadic herding method, going into the mountains in the summer and winter months and only staying in the permanent settlement during spring and autumn.

These cases suggest that, though herder-settlement strategy was originally designed to help herders out of their poverty situation which were partially caused by degradation of grassland, most settled herder households are not able to escape poverty. On the contrary, their poverty condition is deepening due to the reasons mentioned above.

GOVERNMENT MEASURES TO RESTORE THE GRASSLANDS

Since 1990s, China has taken integrated measures to improve and restore the degraded grassland eco-system and to reduce the poverty of herder households in the grassland areas of north and northwest China. The Chinese government has made many policies for this purpose.

- West China Development Strategy (1995), in which the protection and restoration of damaged environment of grassland is decided as the first target of the strategy, and about 10 billion yuan has been planned for this target. The strategy calls for rebuilding a green environment in west China.
- Regulation for Converting the Farmland for Forestry and Pasture (Issued by the State Council in 2002), which specifies the policies and measures, and plans to put 3,400 billion yuan for implementing the project which will last for seventeen years.
- Supplementary Policies on Converting the Farmland for Forestry (issued by the State Council in 2005), which further specifies the measures for offering funds and technologies to individual herder

household to practise converting the farmland for forestry and pastures. According to the new measures, more than 80 per cent herder households in grassland areas of north and northwest China obtain cash compensations and technologies for giving up cultivation and returning their land to forestry and pastures.

- Implementation Measures for Regulation on Converting the Farmland for Forestry and Pasture issued by the local governments of the area (from 2003–2008). The local governments (at province and county levels) have made their own measures to ensure and promote the implementation of the project, and more funds are offered by them for specific key areas.
- Project for Restoration of Damaged Grassland Environment. This project jointly-initiated by Ministry of Environment Protection, Ministry of Agriculture, Ministry of Forestry aims to restore the mostly damaged grassland environment of China, most of which is located in north and northwest China. Up to now, hundreds of billion yuan have been allocated for the project.
- Project for Construction of Sanbei Protect Forest covering northeast, north and northwest China. This project aims at growing a grand forest belt from northeast China, via north China and to northwest China to protect the environment and to stop the movement of the desert). The first and second phases of the project have been completed.

Beside the above policies and measures, China has taken other measures to help the herder households of the areas to reduce and alleviate poverty, including:

- improvement of infrastructure of grassland areas;
- implementation of anti-poverty projects at provincial, county and town levels;
- making and implementing poverty relieving policies;
- promotion of small town development in grassland areas; and
- improvement of education in grassland and offering training programmes to help herders access new resources for development.

All these policies and measures have proved effective in reducing poverty conditions of the areas as they have obviously improved the grassland environment. For instance, with the implementation of the

Regulation for Converting the Farmland for Forestry and Pasture, about half a million herders have moved to better environment of the grassland in Xinjiang. Their living condition has improved as the local infrastructure has improved and the grassland environment is better than ten years ago in some areas.

CLIMATE CHANGE'S CHALLENGES TO POVERTY REDUCTION

In 2008, the Altay Steppe area of Xinjiang was hit by a serious drought disaster which, as some aged local herders said, had never been seen in this areas in the past. The disaster, called "black disaster" by the local Kazak and Mongolian herders, caused great damage to the pastures and livelihood of herders. According to the local statistics, on average, there was about a 15–20 per cent decrease in income for each herder household. One of the effects of the drought was that many herders spent more money on fodder and hay for their animals during the long winter (about five months).

In the winter of 2009, the same area was hit by a "big white disaster", an unexpected snowstorm that caused even greater damage to livestock production than the drought in 2008, and more than 12,000 animals died and more were injured. In the spring time of the following year, Xinjiang Altay Steppe area was hit by floods from melted snow, which lasted for nearly two months. The floods caused the starting time of seasonal migrating of herders and their animals to be postponed, and they reached the spring pastures about one month later than usual. Therefore, the herder households had to buy fodder and hay for their animals. Those settled herder households had their farmland flooded; and irrigation channels and ditches were damaged. Some houses in the lowland or river valleys were badly damaged. The seed-time had to be postponed for more than a month, which affected their income in 2010.

It is not clear whether the successive disasters were related to the effects of climate change. More meteorological research has to be carried out. But it is no doubt that they brought about profound effects on livestock production and livelihood of the local herders, deepening the poverty that already existed in the area.

According to research of Chinese scientists (Zhai 2006; Han 2008) and the ethnographic data I collected from the field surveys, the effects of climate change on the grassland environment are mainly the following.

- Visible increase in the times and influences of droughts, which bring about complex effects on the ecosystem of pastures with reduction and disappearance of species of fine quality forage grass and increase in abundance of species of poisonous grass and other unedible herbage grass for animal. The result is clear: with this change, the productivity of pastures is greatly reduced.
- Constant dry climate resulting in shrinking, even dry-up of rivers and lake and disappearance of wetlands. This will further deepen the eco-crises of semi-arid and arid grassland environment, and might endanger the whole ecosystem to the extent that desertification will speed up.
- Fragmentation of pastures with more and more herders turning to farming through reclaiming grassland.
- Increase in the frequency of natural disasters, such as droughts, sandstorms, insect plagues, locust plagues, mouse plagues and snowstorms.

Ethnographic data collected by the author, Wang Xiaoyi, Haishan, and others (Zhai 2006; Tsui 2007; Du 2008; Hai 2009; Wang, Xiaoyi 2009; Wang, Yunxia 2010) also reveal that the above effects of climate change on the environment of grassland have in turn induced the challenges for poverty reduction of these areas.

- Measures to reduce poverty of herders taken by the government have lost efficacy to some extent due to further grassland degradation as the damaged pasture environment is irreversible.
- Herder households' efforts to convert farmland to forestry and pasture become more difficult, or even impossible, due to the consequences of climate change, such as lack of water, desertification and constant rise of temperature.
- Projects for eco-protection and eco-environment restoration will bear no results as the eco-environment conditions for them no longer exist due to climate change.

- Herders returning to poverty because of eco-environmental crises that are caused directly or indirectly by climate change is a "social factor" in grassland areas. The number of herder households that were out of poverty but returned to poverty is about 30–35 per cent of "new poor households".

The grassland areas are located in one of China's high eco-sensitivity and eco-fragility zones, and the areas where most of herders live are eco-fragile. These areas are easily influenced by climate change. This explains why most of the national poverty-stricken counties are in the eco-fragile areas and 90 per cent of poor population of the country live in these areas. In comparison with the number of national poverty-stricken counties in most farming areas, the number of national poverty-stricken counties in the grassland areas of north and northwest China is larger.

POLICY

Climate change may be a powerful force that will remap poverty and poverty reduction in grassland areas. These areas are more sensitive to change than the farmland areas; so it is possible that the pasture ecosystem has been seriously damaged. With the unprecedented challenges, it is time to reconsider the strategies for development and poverty reduction in grasslands and to develop new, integrated development strategies for which the social, cultural, eco-environmental components are to be put into the context of climate changes and its complex effects on the areas. By "integrated development strategies" I mean that in order to change the situation and to face the challenges, the policy-makers of the area should change the present policy-making process from an up–down process to a down–up process. They should put social, eco-environmental, and cultural factors into policy-making, of which the local knowledge of climate and pasture management are two key elements. Participation by the local communities, herders in particular, in the strategy-making will be essential as they are the victims of the change, but have both their own experiences and community-based or household-based strategies. The new integrated development strategies for sustainable pastoral development in the area takes a special position. The present development strategies implemented in the area overemphasize growth of GDP and household income. The defects of the strategies have been more and more visible in the past years.

The following may be important in creating the new strategies:

- Reconsider and adjust development strategies for the grasslands away from focus on economic growth towards a focus on sustainable development.
- Change the policy-making for poverty reduction away from government-orientation towards the interaction between governmental and local participation.
- Cooperation between modern technologies and local knowledge in grassland management and the protection and restoration of pasture eco-system.
- Develop various integrated green economy models to meet the needs of different herder communities in different eco-environment areas and cultural settings.
- Change the strategies for input on poverty reduction away from reducing income poverty to reducing climate poverty. "Climate-poverty" is a somewhat ambiguous term. The causes of the herder poverty are complex, though the effects of climate change are more and more important and obvious. It is impossible to measure climate poverty without considering other causes, such as policy-making at institutional and household levels, market demands and local responses to them, and changes in eco-environmental concepts and behaviour of the local herders. More multi-disciplinary research will be needed to work out ways to measure climate poverty reduction.
- Develop global network for poverty reduction and change from area efforts to global efforts.

The semi-arid and arid belt of the east Eurasian grassland extends into neighbouring Mongolia, Kazakhstan, and Russia. Those countries have the same problems with grassland development, in particular, with climate change in pastoral areas. In recent years, Inner Mongolia and Xinjiang have cooperated with Mongolia, Kazakhstan, and South Siberia of Russia in regional development. Meeting the challenges of environment deterioration of the dryland grassland areas has been an important item on the agenda. But the present cooperation is far from enough in taking measures against the social and environmental problems resulting from climate change. Strategies for regional poverty reduction with an emphasis on the effects of climate change are needed. This could be expanded further to a global network for poverty reduction.

CONCLUSION

Due to drought, rising temperature, and unsustainable development, there have been drastic changes to the ecology and environment of the vast grasslands of north and northwest China over the past fifty years. Of the 70 million people who live there, seven or eight million are herders. Environmental change is affecting their means of survival.

In this essay, I analyse the herders' poverty in connection with environmental, social, and cultural aspects of grasslands. I report on local knowledge about climate change and assess measures taken by the national and local governments to deal with the problems.

I describe the changes to the environment and how they affect the poor. I report on the local understanding of climate change (based on my interviews) and how it affects the way herders make a living. Based on data from my field surveys, I describe the environmental, social, and cultural aspects of the poverty among herders. I start with a description of the national and local governments' attempts to address dryland poverty, reduce the effects of the climate changes on the environment and the livelihood of the people. I discuss the successful and unsuccessful aspects of the measures that have been taken to reduce poverty in the areas.

I recommend that poverty should be understood as being not merely an economic issue. Social and cultural factors should be considered in the strategies for poverty reduction.

Notes

1. In this section, some ethnographic data about the responses of the herders in the areas to the climate change and its effects on their production and life will be used for the topic. The data come from two sources. First, most of them are from the author's field surveys from 1999 to 2009, which

were done in the grassland areas of Tianshan Mountains, Altay Steppes and Ordos, Inner Mongolia, and the methods of individual interviews and questionnaires were used in the questions to the surveyed herders included that concerning the climate change and environmental changes in the different sites. Second, some of the data from the other anthropologists and ecologists who did similar surveys from 1994 to 2008 in the grassland areas of Gansu, Qinghai and Tibet, and in particular, the data obtained by Du Fachun, Du Guozhen, and Li Jin are extremely useful. In total, about 140 herders were interviewed.

2. Wang Xiaoyi offered a very convincing case about this "herders returning to poverty" based on his surveys in Inner Mongolia; and his finding are supported by Hai Shan and the author of the paper who surveyed other parts of the area.

References

Banks, Tony, Camille Richard, and Yang Zhaoli. "Community-Based Grassland Management in West China-Rationale, Pilot Project Experience and Policy Implications". *Mountain Research and Development* 23, no. 2 (May 2003).

Drought Monitoring and Forecasting Section of Lanzhou Arid Meteorology Institute. "Drought Situation in the 2009 Summer." *China Journal of Arid Meterology*, no. 2 (2009).

Du, Fachun. "Pasture Degradation and Eco-migrant: A Case of Qinghai Maduo County". Paper presented at the Conference for Environmental Changes of Grassland and Social and Economic Problems, organized by China Academy of Social Sciences, 2008.

Greenpeace and Oxfam. "Climate Change & Poverty in China: A Case Study of China," A report published by Greenpeace and Oxfam (China Office in Beijing), Beijing and Hong Kong, March 2009.

Hai, Shan. "Poverty in Pastotral Areas of Inner Mongolia and Poverty-aid Strategies" (in Chinese). *Animal Husbandry Economy*, no. 10 (2009).

Han, Xinhui. "Research on Ecological Effects and Mechanism of Forestry (Pasture) Project in Loess Plateau". Ph.D. dissertation. Northwest University of Agriculture and Forestry, Yangling, China, 2008.

Hansen, Art, and Anthony Oliver-Smith. *Involuntary Migration and Resettlement: The Problems and Responses of Dislocated People.* Boulder, Colorado: Westview Press, 1981.

Ma Jingkui and Shu Qing, eds. *China Statistical Yearbook on Environment. 2008.* Beijing: China Statistics Press, 2008.

Tsui, Yen Hu. "Institutional Reasons and Reforms of Grassland Mangement Institutions: A Case Analysis of Social, Economic and Environmental

Problems in Xinjiang Pastoral Areas". Paper presented at Beijing Seminar for Society, Economy and Environment of North China, 2007.

————. "Environmental Changes of Handgarte Pastures of Altai over Fifty Years: A Case Analysis of Xinjiang Altai Grassland." In *Good Earths*. Kyoto, Japan: Kyoto University Press, 2009.

Wang, Xiaoyi. *Pastoral Communities under Environmental Pressure: Case Studies of Six Villages in Inner Mongolia* (in Chinese). Beijing: Social Science Literature Press, 2009

Wang, Yunxia. "A Positive Study on the Grassland Degradation and Its Determinants in Inner Mongolia". Ph.D. dissertation. Inner Mongolia University, Hohhot, China, 2010.

Zhai, Luxin. "Climatic Variability and Impact on Hydrology in Recent 50 Years in Northwest China". Ph.D. dissertation. Lanzhou University, China, 2006.

3

CLIMATE CHANGE, FOOD SECURITY, AND POVERTY IN THE PEOPLE'S REPUBLIC OF CHINA

Qi Gubo

China's agriculture has grown rapidly over the last three decades. This is due to the liberalization of markets, rapid technological change, and the "household responsibility system".[1] When economies grow, they vary in how much the growth benefits the poor. In the recent growth of the Chinese economy, the growth in agriculture benefitted the poor three and half times as much as the growth of the rest of the economy (World Bank, 2008, p. 6). The growth in China's agriculture has been largely responsible for the decline in rural poverty from 250 million in 1978 to 14.78 million in 2007, according to the official poverty line and income indicator. China has largely eliminated the fear of hunger in the country.[2] But these achievements are being threatened by climate change. Some parts of the country are more affected than others. One type of area that is especially sensitive to climate change is the ecotone, that is, where two different ecological communities (e.g., forest and grassland) border and overlap. Poor people who live in such areas are finding it even more difficult to overcome their poverty. The Chinese government's efforts to mitigate climate change often unintentionally make life more difficult for them.

CLIMATE CHANGE, FOOD PRODUCTION, AND POVERTY

Influence of Climate Change on Food Production

Climate change will cause productivity in the farming of major food crops to decline and be unstable in China. As a result of the increase in temperature and the decrease in water and arable land expected for the next twenty to fifty years, the period of crop production will be shortened and food production will be threatened. The production levels of China's three main food crops (rice, wheat, and maize) are expected to decrease by 14 per cent to 23 per cent, not taking into account possible adaptation measures (Lin Erda et al. 2008).[3] See Table 3.1.

Climate change will have a substantial effect on water resources, an essential factor in food production. Water flow will probably be reduced in northern provinces and in regions such as Ningxia and Gansu in next fifty to hundred years, while in southern provinces such as Hubei and Hunan, the flow will increase. So there will be more drought in some areas and more flooding in others. If efforts are made to use water in a sustainable way, most provinces in China will have enough water; but there will probably be shortages in Inner Mongolia, Xinjiang, Gansu and Ningxia.[4]

Food production will also be threatened by disasters, insects, and disease. Warmer weather will allow insects and diseases to survive the winters more easily and extend their growing period.[5] This will result in more insects and more diseases and a larger affected area. Extreme weather induced by climate change will be accompanied by more droughts, flooding, and high-temperature disasters. These will cause more losses in food production. Collective and individual adaptation however will help to prevent some of these effects.

Influence of Climate Change on Agriculture

With higher CO_2 emissions, rapid population growth, and economic growth, the water available for agriculture will decrease rapidly. The

TABLE 3.1
Predicted Change of Unit Yield of Three Main Food Crops in China
(Yield in 2000 as baseline)

Scenario of climate	CO_2 fertilization	Cropping pattern	Change of unit yield of rice (%)		Change of unit yield of wheat (%)		Change of unit yield of maize (%)	
			2020s[a]	2050s[*b]	2020s	2050s	2020s	2050s
A2 Middle-high emission	Not considered	Rain-fed			−18.5	−20.4	−10.3	−22.8
		Irrigated	−8.9	−12.4	−5.6	−6.7	−5.3	−11.9
	Considered	Rain-fed			15.4	13.3	9.8	18.4
		Irrigated	3.8	6.2	20.0	25.1	−0.6	−2.2
B2 Middle-low emission	Not considered	Rain-fed			−10.2	−11.4	−11.3	−14.5
		Irrigated	−1.1	−4.3	−0.5	−2.2	0.2	−0.4
	Considered	Rain-fed			4.5	6.6	1.1	8.5
		Irrigated	−0.4	−1.2	11.0	14.2	−0.1	−1.3

Notes: A2 scenario of middle-high emission reflects slower speed of regional cooperation and
adaptation to new technologies, and continued population growth, corresponding to
IPCC published data of stable CO_2 concentration of 600 ppm. B2 scenario of middle-low
emission reflects regionally environmental improvement, corresponding to IPCC published
data of stable CO_2 concentration of 450–500 ppm.
(a) 2011–40; (b) 2041–70.
Source: Lin et al. (2005).

area of rice production will decrease by 40 per cent and the area
of rain-fed maize will increase by more than 40 per cent. Increasing
temperatures will harm crops planted in cool ecotones. For example,
potato production in southern mountain areas of Ningxia has decreased
(Sun Fang 2008). Planting methods are changing rapidly: the proportion of grain-planted areas to the total arable land declined from
80 per cent in 1980 to 67 per cent in 2005, with grain output increasing
from 321 million to 484 million tons.[6] In response to climate change,
crop production will change in four ways: (1) the multiple planting
area will be extended northward and into high altitude areas, (2) the
area for planting winter wheat will be extended north and west,
(3) maize that is now grown in the northeast will be moved farther
north and farther east, and (4) the planting area of late maturing

varieties will be extended (Li Yijun and Wang Chunyi 2010). Farmers can adapt to climate change by producing drought-resistant crops or greenhouse crops, or by leaving land that is no longer arable to do off-farm work.

Food availability increased from 317 kg/person in 1980 to 379.6 kg/person in 2007. Per capita grain production reached 285 kg per year by the late 1970s and early 1980s and then exceeded 300 kg after that, except for 2003, when production decreased to 286 kg. As measured by the Food and Agriculture Organization's food security standards, China's grain output totaled 501.5 million tons in 2007. Net cereal exports were 7.96 million tons and net soybean imports were 30.82 million tons. The self-sufficiency ratio for grains (including soybean) exceeded 95 per cent, meaning that per capita grain supply (including production and storage) would be 400 kg when divided into a population of 1.3 billion. The stock consumption ratio stood around 45 per cent at the end of 2007. China's cereal imports had accounted for a high percentage, reaching 34 per cent of total agricultural imports from 1979 to 1981. However, the percentage of cereal imports in China's total agricultural imports dropped to 8.68 per cent in 2004. Cereal's percentage in China's total agricultural exports has fluctuated according to the production cycle of cereal in China. See Table 3.2.

How Climate Change Influences Livelihoods

The people in ecologically sensitive areas are less able to adapt to climate change, and thus are more likely to have problems making a living. In 2005, there were 23.65 million people living below the

TABLE 3.2
Cereals Import and Export of China

		1979–81	1989–91	1999–2001	2003	2004
Percentage of cereals in total agricultural imports	China	34.15	19.98	6.91	5.19	8.68
	World	17	11	9	8	8
Percentage of cereals in total agricultural exports	China	8.44	5.62	8.15	13.01	4.01
	World	17	11	9	8	8

Source: FAOSTAT, http://faostat.fao.org.

poverty line established by Chinese government (683 yuan of annual per capita net income in 2005, equivalent of US$84.63 at 2005 exchange rate), more than 95 per cent of whom lived in remote or frontier areas inhabited by ethnic minorities. The poverty-stricken areas all have extremely fragile ecological environments.[7] Climate change will affect poverty directly and indirectly. The direct effects are extreme weather disasters causing losses to agriculture, livelihood assets, and infrastructure. The indirect effects are through economic growth. Poor areas will have more problems since they rely more on rainfall and other natural resources. Their finances, technology, and institutions also have little capacity to adapt to climate change. Ecotones are affected in additional ways because of their higher sensitivity to climate. Rural poverty incidence will increase by 2–3 per cent for every 10 per cent increase in damage to agricultural production by floods and drought.[8] In famine years, the rate of relapse into poverty in rural areas in Guizhou Province is as high as 20 per cent. In certain kinds of extreme weather, it may not be possible to secure healthy food and water, even with quick rescues as with the sustained, serious drought in five provinces of southern China in 2010. So the health of poor population would be threatened. As a result of lower resistance and malnutrition, diseases could spread.

POVERTY ALLEVIATION AND THE RESPONSE TO CLIMATE CHANGE

Poverty Alleviation and Climate Change

Recently, government plans for reducing poverty have included industrialization, integrated village planning, and agricultural and rural development funds. But climate change has not been factored into poverty alleviation plans. Poor people tend to be more exposed to the environment, especially those living in fragile areas. Climate change is affecting the poor more than others.

One attempt to reduce poverty is through loans of various sorts. The microfinance loans made directly to poor farmers can be used to diversify their sources of income (by technological support, such as guidance of functioning of fund, doing business and production innovation) and accumulate capital. Diversification of livelihood is a way for farmers to avoid smaller risks. Capital accumulation can help them deal with bigger risks. Farmers cannot avoid the loss of material assets when unexpected disasters strike. Under such circumstances, the inability to engage in capital accumulation prevents them from forming new groups.[9] Therefore, without the diversification and capital accumulation made possible by small loans, the livelihood vulnerability of farmers cannot be reduced and these farmers will remain poor.

As a way of limiting the risks caused by climate change, poverty alleviation in industrial sectors can also provide farmers with alternative livelihoods similar to those discussed above. But these activities cannot reach the poor without being adapted to social, economic, and political conditions. Moreover, microfinance funds are too limited to support alternative livelihoods. Besides, industrial poverty alleviation promotes economies of scale. Economies of scale can, on the one hand, increase the ability of farmers to respond to natural risks, including those from climate change, if the scale of production is guaranteed by agricultural facilities, such as greenhouses for vegetables. On the other hand, economies of scale may reduce the diversity of production, and farmers will be more easily exposed to risks from unpredictable weather or price fluctuation.

Nevertheless, some poverty alleviation measures increase the adaptation of the society to climate change; for example, the poor can be paid to build structures that protect against extreme weather. Small-scale irrigation, water conservation, and farmland capital construction compensate for the uneven distribution of rainfall and temperature. They also allow poor people to more efficiently use natural resources, such as land, water, and accumulated temperature. Road construction enables counties, townships, and villages to have access to markets. Drinking water projects for humans and livestock improve the living conditions of poor households directly.

The following is an example of the role of water conservation facilities in reducing vulnerability to climate change. Compared to villages without irrigated arable land, Guantan Village of Ningxia Hui Autonomous Region can respond more adequately to the changing climate with water channelled from the Yellow River since 1998. Villagers use the maize grown on irrigated land as feed for livestock and poultry, thus saving around US$8,00 per household on feed costs every year, which can make up their shortage of cash income and help them develop animal husbandry.[10]

Policy Responses to Climate Change and Poverty

The People's Republic of China's National Development Reform Commission is the country's economic planning agency. As this includes coordinating the national response to climate change, the commission has assembled an advisory group made up of representatives of various of sectors of the economy and ten national ministries. It is called the National Leading Group on Climate Change. This group contributed to the drafting of the National Strategy for Coping with Climate Change, which was released by the National Development Reform Commission in June 2007.[11] In that strategy document, the group recommends many responses to climate change, including bio-gas projects in rural areas, restoring forests on farmland, paying for forest ecological services, the restoring grasslands on pastures, protecting wetlands, and constructing nature reserves. However, these policy makers sometimes appear to be unaware of how their policies affect poor people. I will illustrate this lack of awareness by looking at one case concerning nature reserve policy, which gives little consideration to the livelihood vulnerability of the poor. Here is an example of ecological protection and opportunity cost for farmers' living in nature reserves. In a nature reserve in the Sanjiang Plain, where the villagers lost both their income from crop farming and their subsidies for growing grain a villager said,

> The nature reserve has nothing to do with us. There are no benefits at all. In the past, people from Yongfeng village and Jiahe town farmed in the nature reserve. They could plough after paying a small amount of money for permission to Raohe Land Administration.[12]

As approved by the land administration, the land was unrecoverable and could also receive "two subsidies" (direct and comprehensive grain). But now the wetland is under the management of the forestry administration, and farmers are not allowed to plough the land.[13]

The policy that promises to mitigate climate change has new requirements that affect rural livelihoods. The policy of reducing carbon sources by promoting biofuel and clean energy in rural areas may put the livelihood of the poor at greater risk. Therefore, transfer payments and technical support for the poor should be considered.

Adaptation to Climate Change by Poor People Themselves

Not all climate change adaptation and mitigation come from above. Some come from communities and households. Poor people adapt to climate change all the time, but they are limited in their ability to reduce their exposure to risk, given the condition of their assets. Poor people often take the following measures to reduce the vulnerability of their livelihoods to the effects of climate change:

- Responsive measures based upon the traditional ways of making a livelihood. For example, collecting rain water, changing the farming cycle, preserving soil moisture, water-saving irrigation, and so on.
- Alternative livelihoods. Examples of changes with smaller scope are alternative crops, livestock, and poultry. Examples of changes with wider scope are changing from fishing to planting and animal husbandry, developing an orchard, or travel for employment opportunities. They might not be permanent emigrants, but only temporary, say for several months in a year.
- Adaptation involving a combination of external interventions and traditional ways of living, for example, state-funded construction of irrigation, water conservation facilities, and water-saving irrigation technology. In agriculture-animal husbandry areas, technological and financial aids are used to adjust grazing times and livestock carrying capacity, together with stable breeding.
- Adjustment to alternative livelihoods via external interventions. For example, poor women in arid areas could start small businesses or engage in animal husbandry with the aid of a microfinance project. People in areas where ethnic minorities live and economic activities are limited could develop tourism or sell handicrafts. People in areas that are too harsh for living could migrate to find jobs in new places.

The following are examples of adaptation from below in three ecotone-type areas. In Ningxia Hui Autonomous Region, climate-change effects, especially drought, affect the normal production and life of farmers. In addition to looking for non-agricultural job opportunities, farmers try their best in agriculture. Their main measures for adaptation are preserving soil moisture (covering with plastic film, ploughing and grinding the soil, and sand pressing), collecting water, and water-saving irrigation (Wu Yanjuan 2008). Furthermore, farmers reduce livestock carrying capacity. The self-management of grassland adopted by some cooperatives reduces the pressure on grassland and promotes the sustainable development of livelihoods. In Inner Mongolia, the dry climate threatens local grain, resulting in the locals' vulnerability to drought (Brogaard et al. 2005). Only a small part of rural land can be irrigated. If drought hits in spring, the major response for rainwater-irrigation agriculture is to plant broomcorn instead of maize, and sunflower instead of chestnut. In cases of severe drought, farmers are unable to plant any crops at all.

In Wuming in Guangxi Zhuang Autonomous Region, farmers view drought and floods to be the biggest difficulty they have ever encountered. The area of irrigated land has dropped from 300 mu to 64 mu, due to the loss of water in the reservoir. Many farmers have adapted by planting cassava (a cash crop) instead of cereal. Farmers pump water from the reservoir or wait for rainfall when they suffer drought and water shortages (Wang Xiufen 2007).

In the measures taken by farmers in Zhongdian, Yunnan Province, to reduce damage from floods, misty rain, and hail, the rich could depend on loans, while the poor could only rely on aid from neighbours and the government. And in serious situations, poor farmers had no choice but to sell assets, mainly livestock (Hui Xue 2006). Farmers thought that of all the risk-reducing activities, community safety-net building was the most effective short-term programme, while education for their children was effective for the long term. Training in how to use new farming technologies, joint decision-making, and increasing the number of grazing herds were considered to be effective long-term choices that could reduce damage. Farmers also considered diversifying sources of income and strengthening family ties to be effective in the short run.

Experiences in Increasing Poor People's Adaptability to Climate Change

Farmers need external assistance to improve their ability to adapt. In the northern irrigated area they hoped the government would support the construction of farmland capital, transfers of cash, and the input of agricultural material for locals engaged in agriculture and animal husbandry.[14] Though the farmers in the middle arid area of the country also expressed hopes for the above-mentioned assistance, what they needed most was direct cash payments from the government. This is because a large proportion of their agriculture has been affected by drought, and many farmers thought the problem could not be solved by farmland capital construction or increased input of agricultural material. They thought cash subsidies would more effectively ensure their food security (Wu Yanjuan 2008). In the dry northwest region, farmers have been encouraged to shift from rain-fed agriculture to greenhouse production. The use of simple plastic greenhouse technology reduces evaporative losses from the soil and permits the cultivation of high-value vegetable crops. But these require intensive irrigation, so water use increases.

There has been an increased use of insurance policies issued by the government or by mutual insurance associations. In 2007, the China Insurance Regulatory Commission issued a statement that emphasized the need to prepare for more frequent extreme weather by innovations in insurance products. With this policy, all farmers could buy insurance for breeding sows, milk cows, and rapeseed; and specialized farmers could buy insurance for rice, greenhouse vegetables, watermelon, oranges, forest, pigs, chickens, ducks, geese, and fish. Hazard coverage includes tropical cyclones, rainstorms, floods, frost damage, common insects, and disease. Though agricultural insurance for farmers is a good way to improve their resilience in the face of disasters, it is always difficult to implement in practice through a purely commercial approach. There have also been efforts to provide better warning systems for floods or typhoons. The local government and weather bureaus make use of more advanced communication technology to help farmers and fishermen prepare for weather-related disasters.

BOX 3.1
Role of Microfinance in Reducing Livelihood Vulnerability
of Farmers

The following is an example of the role of microfinance in reducing livelihood vulnerability of farmers. Farmers in the village of Zheguyuan in Guizhou province reclaimed wasteland and planted over 3,000 yews in 1993. Before they received any small loans, they had to cut down and sell trees as their main source of income. Each yew could be sold at a price of RMB50–200. But the price increases to RMB1,000 if the tree are 20 years old or more. Thanks to small loans, the farmers were able to begin planting vegetables in 2005. This has gradually become the main source of income. The farmers no longer had to cut down trees, but they reserve the yews as a source of future income. They can fall back on cutting down yews if the yield of vegetables is lowered by disease and insects—as could happen as a result of temperature changes.

RECOMMENDATIONS

I recommend that research be done on local activities that are already lowering people's vulnerability to climate change damage. This would involve studying the combination of external support, indigenous knowledge (particularly of how to disseminate predictions), micro-insurance, and alternative livelihoods.[15] This research would also include the participation of the relevant government departments. The results should be made immediately available to policy makers. Based on the current food subsidy policy, an awarding approach and support for incentives to apply new technology would provide incentives to local people for food production. Since 2010 the National Reform and Development Committee has been preparing policies in which people are paid for their ecological services. It is expected that the implementation of those policies will start by 2012. They provide an opportunity to integrate considerations of food security, livelihood development for the poor, and environmental protection. Natural migration with support from the state in China has been considered an important alternative for those living in the areas to adapt to climate change.

The poor can contribute to climate change mitigation by living in nature reserves/areas where cultivation is prohibited, and where there are grassland ecological construction projects, afforestation and reforestation projects, food security projects, and bio-energy projects. Their contribution should be fully compensated. The compensation should be made along with the development programmes that improve their livelihood. The goal should be for the compensatory measures to promote asset accumulation and sustainable livelihoods. Special poverty alleviation measures, financial budgets, and transfer payments should be established for ecotones.

Climate change threatens food security, for some more than others, since some communities are more exposed to natural disasters and land degradation. However, current poverty alleviation policies integrate climate-change considerations in only a limited way. Poor people have their own ways of adapting to climate change — through agricultural production adjustment, production development strategy, and alternative livelihood activities. But since their adaptability is limited by a low level of assets and insurance, they need external support of the sort that the government can provide. The government's poverty alleviation policies should integrate climate-change considerations, introducing elements of mitigation and adaptation. The government can play an important role in providing this external support. In order to ensure food security amidst climate change in China, it will be necessary to adopt a new way of looking at the relationship between the environment and poverty. In order to deal with the threat that climate change poses to agricultural production and food security, China must accept the long-term challenge of adapting agriculture to the changing climate and develop the capacity to cope with disasters caused by climate change.

Notes

1. Small-holders have had long-term land-use rights since the institutional innovation of the household responsibility system in 1978, and the share of agricultural production by small-holders is more than 85 per cent of total agricultural production.
2. Food security is a lack of anxiety over whether one will have continued access to sufficient nutrition for a healthy life. The most extreme form of food insecurity is the strong possibility of starvation, for example, because of living in circumstances where droughts have the ability to completely remove any chance of eating enough to survive.

3. Climate change, in particular the precipitation change in northern China, and intensive human activities in the future could exert far-reaching effects on desertification. The area of desertification is 2,636.2 thousand km², accounting for 27.46 per cent of total national area in 2004 (State Forest Bureau 2005). Some researchers have analysed the relationship between climate change and desertification (e.g., Su Zhi-zhu et al. 2006). The warm-drying trend may speed up desertification development, but regionally rising precipitation could be in favour of the reverse of desertification.

4. China National Development and Reform Committee (2007).

5. Justin Gillis, "Temperature Rising: With Deaths of Forests, a Loss of Key Climate Protectors." *New York Times*, 1 October 2011, p. 1.

6. Chinese Academy of Sciences and ISET Associate (2008).

7. Ministry of Environmental Protection (2008).

8. See studies by Zhang Xiao and others on the relationship between rural poverty and floods and drought.

9. Forming a group is precondition for getting the loan. Those who damage their assets and influenced other group members are not trusted by others to be accepted in a group again.

10. "Social Adaptation to Climate Change", Survey conducted by College of Humanities and Development Studies, China Agricultural University in 2010.

11. Chinese Academy of Sciences (2008), p. 14.

12. From 1989 and 1994 farmers could bring wetlands under cultivation after paying the reclamation fees of RMB50/mu.

13. Interview with a villager of Yongfeng Village in Wang Libin et al. (2009), pp. 107–08.

14. Studies in Ningxia Hui Autonomous Region.

15. There have been several experiments on crop insurance, but they are not purely commercial as they may still be unprofitable. They would require government spending or community self-organization.

References

Brogaard, S., M. Runnstrom, and J. A. Seaquist. "Primary Production of Inner Mongolia, China between 1982 and 1999 estimated by a satellite-driven light use efficiency model". *Global and Planetary Change* 45 (2005): 313–32.

China National Development and Reform Committee (NDRC). *China National Project of Coping with Climate Change*. Printed in June 2007 (in Chinese).

Chinese Academy of Sciences and ISET Associate. "Climate Adaptation in Asia: Knowledge Gaps and Research Issues in China". Final Report to IDRC and DFID. September 2008.

Hui Xue. "Assessing the Role of Risk in the Agro-pastoral Systems of Northwest Yunnan Province, China". Report No. 408. Simon Fraser University, 2006.

Li Yijun, Wang Chunyi. "Impacts of Climate Change on Crop Planting Structure in China. Chinese Academy of Meteorological Sciences". *Advances In Climate Change Research* 6, no. 2 (2010): 123–29 (in Chinese).

Lin, E. D., Xiong W., Ju H. et al. "Climate change impacts on crop yield and quality with C02 fertilization in China". *Philosophical Transaction of the Royal Society B.* 360 (2005) 2149–54.

Lin Erda, Ju Hui, Xiong Wei et al. *Climate Change and Food Security in China.* Beijing: Xueyuan Press, 2008 (in Chinese).

Lin Erda, Xu Yinlong and Jiang Jinhe et al. "National Assessment Report on Climate Change (II): Climate Change Impacts and Adaptation". *Advances in Climate Change Research* 2, no. 2 (2006): 51–56 (in Chinese).

Ministry of Environmental Protection of the People's Republic of China. "Program for Protection of the National Ecologically Fragile Zones". September 2008 (in Chinese).

Parry, M. L., O. F. Canziani, J. P. Palutikof, P. J. van der Linden, and C. E. Hanson, eds. *Climate Change 2007: Impacts, Adaptation and Vulnerability.* Contribution of Working Group II to the Fourth Assessment Report of the Intergovernmental Panel on Climate Change. Cambridge: Cambridge University Press, 2006.

Sun Fang. "Study on Adaptive Capacity of Agriculture to Climate Change: Cropping pattern and technologies perspectives". Ph.D. Dissertation. China Academy of Agricultural Sciences, 2008 (in Chinese).

Su Zhi-zhu, Lu Qi, Wu Bo, Jin He-ling, Dong Guang-rong. "Potential Impact of Climate Change and Human Activities on Desertification in China". *Journal of Desert Research* 26, no. 3 (May 2006): 329–35.

State Forest Bureau. "The Third Bulletin on Desertification and Sandy Desertification in China". June 2005.

Wang Libin, Jin Leshan, Cheng Shaoxia, Li Xiaoyun, and Quan Wuxian et al. *Conservation and Alternative Livelihoods: Study on the Sanjiang Plain Wetlands.* Social Sciences Academic Press (China), 2008 (in Chinese).

Wang Xiufen. "Studies on Livelihood Vulnerability of Farmers: An Example from Changgang Community in Guangxi Zhuang Autonomous Region". Dissertation for China Agricultural University, 2007 (in Chinese).

World Bank. *World Development Report: Agriculture for Development*, 2008.

Wu Yanjuan. "Impacts of Climate Change on the Farmers in Ningxia Hui Autonomous Region". Dissertation for the Chinese Academy of Agricultural Sciences, 2008 (in Chinese).

4

THE PHYSICAL AND SOCIAL ENVIRONMENT OF THE CHINESE URBAN POOR

Wendy Walker, Madhumita Gupta, and Daniel Roberts

Over the past thirty years, China has witnessed an explosive growth of its cities. By 2008, the urban population of China had risen to 607 million (45.7 per cent of the population).[1] Two-thirds of the urban population growth is attributable to rural-to-urban migration. By 2015, the urban population is projected to be 700 million, exceeding the rural population for the first time. By 2030, one billion people will live in China's cities.[2] This growth is being accompanied by a rapid expansion of urban land: between 1990 and 2005, China's urban land area grew by an average of 24,727 square kilometres per year, reaching a total of 2,600,000 square kilometres.[3] In this essay, we examine the history of urbanization in China and explore the effects of the related spatial, physical, and social changes on the environments of the poor. In order to create sustainable urban environments in the coming years, it will be necessary to address the challenges these changes bring with them.

URBANIZATION IN CHINA

Rapid urbanization has contributed to China's economic growth and improved living conditions. From 1981 to 2001, 400 million people escaped poverty and 200 million of those who continue to live below one dollar per day have been provided with assistance. These successes have created new challenges for local authorities in urban areas. They have had to concern themselves with providing housing, improving access to services, and addressing growing inequality. "China has recorded the most spectacular progress in the world, with improvements to the day-to-day conditions of 65.3 million urban residents who were living with one or more factors of shelter deprivation."[4]

In 1949, China was a predominantly rural society. Only 11 per cent of the population lived in its 69 cities.[5] China's urbanization has passed through three distinct phases: moderate growth, a plateau from the late 1950s to the early 1980s, and accelerating urbanization in recent years. In the 1950s, a natural growth of urbanization took place without restrictions as people moved freely from the countryside to the cities. The urbanization rate was 10.6 per cent in 1949 and rose (by an average of 0.6 per cent per annum) to 15.39 per cent in 1957. From 1957 to 1978, urbanization was restricted by measures that supported a centrally planned economy geared towards industrial production. The establishment and gradual implementation of the *hukou* registration system during the 1950s divided the population into rural farmers and urban workers. Urban household registration brought the guarantee of daily necessities — such as staple grains and cooking oils, clothing, and other rationed goods — as well as access to urban services, such as state education, medical services, jobs, and housing. None of these benefits were enjoyed by those with rural household registrations. Initially, the political demand to increase industrial output during the Great Leap Forward ensured continued migration from the countryside to the cities. During the early 1960s, around 26 million farmers returned to the countryside,[6] followed by millions of urbanites and intellectuals "sent down" during the rustication movements of the

Cultural Revolution. Throughout this period, urbanization stagnated, with little or negative growth. The central government was solely responsible for urban development, leading to inadequate investment in infrastructure and limits on the growth of small cities and townships.[7] The rate of urbanization remained at a stand still from 1962 (17.33 per cent) to 1978 (17.92 per cent).

Following the adoption of economic reforms in 1978, the urbanization rate gradually increased, reaching 27.63 per cent in 1992. Strict controls on rural-urban migration were maintained during this time. In 1984, the government allowed rural people to live and work in townships as long as they could feed themselves. In 1985, they were permitted to register in urban areas on a temporary basis. Stability and growing prosperity made food rationing less important in the cities, and increasing numbers of rural migrants arrived. By the 1990s, millions were flocking to China's cities to work in the construction and service industries. In 1992, a number of local authorities — including those in Shenzhen, Shanghai, and Guangzhou — allowed migrant workers to apply for "blue" *hukou* registrations, provided that they could afford to buy a house and pay a one-time fee for the use of urban infrastructure. For a small number of well-off migrants, it became possible to join China's burgeoning urban society.

Today, urbanization continues to grow at around 1 per cent per annum, resulting in significant effects on land, the environment, and people. The Ministry of Housing and Urban-Rural Development notes that "the built up area for urban localities expanded from 7,438 km^2 in 1981 to 36,295 km^2 in 2008, representing a 4.88 times increase within 27 years."[8] Thanks in part to the growth of megacities such as Shanghai and the urban agglomerations of the Pearl and Yangtze deltas, urbanization is, as mentioned earlier, expected to pass 50 per cent by 2015.[9]

Roughly one in four urban dwellers in China today is a migrant,[10] most of whom live as a "floating population" without official urban *hukou* registration. Urbanization in coastal areas has been largely due to increased migration across regions but rising rates in the inland areas are primarily due to an exodus from rural areas, most often in the same province and resulting decrease in the rural population.[11] The emphasis of economic growth has led to growing social vulnerabilities associated with the rise of "new urban poverty" (see below) in many Chinese cities.

Structurally, China's urbanization has been concentrated in a few regions and provinces: a small number of megacities attract enormous populations, while many prefecture-level cities are about half of their efficient size. These smaller cities can neither benefit from the clustering of economic activities, nor develop a sufficient concentration of specialized industries. They therefore have limited capital for new investment.

OLD AND NEW URBAN POVERTY

Prior to the market reforms of 1978, the urban poor were identified as those suffering the "three no's": no relatives or dependants that could support them, no ability to work, and no other source of income. Urban poverty is a relatively new concept in China: it is only recently that phrases such as "weak social and economic groups" (*ruoshi qunti*) and "urban poor residents" (*chengshi pingkun jumin*) have gained acceptance in government publications.

The emergence of vulnerable urban groups is closely tied to the particular history of economic and social policies in the country. Shortly after 1949, the approach of China's new government to private enterprise ensured that the 4 million unemployed urban residents found work in factories and services, which also attracted many rural labourers.[12] During the economic difficulties of the early 1960s, urban employment fell dramatically and many workers left the cities.

In the 1960s and 1970s, new categories of urban poor received state assistance: those who had lost jobs after the Great Leap Forward, unemployed youths returning from the countryside, and those who had suffered during the Cultural Revolution. By 1985, 3.8 million urban citizens received support from a government relief fund, as did another 534,000 who could not work due to illness or disability.

The 1990s led to new forms of urban poverty, which persist in China today. Although the unemployment rate remained steady at around 3 per cent, the actual number of people listed as unemployed doubled to 6 million. Restructuring across state and collective sectors was designed to improve efficiency through a reduction in the work-force. From 1997 to 2000, 6 million workers were laid off each year. They became the main victims of poverty in urban China.

The classification and composition of the urban poor in China has therefore changed drastically in the last twenty years. Perhaps most significant has been the explosive growth in the number of registered urban poor — up from 0.85 million in 1996 to 22.32 million in 2005 (4.1 per cent of the total urban population).[13] Today the urban poor can be classified into roughly five categories: (1) the laid-off and the unemployed (around 30 million in 2001); (2) pensioners and retirees (42 million in 2002, a thirteenfold increase since 1978); (3) landless farmers; (4) smaller groups with particular difficulties, such as ethnic minorities and impoverished students; and (5) rural migrant labourers. To understand the social and physical effects of Chinese urbanization, landless farmers and rural migrants deserve special attention.

Landless Farmers

As China's cities grow and take control of more land, villages are being absorbed into the urban fringes and rural farmers gradually become urban dwellers. New economic development zones and industrial parks create more job opportunities, but have led to the expropriation of large amounts of farmland. The construction of dams to supply water and electricity (via hydropower) to the new urban areas has also displaced many people. Over the past few decades, China has tackled the displacement of communities resulting from the boom in infrastructure building with (1) regulations to safeguard the rights of people, (2) compensation for lost assets and housing, and (3) opportunities to earn income and thereby restore or improve their livelihoods.

Land in the rural area is state-owned and allocated to rural farmers and managed by the village collective. This system allows the local government to acquire land from farmers easily and at low prices. The local governments sell the land at higher prices to property developers and they generate revenues and benefit from levying taxes on the land acquisition.[14] The profits are then invested in infrastructure that supports urban and economic development. This process has resulted in increased social conflict, with protests from farmers who demand that rural land be privatized. In theory, with the current system of land ownership there should not be any landless farmers in China. However, the official estimate for landless farmers in 2006 was 70 million,[15] with an incremental growth of 3 million per year. Rural farmlands are not being privatized, but there is talk about permitting farmers to sell their land use rights to other farmers.

China has good land acquisition regulations, procedures, and institutional mechanisms in place. But there are situations where people receive inadequate cash compensation, suffer severe loss of livelihood, and are forced to leave their hometowns to find migrant work. Thus, a large number are excluded from the benefits of the urbanization when they move to cities as migrants and are prevented from accessing various social benefits offered to other residents in the city.

Rural Migrant Labourers

In 2000, there were 175 million international migrants throughout the world. By contrast, in the same year, there were around 180 million rural migrants working in urban China.[16] Labour migration is subject to both regional and sector income inequalities.[17] Rural migrants moving to China's cities are institutionally excluded from healthcare and educational services. They are also ineligible for programmes designed to alleviate urban poverty, such as social security and housing benefits. This is because entitlement is linked to one's place of residence, as determined by the *hukou* registration system.

The category of rural migrant labourers is excluded from official urban poverty statistics, but may now represent as many as 200 million of China's citizens. The *hukou* household registration system was designed, in part, to prevent the sort of mass rural-urban migration that has led to slum formation in many developing countries. But the system has resulted in restrictions on mobility and access to opportunities for rural citizens.

ENVIRONMENTS OF THE POOR

In pre-reform China, most urban workers were connected to work units (*danwei*), which — beyond providing employment — offered housing, medical care, pensions, and education for children. Their role was to organize and manage the urban population, as "Chinese work units were also social organisations and the basic cells of the socialist urban structure,"[18] Cities were planned in accordance with socialist principles. Urban districts were designed to be largely self-sufficient.

During the first stages of the reform era, in the 1980s and early 1990s, work units remained an important part of urban development as private and foreign businesses began to compete with state-owned enterprises. In place of the self-sufficient districts created by socialist planning, cities in the reform era have developed specialized districts such as central business districts, residential zones, and high-tech parks. Socio-economic organizations in areas such as individual mobility and transportation requirements have also increased. As a result, clusters of housing based on market value, income, and status have emerged, leading to new forms of social and spatial organization and land use. City centres have been transformed from narrow alleys, traditional housing, and small shops into high-rise residential and commercial office buildings. Isolated housing estates on urban peripheries have also emerged, with few services in the immediate vicinity. The former work units on the urban periphery were redeveloped or sold to developers. Farmland bordering Chinese cities is consumed by urban expansion, leading to the phenomenon of "urban villages" (*chengzhongcun*). The traditional urban centre typically housed both government officials and professionals, alongside the urban working class. As these areas have been redeveloped to provide exclusive residential compounds and offices, residents have been relocated to apartment complexes and government-supported workers' housing. Since the 1990s, urban villages and migrant enclaves have appeared.

The diverse groups who constitute today's urban poor are concentrated into various types of neighbourhood, distinguishable by the housing: traditional, poor-quality public, urban village, and migrant. Neighbourhoods with traditional housing are generally populated by low-income urban families and migrants from the countryside. These areas were not substantially redeveloped during the early socialist period, and they often suffer from poor drainage and fewer modern conveniences, such as indoor kitchens and toilets.

Poor-quality public housing was built during the early years of socialist urban planning. During the movement to improve urban worker housing in the 1980s, the state constructed housing in the inner suburbs to maximize access to work. But to minimize cost, this high-density housing often used poor designs and low-quality materials. Due to the poor quality and lack of maintenance, "these workers' communities are now deteriorating into degraded residential areas".[19]

Urban villages (*chengzhongcun*) are a result of the co-existence of two systems of land use — urban leasing and rural collective ownership. In these villages, villagers maintain ownership of their houses and may seek to build extensions and lease rooms to migrants seeking proximity to urban jobs. Liberalization of the urban housing market allowed migrants to buy their own housing, but this is often outside the reach of those with low-paying jobs. Since migrants are excluded from the urban housing allocation system, urban villages have provided both relatively affordable housing and an income to farmers who have lost their land due to urban expansion. In Guangzhou City, researchers found that the average monthly rental price was 7 yuan per square metre, which was one-fifth to one-tenth the price of regular commercial housing. Even though the rent is low, the quality of housing is generally poor and the rooms are often shared with strangers. Privacy is limited and basic amenities, such as heating and running water, may be limited or non-existent. The potential for organized crime and social unrest within these concentrations of "outsiders" is viewed with considerable concern by municipal authorities. Such arrangements may be seen in cities across China. Within 190 km² of Xi'an, there are 187 such villages,[20] and in Guangzhou they house most of the city's 3 million migrant workers.[21] Zhejiang Village (*Zhejiangcun*) in Beijing was one of the best-known urban villages, housing over 100,000 migrants from the coastal province in 1995.

Migrant housing appears when many rural migrants seek shelter on the construction sites where they work[22] or in distant suburban areas. The Fifth Population Survey on the housing status of migrants in Pudong New District found that whereas 69 per cent of the registered local population had bought their own houses, 69 per cent of migrants rented. Migrants tend to live on the suburban fringes of cities: "in 2003, among migrants who came to Beijing from other provinces, 55.9 per cent lived in the nearby suburbs and 35 per cent in more distant districts and counties."[23] The quality of housing and space are key issues. Rooms tend to be small (45 per cent are under 8–12 m²) and shared by many migrants. A recent ADB study of four cities[24] found that 90 per cent of migrants did not have private rooms: 30.4 per cent shared a single room with two to four people, 31 per cent with five to eight people, and 20 per cent with nine or more people. Toilets are generally shared and even basic services such as heating can be scarce: 60 per cent of migrants surveyed in Lanzhou had no heating

Efforts are being made to address these housing problems for low-income and migrant populations. Chongqing administrators — who aim to increase the urban residence to 70 per cent of the overall population by 2020 — are working to prevent slum development by building low-income housing with government investment and community management. These units are accompanied by the public spaces, libraries, social networks in sports and arts and a have often initiated networking tools such as community websites. Similarly, the city of Haerbin has started experimental migrant housing schemes. These include apartments, building standards for temporary migrant housing, and a housing provident fund for migrants. These initiatives are welcome, but are often stymied by insufficient funds from local resources.

While the spatial distribution and social composition of neigh-bourhoods in urban China may have changed in response to rapid urbanization, the urban poor continue to face challenges in both their physical and social environments, which are inextricably linked. The challenge for local communities and municipal authorities is to remove the social, institutional, physical, and financial barriers to social inclusion.

CHALLENGES FACED BY THE URBAN POOR

The implementation of the *hukou* registration system has facilitated the physical and social management of urbanization, allowing cities to develop without slums of the sort found in many other parts of the world. This is a great achievement, but not without social costs. The creation of new urban spaces has been accompanied by environmental degradation and new forms of social exclusion. The challenges faced by the Chinese urban poor extend beyond their physical environment to include access to services, the provision of welfare support, and the creation of sustainable urban communities in rapidly developing cities with constantly circulating populations of migrant workers.

Physical Challenges

China is now home to sixteen of the world's twenty most-polluted cities.[25] Reliance on dirty coal-powered energy supply has led to rising rates of cancer and respiratory diseases and acid rain falling on one-third of China's agricultural land. The problem of air pollution is compounded by pro-growth municipal planning. Urban expansion into farmland reduces green cover and leads to urban heat islands, causing higher ambient temperatures within cities and a greater demand for energy.

Untreated waste and water shortages — which affect two-thirds of China's cities, one-sixth critically — are constantly encountered. Sixty per cent of China's cities are located along the densely populated eastern and southern coastal provinces, where both agricultural and industrial production is concentrated in areas less than 2 metres above sea level (which is rising by 2–3 mm per year). Along these coasts, the increasing incidence of tropical storms and flooding has led to salinization of water supplies, reduced industrial output, and damage to infrastructure, such as harbours and airports. While these environmental factors affect all of the population in urban areas, important research still needs to be undertaken to identify the specific differential effects and risks of environmental degradation on the urban poor.

In August 2010, China's National Development and Reform Commission launched a pilot project that began the implementation of a low-carbon development strategy.[26] This project aims to restructure industry in a way that results in lower carbon emissions. The means are incentives and guidance that promote low-carbon lifestyles and consumption. This is part of China's efforts to tackle the causes and effects of climate change.[27] While understanding climate change and perceiving its risks remains low among the Chinese population,[28] there is an increasing consensus that future urbanization must incorporate both environmental and social concerns.

Social Challenges

The implementation of the *hukou* household registration system limited rural-urban migration and slum formation by restricting people to their places of birth. Paradoxically, the very populations who have initiated and sustained industrial growth and urban expansion are those most vulnerable to the environmental and social risks of such development. While the physical environment of the urban poor has been improving in recent years, the political architecture necessary to ensure social inclusion, the strengthening of social networks, and the provision of social protection has not kept pace with demographic changes. In particular, the *hukou* household registration system's distinction between rural and urban citizens creates and perpetuates social exclusion in urban areas. There are now many initiatives underway to modify the *hukou* system and expand both the coverage and portability of different forms of social assistance. The central authorities are seeking new models for the targeting and provision of social protection; but implementation will require support, resourcing, collaboration, and enforcement from national government.

FROM HOUSING TO LIVEABLE CITIES

A major challenge in developing liveable cities is to address environmental degradation and social exclusion. Under the 12th Five Year Plan, China plans to build 10 million low-cost housing units by 2011 and about 36 million by 2015. The government made RMB1.3 trillion available for this purpose in 2011. In March 2010, the Ministry of Land Resources stated that no less than 70 per cent of the supply of new land should be dedicated to the construction of this housing. Urban land sales in China form a large portion of the revenue for local governments. The supply of land for the construction of low-cost housing and financing is a challenge. Cost-sharing arrangements between local government and developers are complicated: local are is expected to bear a large part of the construction cost as subsidies for developers. Today, cities such as Chongqing — one of the largest and fastest-growing in the nation — recognize the benefits of adopting environmental measures such as incorporating green space into urban planning and social measures such as creating low-cost housing targeting migrants.

There is a tremendous potential for China to ensure long-term sustainability by combining economic growth with responsible environmental stewardship and inclusive social policies. There is an increasing appreciation within Chinese literature of the need to foster a more balanced approach to urbanization. While economic growth remains central to poverty alleviation and national development, Chinese and other scholars stress the importance of achieving a balance between environmental protection, social inclusion, and the growth of cities. Physical and financial constraints pose serious challenges to creating liveable and inclusive cities capable of addressing the growing social vulnerabilities of the urban poor.

Notes

1. National Bureau of Statistics of China (2009).
2. Ibid., p. 6.
3. McKinsey Global Institute (2009), p. 61.
4. UN Habitat, "State of the World's Cities 2010", p. 39.
5. Wang (2004), p. 25
6. Zhou (2010).
7. Three types of city administration are recognized in China: Municipality (e.g. Shanghai, Beijing); Prefecture-level City (governed by the province or autonomous region); County-level City (sub-unit of a prefecture-level administrative division). Small cities are generally defined as cities with non-agricultural populations under 100,000 living in urbanized areas. Townships are defined as: (a) areas hosting a county-level government; (b) a township of fewer than 20,000 people and 2,000 or more of whom are not working in agriculture; or (c) a township with more than 20,000 people and more than 10 per cent of the population not engaged in agriculture; or (d) if in a remote area, mountainous area, small-sized mining area, small harbour, tourism area, a settlement with fewer than 2,000 people employed in non-agricultural work may also be approved as a town.
8. Li (2010).
9. Xinhua (2010).
10. Jun (2010).
11. Ibid.
12. Wang (2004), p. 56.
13. Shunfeng et al. (2009).
14. *Global Times* (2010).
15. Bajoria (2008).
16. Murphy (2009).
17. Ibid.
18. Wang (2004).
19. Liu and Wu (2006).

20. Wang (2004).
21. Liu et al. (2010).
22. 45 million rural labourers work on China's urban construction projects and usually live in temporary onsite dormitories
23. ADB (2008), p. 100.
24. Beijing, Nanjing, Guangzhou, and Lanzhou.
25. Blacksmith Institute (2007).
26. The five provinces are Guangdong, Liaoning, Hubei, Shaanxi, and Yunnan; the eight cities are Tianjin, Chongqing, Shenzhen, Xiamen, Hangzhou, Nanchang, Guiyang, and Baoding.
27. People's Daily (2010).
28. Pugliese and Ray (2009).

References

ADB. *TA 4964: Urban Poverty Strategy II Final Report*. Manila: Asian Development Bank, 2008.

Bajoria, Jayshree. "China's Land Reform Challenge". 10 March 2008. Council on Foreign Relations <http://www.cfr.org/publication/15699/chinas_land_reform_challenge.html>.

Blacksmith Institute. The World's Worst Polluted Places. 12 September 2007 <http://www.worstpolluted.org/reports/file/2007%20Report%20updated%202009.pdf>.

Global Times. "China Plans to Make Law on Collective Land Acquisition". 18 September 2010 <http://www.china.org.cn/china/2010-09/18/content_20959732.htm>.

Jun, Han. "Study on Social Service Delivery in Rapid Urbanization of the People's Republic of China". ADB working paper (unpublished), 2010.

Li, Tie. "Urban Development Strategy in the People's Republic of China". Paper presented in Senior Level Workshop for the 12th Five-Year Plan of the PRC. Beijing, 20 April 2010.

Liu, Yuting, and Fulong Wu. "Urban Poverty Neighbourhoods: Typology and Spatial Concentration Under China's Market Transition, a Case Study of Nanjing". *Geoforum* 37, no. 4 (July 2006): 610–26.

Liu, Yuting, Shenjing He, Fulong Wu, and Chris Webster. "Urban Villages Under China's Rapid Urbanization: Unregulated Assets and Transitional Neighbourhoods". *Habitat International* 34, no. 2 (April 2010): 135–44.

McKinsey Global Institute. "Preparing for China's Urban Billion". March 2009 <http://www.mckinsey.com/mgi/publications/china_urban_billion/>.

Murphy, Rachel, ed. *Labour Migration and Social Development in Contemporary China*. Comparative Development and Policy in Asia series. London: Routledge, 2009.

National Bureau of Statistics of China. 2009. "China Statistical Yearbook 2009" <http://www.stats.gov.cn/tjsj/ndsj/2009/indexeh.htm>.

People's Daily. "China Launches Low-Carbon Pilot in Select Cities, Provinces". 19 August 2009 <http://english.peopledaily.com.cn/90001/90778/90862/7 110049.html>.

Pugliese, Anita, and Julie Ray. "Top-Emitting Countries Differ on Climate Change Threat". 7 December 2009 <http://www.gallup.com/poll/124595/ top-emitting-countries-differ-climate-change-threat.aspx>.

Shunfeng Song, Erqian Zhu, and Sankar Mukhopadhyay. "Urban Poor in China". *Chinese Economy* 42, no. 4 (July 2009): 44–62.

UN Habitat. "State of the World's Cities 2010/2011 — Cities for All: Bridging the Urban Divide". 2010 <http://www.unhabitat.org/pmss/listItemDetails. aspx?publicationID=2917>.

Wang, Ya Ping. *Urban Poverty, Housing, and Social Change in China*. London: Routledge, 2004.

Xinhua. "China's Population to Near 1.4 Billion by 2015". *China Daily*, 4 July 2010.

Zhou, Yixing. *Urbanization in the People Republic of China* [sic]. Peking University, 8 December 2009.

5

BENEFITING THE POOR, THE ENVIRONMENT, AND THE PRIVATE SECTOR WITH SMALL ENTERPRISES AND GREEN JOBS IN THE PEOPLE'S REPUBLIC OF CHINA

Satoshi Sasaki

China is shifting its development policy towards creating a low-carbon economy and a more equitable society, departing from the rapid economic growth policy started by Deng Xiaoping three decades ago. Drastic changes in production and consumption are required to make development responsive to climate change and environmental degradation. Environmental protection and a transition to a low-carbon economy are imperatives with no leeway for China. In the coming decades, government departments will have to adopt new laws and regulations that guide changes in industry and the lives of the Chinese people. Efforts have been made in many companies to make their production processes and services greener. Green enterprises already exist and their number is increasing.

However, are the poor left behind in the transition process? Green jobs can benefit the environment as well as the worker. As most of the poor who are employed work for micro and small enterprises, it is critical to promote micro and small enterprises in a green economy, if the greening process is to be pro-poor. Also, it is likely that small businesses could provide green products and services for the poor and contribute to the local economic development. Green small enterprises would be promoted effectively if the economic, environmental, and social aspects of sustainable development are integrated.

It is a crucial concern of the International Labour Organization (ILO) to make the transition to a green economy by ensuring that the new jobs created in green enterprises are decent and socially acceptable. For the last two years, the ILO has been introducing the concept of green jobs to its three constituents — government, worker, and employer organizations — in China, and alerting them to the changes that will be coming in the world of work. At the same time, the ILO has tried to create new employment opportunities in emerging green industries. The ILO has been promoting the Green Jobs Initiative, which supports the process of a just transition for the workers who are affected by the ongoing changes in the green economy. It also supports the creation of enabling environment for green businesses to grow in.

The ILO also has an entrepreneurship training programme in China called Green Business Options (GBO). It explores the potential of individuals who intend to take advantage of the business development opportunities of the green economy. Since the GBO pilot programme officially started only in March 2010, it is too early to evaluate its effectiveness in creating small green businesses. But the green business ideas developed by the students who have participated in the GBO pilot training in Chengdu suggest there is ample possibility for micro enterprises to capture emerging green markets and employ more people as business expands. This essay reviews the 2010 pilot training programme of GBO and summarizes the experiences to date. Based on the findings from the pilot programme and the ILO's experiences in micro and small enterprise development in China, suggestions are made for the development of future projects involving the private sector in the promotion of environment protection and a just and pro-poor transition to a low-carbon economy.

GREEN JOBS INITIATIVE IN CHINA

During the 11th Five-Year Plan period (2006–10), the Chinese government promoted the concept of "harmonious society". It aimed to reduce gaps in wealth and services between regions and individuals, which had increased of recent. Recent discussions on the formulation of the 12th Five-Year Plan (2011–15) have focused more on the transformation of growth patterns leading to better economic prospects in the long run. The Government work report for 2010 highlighted *sound* development rather than *fast* development for the first time.[1] While maintaining relatively high economic growth, the Communist Party of China (CPC) committed itself to increasing its efforts to save energy and resources and build an environmentally friendly society.

However, there is no complete analysis or projection of green jobs in China. The ILO and the China Academy of Social Sciences organized a study in 2009, trying to estimate the potential green jobs in selected sectors.[2]

The figures in Table 5.1 show huge employment gains expected in forestry and power sectors, while net employment loss is seen in iron and steel industries. The result of the study suggests that the Green Jobs Initiative should support the emerging green industries. At the same time it is important to take care of the workers who will lose their jobs.

Retrofitting buildings saves energy, reduces emissions, and protects the environment and natural resources. It creates many job opportunities due to the labour-intensive nature of the work. If one-third of the 42 billion square metres of existing buildings in China were to be retrofitted at RMB200 per square metre, there would be a market potential of RMB2.6 trillion. In 2009, building energy efficiency retrofits can create 12.6 million jobs.[3]

In the meantime, ILO's promotion of green jobs has been conducive to the creation of sustainable enterprises in three ways:

(1) In terms of job creation, the ILO supports its country constituent's development of enterprises that solve climate and environmental problems through the market mechanism. Particularly, stronger focus should be put on developing micro, small and medium-sized enterprises. It is these enterprises that create most employment opportunities, including for migrant

TABLE 5.1
Total Employment Effects of Low-carbon Development in Major Sectors in China
(1,000 jobs)

Sectors	Sub-sectors	Direct Employment	Indirect Employment	Sub-total
Forestry (2005–2020)	Afforestation & Reforestation	7,600	11,085	18,685
	Sustainable Forest Management	188	61	249
	Forest Tourism	3,154	3,616	6,770
Power Industry (2005–2020)	Thermal Power	251	29	279
	Wind Power	848	2309	3,157
	Solar Power	50	1,237	1,287
Core Industry	Iron and Steel (2007~2011)	−200	—	−200
Green investment (2008~2011)[a]		175	357	532
Total[b]				30,759

Notes: (a) Part of investment made through 4 trillion yuan stimulus package after the financial crisis in 2008.

(b) Here the simple measurement of sum total is only for reference. Similarly data comparison on sectors like forestry and iron and steel are indicative and should only indicate different methodology and data resources. Furthermore, some of the employment data in this table is average value.

workers. Efforts should be made to promote sustainable enterprises by:

- nurturing entrepreneurship,
- coping with the increasing needs for skilled workers,
- improving the business environment, and
- providing financial support for the entrepreneurs to start and expand their businesses.

(2) Many green businesses already exist in China, but workers in these businesses are not always well protected. For example, toxic chemicals used in e-waste recycling are harmful to workers if they do not have protection gear or ventilation. Many such jobs in small enterprises are held by migrant workers who have limited

health and injury insurance. Irregular or delayed payment and a lack of dialogue between employers and workers are common in these enterprises. The ILO green jobs programmes will foster the Decent Work Agenda,[4] which will pursue not just any kind of employment, but better quality employment that is protected and sustainable.

(3) The promotion of environment protection and a low-carbon economy requires changes in industrial structures and their process of operation. Some industries that cause pollution have been forced to close by government order. This has happened to small coal mines that produce low-grade coal and contribute to air pollution. These small coal mines also have hazardous working conditions for the mine workers. Several thousand miners are killed every year. Workers who lose jobs in such enterprises have to find alternative jobs. But apparently, emerging green industries do not exist where brown enterprises are closed down. Also, the skills of workers from closed enterprises are not compatible with the new jobs created in green industries. The ILO copes with the transition needs of workers from brown industries and minimizes the effect of an industry by supporting government efforts to provide them with social security[5] and the opportunity to gain new skills.

Though no official guidelines have been established by the Ministry of Human Resources and Social Security (MOHRSS) on the employment aspects of developing green economy in China, the August 2010 speech by Zhang Xiaojian, Vice Minister, MOHRSS, well summarized the current view of the Ministry on the promotion of green jobs as part of employment promotion in China.[6] He made five main points:

- Eliminate "backward production capacity"[7] and create new employment opportunities through public employment services[8] in forest protection, sand prevention, energy-saving activities, and renewable energy;
- Take measures against job loss; for example, re-employ laid-off workers and unemployed persons. Also improve the social security system to mitigate unemployment risks;
- Train workers for skills needed for green economy;

- Promote green small enterprises: encourage business start-ups in priority industries, such as those with "comprehensive resource utilization";[9]
- Conduct research in support of green employment policy formulation.

He also emphasized the importance of coordination between employment, environmental, and industrial policies.

Based on the Employment Promotion Law established in 2008, MOHRSS is in the process of developing the Guiding Opinions for Promoting Green Jobs. This policy guidance will explain how to adapt employment services at the local level and facilitate a green economy at provincial and municipal levels. It could also be used by MOHRSS as a position paper to show how the ministry would promote a transition to a green economy at the national level.

GREEN BUSINESS OPTIONS TRAINING

Objectives

The idea of Green Business Options (GBO) training was conceived as part of the Millennium Development Goal Achievement Fund Programme on Climate Change in 2008.[10] It addresses the need for small enterprises and self-employed people to grasp business opportunities in environmental protection and reduction of greenhouse gas emissions. The programme became the first opportunity for the ILO to introduce the concept of green jobs in the transition to a low-carbon economy in China. GBO is a training tool for sustainable enterprise development, embodying the three pillars of development, namely, business development (economic), job creation (social), and environmental protection (environmental). It has been developed based on the national entrepreneurship training platform owned and operated by the Ministry of Human Resources and Social Security (MOHRSS).

Small and medium-sized enterprises (SMEs) provide 80 per cent of the employment in Chinese cities.[11] The economic and social stability of China largely depends on the capacity of SMEs, in particular small enterprises, to absorb the labour force and make economic growth conducive for the poor to increase their income level and thus improve their livelihood conditions. It is of strategic importance for the government to support small enterprises in exploring emerging business opportunities in the transition to a low-carbon economy. The ILO decided to develop a new entrepreneurship training programme that supports entrepreneurs in developing business ideas for climate change adaptation and environmental protection.

After the pre-testing of the training materials in 2009, eleven institutions organized the first pilot training from March to June 2010. The second pilot training began in August 2010 in Jiangsu Province and the city of Chongqing.[12]

Many entrepreneurs and potential entrepreneurs understand there are different kinds of environmental problems in China, but few of them view the problems as business opportunities. GBO training intends to provide entrepreneurs with a big picture of climate change and environmental issues with tools to analyse emerging green markets and help them develop new business ideas.

The contributions of green jobs towards the realization of a low-carbon economy could be made mainly in the following areas:

- Supplying the skilled people needed to start green businesses, that is building the skills of workers to facilitate the existing enterprises' transition to a cleaner and low carbon production system.
- Protecting workers in green businesses by maintaining occupational safety and health standards.
- Helping workers in enterprises closing due to the environmental protection find new jobs in other sectors.

GBO contributes to the first point.

Training Programmes

For the last thirty years the ILO has run a programme worldwide for training people on how to start a business and how to manage its development, called Start and Improve Your Business (SIYB). It has four sections, for different stages of enterprise development: Generate Your Business Ideas (GYB), Start Your Business (SYB), Improve Your Business (IYB), and Expand Your Business (EYB). GBO training programme was developed using GYB as the platform to accommodate climate change and environmental issues. It explains new business opportunities in climate change and environmental issues and leads the learners to come up with their own business ideas.

GBO is designed as learner-centred participatory training, using case studies, brain storming, and small-group discussions. The size of a GBO class is limited to twenty. It takes three to four days to complete the course.

GBO was initially designed for young people, especially university students and recent graduates who are thinking of going into business as a career option. It was expected that those students and graduates who already have scientific knowledge and skills might have better prospects in environment-related businesses. When the pilot training programme was launched, it was found that private business owners who are thinking of expanding their businesses also showed high interest in GBO training.

At present, GBO is still suitable for people who are thinking of starting businesses in climate change adaptation and environmental protection, although existing entrepreneurs are not excluded.

The initial idea of GBO was to make it generic training, not addressing issues of specific sectors. There are advantages to this, from the view point of enterprise development:

- The very nature of GBO is as a means for trainees to create unique business ideas. The selection of specific economic sectors in training may cause a number of people to end up with similar business ideas.
- GBO should be an opportunity for trainees to learn about business possibilities in various green sectors. This is particularly important for students and recent graduates who do not currently own businesses to find the sectors that they could use their knowledge and skills in.

Unlike students and graduates, existing entrepreneurs who wish to expand their businesses need more information that is more specific to the sectors they may explore. To meet their needs, GBO training has developed two resource books, on "circular economy" and energy conservation. Resource books will be written about other green sectors to meet trainees' varied needs for information. Resource books will be adopted in GBO training courses on a case-by-case basis.

Training Management

The development of GBO training is largely based on the SIYB entre-prenurship training programme. In 2001, MOHRSS became the first to adopt the SIYB training programme in China. It did so as a way of facilitating alternative employment opportunities for self-employment and small-enterprise development, particularly for people having difficulty in finding jobs (laid-off workers, migrant workers, graduates, people with disabilities, retired military personnel, etc.). The SIYB programme has expanded through the national network of vocational training institutions and certified SIYB trainers nationwide. The SIYB programme has been given a solid legal foundation by the Employment Promotion Law of 2008. The SIYB network has been administered by the China Employment Training Technical Instruction Center (CETTIC) under MOHRSS. It has 142 master trainers and 18,900 regular trainers around the country.[13]

Based on the results expected from the ongoing pilot training in Jiangsu and Chongqing, GBO training is expected to be extended to the whole country using SIYB training as a platform. High participation is expected for GBO training in cities that are facing environmental problems and in old industrial bases in the northeastern provinces. The latter are required to develop alternative economic development strategies.

Since it can use the extensive network of SIYB training institutions and trainers as the platform for rolling out GBO training, ILO has been able to concentrate on training SIYB trainers to be GBO trainers. Typically, it takes one week for the trainer trainees to understand the technical material and engage in micro-teaching sessions that allow them to demonstrate their ability to organize GBO sessions. Currently, the ILO Beijing Office has two GBO master trainers who have been involved in the development of GBO training. MOHRSS and the ILO expect to develop a core team of GBO master trainers in the next two years.

Initial Achievements of Pilot Training

Some of the those who took the GBO pilot training in 2010 have started their own businesses in various areas of the green economy. Two cases are presented below.

The Chengdu Vocational and Technical College is one of eleven training institutions where the ILO tested GBO in April 2010. The college has 41 majors and 10,000 students. The students from various majors participated in the GBO pilot training, allowing them to use their own skills and experiences in creating green business ideas.

Some of the twenty participants came up with practical green business ideas and are now developing new businesses on a small scale. For example, the ideas include:

- Energy efficiency in school lighting
- A/C adapter for multiple purposes
- Stuff toys produced from used children's clothes
- Rental bicycle
- Eco-tour

The college, through its Entrepreneurship Department, encourages students to consider starting a business as part of a career option. Students can apply for financial support to test their business ideas and be given a small space for incubating their business. The college also works closely with the local enterprise association, connecting students' activities with a network of local enterprises.

ENERGY EFFICIENCY THROUGH LED AND ELECTRICITY CONTROL DEVICE[14]

Yang Shunbo is a third-year electronics major at Chengdu Vocational and Technical College. He participated in the GBO pilot training in April 2010. The business idea he developed was to provide a service of replacing electric bulbs with light-emitting diodes (LEDs) and installing a small controller that he developed to further reduce electricity use. He found that many electric bulbs are used in the college, an average of thirteen bulbs per lecture room. In addition, he had an idea of adding a small electricity control device that minimized the electricity consumed. Since he was studying electronics, he was confident that he could develop such a device by himself. When participating in GBO training, he confirmed that his idea conformed to the government policy of reducing energy use in the maintenance of school buildings.

Obviously, his idea could be applied beyond lighting schools, but he decided to test it in his school first. He established the Yu Chen Cheng Electronic Technology Company with two other students. The Chengdu Vocational and Technical College supported his business plan and provided 5,000 yuan for the project. With this he entered into a contract with the college to install 100 LEDs. The contract allowed him to share in the college's savings from the reduction of the electricity use. He has now developed the electricity controlling device. With his colleagues, he is now producing 1,000 units, which will add profit to his business and further reduce the energy consumption in school lighting.

Yang is expecting graduation in 2012. He is thinking of continuing and expanding his business to other areas. In his business plan, his primary target is colleges and universities, which have similar needs for energy reduction. He is also thinking of expanding to interior illumination, pedestrian lights, and street advertisement equipment in large cities. He is also looking into similar needs in the rural areas. He expects to consolidate his business in the first five years, improve his technology, and expand to southwest China in the next ten years.

Selling Used Books in the Universities of Nanjing[15]

Often called China's third city of science and education after Beijing and Shanghai, Nanjing, with over 700,000 college students on campus, has a variety of schools of higher education and research institutes. The Xianlin University Town section of Nanjing is home to many universities and a total of 180,000 students. According to the 2009 Report on the Work of the Nanjing Municipal Government, the city will be made low carbon, green, and intellectual. All people are encouraged to actively lower their consumption of carbon in the process of the transformation of the industrial structure.

In April 2010, Fan Songwei attended a GBO training course. Afterwards, he found in a consumer behavior survey of college students that they consume an enormous number of books each year. As 18 million twenty- to forty-year-old trees are annually consumed for textbooks in China, the country is the world's largest pulp importer with its college students consuming over 35 kg of paper per student during their college education. As more than 6 million college students graduate each year, they throw away used textbooks which were originally worth 720 million yuan. If twenty used books were recycled, a fifteen-year-old tree could be saved from being felled. Therefore, Fan came up with the idea of recycling second-hand books by selling them. He registered Jiangsu NUC Renewable Resources Co. Ltd.

Every year when they leave school, college graduates have to decide whether to sell their used books for scrap or just put them on bookshelves at home. Eighty per cent choose to scrap them, gradually forming a simple second-hand book market. As the buyers are mostly scrap collectors, their value as books is wasted. For a university town with over 180,000 registered students, this waste is huge. The books undergraduates have are not enough to satisfy their needs. Although some may buy books, borrow from the library, or download them from the Internet, it is either expensive or inconvenient. Therefore, Jiangsu NUC is going to open a market for the purchase and sale of second-hand books — and at the same time promote academic and cultural exchange between college students.

The NUC entrepreneurial team aims to build a large-scale, professional platform for second-hand book exchange by college students themselves. By establishing inter-collegiate alliances and a network of second-hand book distributors, market segmentation supplemented with excellent cultural exchange services can be achieved, and then second-hand books can be recycled and reused. A green business is formed.

Based on an analysis of the relevant information gathered, the NUC team came to the conclusion that 2,000 to 3,000 tons of books are sold for scrap each year by graduates inside the Xianlin University Town, among which 30 per cent to 50 per cent can be sold as second-hand books. If half of them can be recycled, over 3 million copies can be circulated among colleges, enough to satisfy the entire University Town's annual demand for secondhand books.

After recycling scores of tons of used books in June 2010, Jiangsu NUC classified them into top-quality, average, and partially defective, and then priced them (except completely defective books) for sale as second-hand books. There is not much difference between a new book and a "top-quality" second-hand book but the price of new books is several times higher. "Average" second-hand books are specialized books and those used in preparation for examinations for various certificates. Commonly used second-hand textbooks are labelled as "partially defective". They can be offered to various majors for reference. "Completely defective" are sold as waste paper. What Jiangsu NUC is doing has had a huge repercussion in colleges. As there is a huge demand for second-hand books among college students, the young company has achieved much more profits than they would have with traditional second-hand book recycling.

Jiangsu NUC now has an office at the practice centre for entrepreneurship of the Nanjing College and Information Technology. It will develop the business-to-consumer interactive platform. In the second half of 2010, the company will invest 100,000 yuan to build the office at the University Town into an exemplar platform and the largest second-hand bookstore in the town, with storage of 50,000 copies of top-quality second-hand books. In the second half of 2011, the company will continue to build up its storage and expand its services to all the colleges in Nanjing. On this basis, NUC will invest to expand its business and carry out a nationwide growth strategy.

Operating for half a year, Jiangsu NUC Renewable Resources Co., Ltd. has won substantial support for the project. It has also encountered problems, such as conflict with the textbook purchase-and-management system of each college and competition from the traditional recycling companies. These problems put higher demands on college students' entrepreneurial teams in the innovation of business model.

Lessons Learned

Green sectors suitable for micro and small enterprise development

GBO training aims to create an enabling environment for micro and small businesses to participate in green businesses. The case of Yang Shunbo's energy saving project showed the potential of individuals to use their own technical skills and develop new green businesses. Obviously they are at a disadvantage compared to the large enterprises, which have strong research and development and financial capacities. However, there are niche green markets for micro entrepreneurs to explore, such as 3R (reduce, reuse, recycle), eco-tourism, and organic agriculture and building, none of which are capital intensive. What is important for GBO is to allow the participants to think flexibly in creating unique business ideas.

Make products and services available to the poor

In the business case of A/C adapter for multiple purposes, the student who produced it sold 160 pieces in ten days through the Taobao,[16] which is a popular auction service on the Internet in China. This case suggests the high potential of using the Internet as a platform for small businesses to penetrate without major investment in the markets where the poor participate. More than 400 million people have access to the Internet and more than 800 million mobile phones are used in China.

In case of Fan Songwei in Nanjing, a small business indicated the huge potential to benefit consumers, students in that case, by providing them with a new service that saves them money, at the same time reducing paper consumption. Fan is considering using the Internet as the business-to-consumer platform for expanding his business nationwide.

Increase knowledge

The obstacle to green business development by micro and small enterprises is the lack of understanding of the potential markets created by climate change and environmental problems. People tend to think of climate change as something beyond their control and have nothing to do with the life of ordinary people. There has not been anything like GBO to provide them with systematic and understandable information about climate change and environmental protection.

In some cases, participants in pilot training wanted to have more specific information about the sectors that they were interested in exploring. Given the non-sector specific approach of GBO, it is necessary to strengthen sector information in the training and follow-up services. This can be done by supplying additional informational materials and linking them to public and private agencies involved in the development of the specific sector. For example, the pollution of Taihe Lake is a major concern for the city of Wuxi. The city government has been supporting GBO strongly and looking forward to the private sector's contribution to solving water pollution problems.

Training needs of existing entrepreneurs

The primary target group of GBO training is students and graduates. Given the low employment of graduates from tertiary education — 67 per cent after graduation in 2009 — GBO was expected to serve the dual purposes of helping the young unemployed to use their skills and knowledge to create green businesses. But once the GBO pilot training was launched, the local training institutions found high training needs among existing entrepreneurs, who were thinking of expanding into green business, capitalizing on their technological advantages and adding new value to their products and services.

In order to make a just transition to a low-carbon economy, it is important that the existing enterprises explore new green markets, and at the same time make their existing services and production processes greener. More green jobs will be secured by doing so.

Existing entrepreneurs need training in more strategic thinking required for management, which goes beyond the capacity of GBO training. The Global SIYB Programme of the ILO is now considering developing a training programme that provides these training needs of entrepreneurs.

Protection of intellectual property rights

Due to the small scale of business operations, GBO trainees who turned out to be entrepreneurs are not yet sure about their business potential. This is why they have not thought about asserting intellectual property rights. For example, the electricity controller developed by Yang of the Chengdu Vocational and Technology College could be a core product for his business. But such a valuable device could be easily imitated by others, unless proper protection is provided for his invention. GBO training may need to add information about how entrepreneurs can protect their intellectual property. Also, it would be a good idea for training institutions and schools that provide business incubation services to GBO trainees to support them in this respect.

Training needs of local government

Through the pilot testing of the GBO training programmes, local governments in various parts of the country expressed a need for GBO training. In order to implement the 12th Five-Year Plan (2011–15), the central government will be requiring local governments to adopt strong measures for solving environmental problems and closing the gap between the rich and the poor. Typical interests expressed by local governments are:

- Training private businesses to solve environmental problems that a city or county is facing, especially water pollution.
- Adopting GBO as a tool to promote environmental protection, in conjunction with officially declaring a "low carbon city".
- Looking for alternative industries in old industrial bases, typically in the northeastern part of the country.

Many of the representatives of cities mentioned the need for increasing the capacity of local training institutions to organize GBO training. They would like to have their own SIYB trainers retrained as GBO trainers. It would be necessary for MOHRSS to make a systematic survey of local government needs for GBO.

SUGGESTIONS FOR PROJECT DESIGN: DEVELOP MORE INCLUSIVE GREEN BUSINESSES

The suggestions made below should be taken into consideration when policy makers develop a project to promote private sector approaches towards pro-poor green economic development. In particular, steps should be taken to create an environment that enables micro and small enterprises to explore green business markets and create employment opportunties for the poor.

Integrated Approach to Sustainable Small-Enterprise Development

The experiences from GBO pilot training indicate the potential for micro and small enterprises taking part in the development of a green economy. Small enterprises could create new employment opportunities, including some that make it possible for the poor to participate in green business. At the same time, small enterprises are likely to make it possible for the poor to be consumers of green products and services.

If a project that promotes green small business is to stop poor workers from becoming more deprived than they already are, its design should have not just economic and environmental dimensions, but also social. The social dimension of sustainable development covers poverty reduction, working conditions, and occupational safety. As this dimension is often neglected, special care should be taken to make sure it is integrated in the promotion of green businesses.

Value Chains Analysis as a Tool to Find Niche Markets Through Upward Connections for Small Enterprises

The indirect effects of employment creation should not be neglected in designing a project. Green businesses cannot exist by themselves. They are connected to other businesses in the local economy. To make the project pro-poor, it is useful to apply Value Chain Analysis (VCA) to identify how the green products and services are produced and consumed and how they could be connected to other businesses and support services. VCA provides an analysis of the participation of stakeholders in the production and marketing of selected products and services. Through VCA, the project may identify opportunities to create new jobs not only in the particular green businesses but also in the businesses connected to them.

Incentives to Create Green Business Markets

The natural demand for green products and services may not be strong enough to allow green businesses to expand in the short term. For example, it takes years to come to the break-even point in replacing fluorescent lights with LEDs, while the initial investment required makes consumers reluctant to buy LEDs. For green enterprises to be able to leapfrog into a low-carbon economy, policy incentives, including financial support and tax reduction, should be available for green entrepreneurs and consumers.

Knowledge Development and Information Dissemination

The poor lack access to information about global trends towards a low-carbon economy. What does environmental protection mean for them, and what are the economic opportunities emerging around them? Education and training should play a key role in this respect. GBO is an example of providing potential micro entrepreneurs and potential self-employed persons with systematic understanding of the green economy and ways to explore business opportunities in it. Given the proliferation of mass media and Internet connections, social media marketing methods for information dissemination to the poor should be considered as an option for knowledge development on green businesses.

Notes

1. "Charting China's New Course". *Beijing Review*, 28 October 2010.
2. Study on Low Carbon Development and Green Employment in China, conducted under the MDG Achievement Fund Programme on Climate Change (March 2010).
3. Information provided by Dr Kevin Mo in the Green Jobs Consultation Meeting organized by the ILO in Beijing on 20 March 2010.
4. The ILO's organizational principles established by Juan Somavia, Director General, and supported by tripartite constituents of the ILO.
5. Convention No. 102 of the International Labour Standards includes following nine branches of social security: medical care; sickness benefit; unemployment benefit; old-age benefit; employment injury benefit; family benefit; maternity benefit; invalidity benefit; and survivors' benefit.
6. The speech was made in the Forum of Green Jobs for a Better Life, organized by the ILO at the Shanghai Expo in August 2010.
7. This term "backward production capacity" is often used by Chinese leaders to represent the characteristics of informal and small enterprises which operate out-of-date production facilities and not applying standard management system.
8. At city/county level, the local employment service centres provide jobseekers with job vacancy information and access to vocational skills training. Also, it provides the unemployed with unemployment benefits.
9. "Comprehensive resource utilization" often refers to enterprises that adopt the three Rs (reduce, reuse, recycle) in their production and services.

10. A technical Cooperation Project funded by the Government of Spain, implemented from 2008 to 2010. It is a UN interagency project, participated by ten UN agencies in China. In this project, the ILO focused on green jobs.
11. "Smaller firms to benefit from new definition of SMEs", Chinadaily.com, 27 October 2010.
12. The ILO and MOHRSS agreed the GBO pilot programme, supporting four cities in Jiangsu and Chongqing to organize training of trainers (TOTs) and training of entrepreneurs (TOEs).
13. Information updated by MOHRSS in October 2010.
14. Information collected by the author in October 2010.
15. A case study reported by a GBO trainer in Nangjing in November 2010.
16. Taobao at <www.taobao.com>.

References

Beijing Review. "Charting China's new course". 28 October 2010 <www.bjreview. com>.

International Labour Organization (ILO). "Conclusions concerning the promotion of sustainable enterprises". International Labour Conference, June 2007.

———. "Report on Forum of Green Jobs for a Better Life". Unpublished internal document, 2010.

———. "Green Business Options Training Book". Unpublished, 2010.

Research Center for Sustainable Development, Chinese Academy of Social Sciences. *Study on low carbon development and green employment in China*, 2010.

UNEP, ILO, IOE, ITUC, Green Jobs Initiative. *Green Jobs: Towards decent work in a sustainable, low-carbon world*. World Watch Institute, 2008.

Wang Weiguang and Zheng Guoguang. *Annual Report on Climate Change Actions 2009* (in Chinese). Beijing: Social Science Academic Press, 2010.

6

ENVIRONMENT, ECONOMIC GROWTH, AND POVERTY IN THE REPUBLIC OF KOREA

Yong-Seong Kim

If environment affects poverty, it is primarily via economic growth. Therefore, it is necessary to investigate how environment affects economic growth. My interest is to find a way to have the environment, economic growth, and poverty reduction interact in a way that results in "pro-poor green growth". In the first section, I briefly review the relationship between economic growth and poverty. Previous studies and experiences from Korea are introduced. In the second section, I investigate the relationship between the environment and economic growth using empirical findings and a theoretical model. The aim of that section is to find a way that the environment and economic growth can get along. I also deal with the relationship between economic growth and inequality. The poverty rate depends on the nature of economic growth. The third section is about government roles in making growth green and poverty-reducing. It reviews findings from the empirical literature and presents conclusions drawn from the experiences of the

Organization for Economic Co-operation and Development. The fourth
section concludes the essay.

ECONOMIC GROWTH AND POVERTY

At the Millennium Summit in 2000, world leaders adopted eight
goals (the Millennium Development Goals, or MDGs). Reducing
poverty and hunger and ensuring environmental sustainability were
among them. Policy makers and scholars search for ways to achieve
economic growth that is "sustainable" and "pro-poor". What is pro-
poor growth? To answer this question, let us look at Figure 6.1. The
figure plots several cases of GDP growth rate and the growth rate
of poor people's income. A possible definition of pro-poor growth is
a rate of income growth for the poor that is higher than the rate of
GDP growth (Kakwani and Pernia 2000). According to this definition,
points A and E would be candidates for pro-poor growth. Another
definition focuses on the status of the poor (Ravallion and Chen 2003).
Specifically, as long as economic growth improves the income of the
poor, it could be regarded as pro-poor. By this definition, points A,
B, C, and D would be examples of pro-poor growth. It is difficult
to decide which definition is superior because both have their pros
and cons.

Does economic growth always reduce poverty? Economic growth
has two conceptually separable effects on poverty. The first is "the
pure growth effect"; the second is "the distributional effect". The pure
growth effect assumes that economic growth always trickles down to
the poor and reduces poverty quasi automatically. Figure 6.2 shows
the pure growth effect — the effect of economic growth on poverty,
holding income distribution constant. Note that the people with income
less than Z are the poor (Z is the poverty line). Since economic
growth shifts income distribution rightwards, increasing the average
per capita GDP from μ_0 to μ_1, the proportion of the population that
is poor should decrease. Economic growth to some extent changes
the shape of income distribution. Figure 6.3 shows the distributional
effect — change in the shape of income distribution, holding income
growth constant. Note that if economic growth increases the dispersion
of income distribution, then economic growth raises the proportion of
the population that is poor.

FIGURE 6.1
The Concept of "Pro-poor Growth"

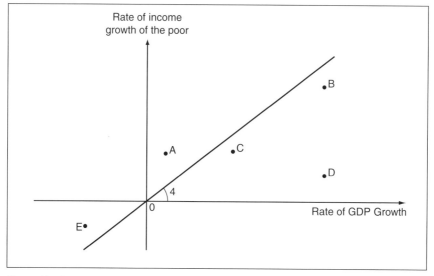

Source: Yoo (2008).

FIGURE 6.2
Effect of Growth on Poverty

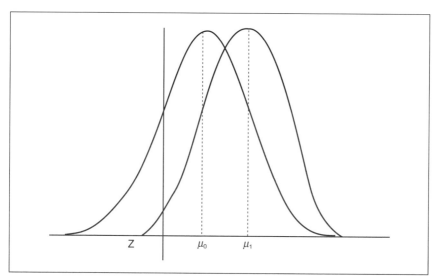

Source: Drawn by the author.

FIGURE 6.3
Effect of Income Distribution on Poverty

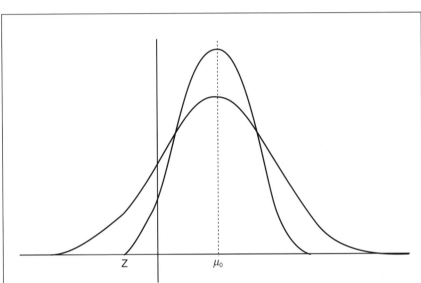

Source: Drawn by the author.

Although the effects of economic growth on poverty are theoreti-
cally inconclusive, it is still possible to draw several stylized facts from
many empirical findings. First, it is known that economic growth tends
to reduce the poverty rate in the long run. This implies that economic
growth is a necessary condition for poverty reduction. Second, it has
been observed that policy attempts to lower income inequality can
reduce the poverty rate in the short run. This suggests that economic
growth is not enough for the reduction of poverty. An effort to reduce
income inequality must be made in order for growth to make poverty
reduction sustainable.

Figure 6.4 illustrates the trend of absolute poverty in Korea since
the early 1980s. Based on the poverty line of year 2000, the proportion
of households below the poverty line appears to have been 82 per
cent in 1982. The proportion of households below the poverty line
had dramatically decreased to 9.2 per cent by 2007. Clearly, rapid

FIGURE 6.4
Absolute Poverty: Korea 1982–2007

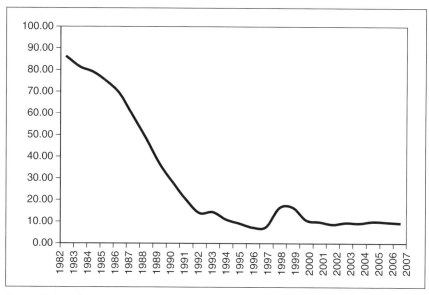

Source: National Statistical Office, Family Income and Expenditure Survey, various years.

economic growth during that time was a main reason the poverty rate declined in Korea.

The relationship between the rate of relative poverty (total income less than 50 per cent of the median income for each year) and income inequality in Korea is presented in Figure 6.5. First, there is salient correlation between the two changes. For example, the relative poverty rate declined continuously until the early 1990s. During this same period, income inequality (Gini coefficient) also declined. Since 1992, relative poverty and the Gini coefficient rose together. In the 2000s, the Gini coefficient rapidly rose. In that time, however, the relative poverty rate remained rather stable. The reason for divergence is due to the introduction of a massive welfare system. It can be said that policy intervention to lower income inequality reduced the poverty rate in the short run.

Table 6.1 breaks down the effects of economic growth on poverty (the growth elasticity of poverty) into the pure growth effect (holding

FIGURE 6.5
Relative Poverty and Income Inequality: Korea 1982–2007

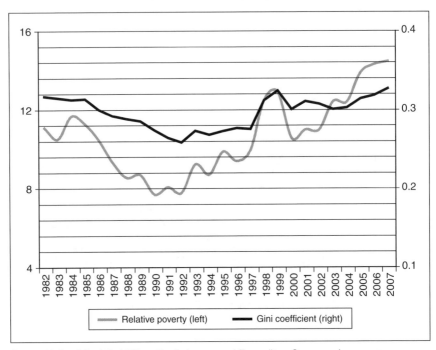

Source: National Statistical Office, Family Income and Expenditure Survey, various years.

income distribution constant) and the distributional effect (holding economic growth rate constant) for the case of Korea (Yoo 2008). As shown in the table, the pure growth effect is dominant in reducing poverty over time. In the past, economic growth appears to have had a favourable distributional effect on poverty. However, since 2003 the distributional effect operates in the direction of raising the poverty rate.

In summary, not only economic growth (or the pure growth effect), but also income distribution (the distributional effect), crucially affects the poverty rate. Economic theory and empirical findings indicate that economic growth is a necessary condition for poverty reduction. But for growth to reduce poverty, income distribution must be improved.

TABLE 6.1
Decomposition of Growth Impacts on the Poverty Rate: Korean Case

Year	Elasticity of Poverty Rate	Pure Growth Effect	Distributional Effect
82/83	−0.55	−0.54	−0.01
83/84	−0.66	−0.67	0.01
84/85	−0.67	−0.76	0.10
85/86	−0.97	−0.94	−0.03
86/87	−1.17	−1.19	0.02
87/88	−1.46	−1.55	0.09
88/89	−2.16	−1.98	−0.18
89/90	−3.31	−2.50	−0.18
90/91	−2.92	−2.65	−0.28
91/92	−3.46	−3.12	−0.33
92/93	0.94	−2.99	3.93
93/94	−3.26	−2.67	−0.58
94/95	−1.87	−2.63	0.75
95/96	−3.32	−2.77	−0.55
96/97	3.04	−3.24	6.27
97/98	−4.11	−2.52	−1.59
98/99	0.36	−2.10	2.46
99/00	−5.48	−2.49	−2.99
00/01	−1.27	−2.61	1.35
01/02	−3.38	−2.87	−0.51
02/03	−6.99	−1.50	−5.49
03/04	−1.15	−1.79	0.63
04/05	3.70	−1.80	5.50
05/06	−1.02	−2.18	1.16
06/07	−0.96	−1.64	0.68

Source: Yoo (2008).

THE ENVIRONMENT AND ECONOMIC GROWTH

What Do Empirical Studies Tell Us?

Many studies have been made about the relationship between the environment and economic growth. A famous conjecture is known as an Environmental Kuznets Curve, an inverse U-shaped relationship between the environment and economic growth (see Figure 6.6). The hypothesis is that environmental pollution at first increases with economic development, but then decreases.

The results of empirical studies are inconclusive. Shafik and Bandyopadhyay (1992, p. 21), using time-series and cross-country data, reported that "many indicators tend to improve as countries approach middle income levels, as evidenced by the negative signs on the quadratic income terms". Grossman and Krueger (1995) also found air pollutants (such as sulfur dioxide and heavy particulates) generally reach peak levels in the low per capita GDP range and then decrease as per capita GDP increases.[1]

On the other hand, several studies cast doubt on the Environmental Kuznets Curve. Stern and Common (2001) reported that the quadratic relationship between the environment and economic development cannot be observed when certain samples are used. Later, Harbaugh, Levinson, and Wilson (2002), using the same data as Grossman and Krueger (1995), insisted that the relationship between the environment and economic growth is sensitive to econometric specifications. They

FIGURE 6.6
Environment and Economic Growth: EKC

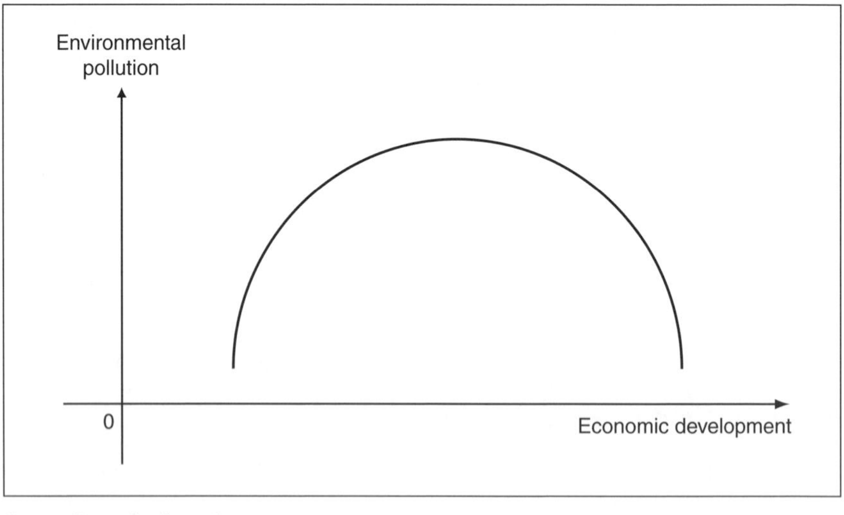

Source: Drawn by the author.

showed that the quadratic form could not be found. In summary, the empirical relationship between the environment and economic development is ambiguous. Depending upon the econometric specifications and the data used in analyses, the conclusions are different and there is no consistent pattern.

What Does Theory Tell Us?

There are debates over the relationship between the environment and the economy in economic theory. In a conventional setting, theoretical models predict that environmental protection measures make the economy operate below its production possibility frontier, lowering economic growth (Ligthart and van der Ploeg 1994). Furthermore, environmental regulations may lower the rate of return on input factors such as capital by raising the cost of production. A few theoretical models show the possibility that an environmentally oriented economy would not necessarily experience a slowdown in economic growth. Gradus and Smulders' (1993) model predicts that a clean environment increases a person's learning capacity. This enables more human capital to accumulate. Bovenberg and Smulders (1996) present a model in which imposing a tax on the environment while lowering distortive taxes would stimulate economic growth.

The model I will be using is the extension of Persson and Tabellini (1994) in Kim (2009). In the latter essay I introduced a pollution tax in a model of overlapping generations. The idea can be expressed mathematically by the following problem:

(1) $$\max_{c,d} U(c_{t-1}^i, d_t^i),$$

where c_{t-1}^i and d_t^i denote a person's consumption when young $(t-1)$ and old (t), respectively. The consumption when young is completely financed by the person's labour earnings (y_{t-1}^i) within a budget constraint $c_{t-1}^i + k_t^i = y_{t-1}^i$ where i is capital (or savings) and $y_{t-1}^i = (w + e^i)k_{t-1}$. Thus, earnings are determined by the average wages, w, and an individual heterogeneity, e^i, coupled by the capital stock of the previous generation, k_{t-1}. On the other hand, the consumption of the person at t is determined by the rate of return on capital (r), a tax on capital income (θ), and a pollution tax (δ), such that $d_t^i = r[1 - \theta_t)k_t^i + \theta_t k_t] - \delta_t x_t^i$. Note that θ_t is an adjustment parameter for a tax on privately accumulated capital. With a higher value of θ_t, capital (hence consumption of the person at t is more evenly distributed around the average level of capital stock (k_t). The pollution tax is levied on the amount of pollutants produced in the use of capital.

The optimal path of consumption in the model is characterized by the ratio of the marginal utility of consumption in two periods being equal to a function of r, θ, and δ. Let $d^i_{t-1}/c^i_{t-1} = D(r, \theta, \delta)$, where $D_r > 0_{D_\theta < 0} D_\delta < 0$.

Solving the optimization problem yields the rate of economic growth given by the following:

(2)
$$g_t = G(w, r, \theta_t, \delta_t) = k_t/k_{t-1} - 1$$
$$= \frac{D(r,\theta,\delta)}{D(r,\theta,\delta) + r} + \frac{\delta_t x_t}{K_{t-1}(D(r,\theta,\delta) + r)} - 1$$

The following points merit noting. First, the equation indicates that the higher the wage the higher the economic growth rate (i.e., $G_w > 0$). Second, the effect that the rate of return on capital has on economic growth is uncertain because of substitution and income effects (i.e., $G_r > 0$ or $G_r < 0$). Third, a tax on capital (θ), or a government's redistributive policy, has a negative effect on economic growth (i.e., $G_\theta < 0$).

A distinctive feature of the model is the effect of the pollution tax on economic growth. According to the model, a pollution tax may or may not assist economic growth. Given that $\partial c^i_{t-1}/\partial \delta_t \leq 0$, a pollution tax has a positive effect on economic growth.[2] In other words, an environmental tax lowers the ratio of marginal utility of consumptions in two periods (i.e., $D_\delta < 0$), implying that the consumption of the person when old should decrease more than the consumption of the person when young. Facing this situation, the person needs to restore the optimal consumption path by accumulating additional capital stock to prevent a sharp decline of future consumption. As a result, an environmental tax may serve to increase capital stock (i.e., $\partial k_t/\partial \delta_t > 0$), resulting in economic growth. The implications are striking. In the model with an environmental tax, an appropriately chosen environmental policy, together with a distributive policy, may achieve economic growth and fair distribution at the same time.

ECONOMIC GROWTH AND INCOME INEQUALITY

Kuznets (1955) argued that economic growth raises income inequality at the early stages of development, but then reduces it as the economy develops further. This is the well-known Kuznets Inverted U Hypothesis. See Figure 6.7.

Some argue that income inequality is inevitable with economic growth because in order to invest capital one must have wealth. Redistribution generally discourages people from investing (Persson and Tabellini 1994). Thus, a policy of reducing income inequality lowers economic growth. Others mention that in an unequal society, the majority favours a progressive tax, which also reduces economic growth. They argue that income inequality causes socio-political instability, reducing investment (Alesina and Rodrik 1994)

Early studies based on cross-sectional or cross-country analyses, such as Kravis (1960), Paukert (1973), and Aldelman and Morris (1973), confirmed the Kuznets Inverse U Hypothesis. However, recent empirical studies using cross-sectional and time-series data report no clear relationship between economic growth and income inequality. This leads many scholars to think that economic growth is distribution-neutral and a country's heterogeneity does matter in determining

FIGURE 6.7
Kuznets Curve: Economic Development vs. Income Inequality

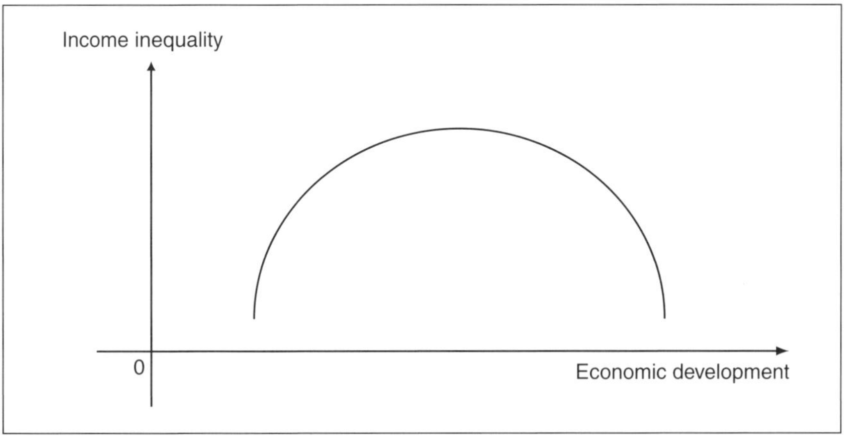

Source: Drawn by the author.

income inequality (Fields and Jakubson 1994; Denniger and Squire 1998; Ravillion and Chen 1997).

Benabou (1996) summarizes various aspects of the relationship between income inequality, economic growth, and capital accumulation. The result in the first column of the Table 6.2 shows that the

TABLE 6.2
Determinants of Growth and Investment

	(1) INEQ on GR, INV	(2) DEM on GR, INV	(3) HUMCAP on GR, INV	(4) INEQ on INSTAB	(5) INSTAB on GR, INV
1. Alesina-Rodrik (94)	⊖	○			
2. Alesina-Perotti (96)			⊕		
3. Alesina et al (96)		○	⊕		−
4. Barro (96)		⌢	M=⊕F=⊖		⊖
5. Benhabib-Spiegel (96)	(−)		⊕	⊕	⊖
6. Bourguignon (94)	⊖		⊕	⊕	(−)
7. Brandolini-Rossi (95)	○				
8. Clarke (92)	⊖		⊕		
9. Deininger-Squire (95)	(−)	(±)	+		
10. Easterly-Rebello (93)			⊕		(±)
11. Keefer-Knack (95)	⊖	(−)	⊕	⊕	⊖
12. Levine-Rebello (93)					−
13. Lindert (96)			⊕		
14. Perotti (92)	⊖		+	⊕	⊖
15. Perotti (94)	⊖		○		
16. Perotti (96)	⊖	○	M=⊕F=⊖	⊕	⊖
17. Persson-Tabellini (92)	⊖		⊕		
18. Persson-Tabellini (94)	⊖	−	⊕		
19. Svensson (93)			⊕	+	⊖
20. Venieris-Gupta (86)	⊖				⊖

Note: symbols: ⊕, ⊖: consistent, sign and generally significant; +, −; consistent sign, sometimes significant; (+), (−): consistent sign but generally not significant, (±): inconsistent sign with significant coefficient; ™: inconsistent sign or close to zero, and not significant; ⌢: inverse U-shaped, significant. INEQ: Measures of inequality DEM: Measures of political rights and degree of democracy HUMCAP: initial stock of human capital INSTAB: socio-political instability
Source: Benabou (1996), NBER Working Paper No. 5658.

coefficient of income inequality on economic growth (or investment) is consistently negative (and statistically significant), meaning that unequal distribution is detrimental to economic growth and capital accumulation.[3]

It is worth noting that in some studies human capital (as indicated by school enrolment rate) has a strong positive effect on economic growth. Moreover, the effect of income inequality on economic growth becomes statistically insignificant when the initial human capital variable is controlled.[4] This result implies that there is a connection between economic growth, income inequality, and human capital. It is possible that high income inequality results in fewer people being able to afford the extent of education they would like; this (lower level of human capital) results in a lower economic growth rate. For example, Korea had high enrolment rate and low illiteracy. And it is believed that a qualified (educated) labour force was an important cause of economic growth and equal income distribution in Korea.

Kim (2004) explores the effects of various socio-economic policies on economic growth (efficiency) and income inequality. Using a stochastic frontier model, the economic efficiency (E_{it}) of a country i at time t can be defined by the ratio of its actual production (GDP) to its maximally achievable level. The income inequality (G_{it}) of each country is measured by the Gini coefficient. Let X be a set of policies that may affect economic efficiency and inequality (e.g., social expenditure and tax policies) and let Z be a set of policies that may affect efficiency only (such as sale tax). One can use the following regression equations to see the effect of socio-economic policies on economic efficiency and inequality.[5]

(3)
$$G_{it} = \gamma_{11}X_{it} + \varepsilon_{it}$$
$$E_{it} = \gamma_{21}X_{it} + \gamma_{22}Z_{it} + v_{it}$$

Table 6.3 shows the results. First, the trade-off between economic growth and inequality can be found for welfare policies. For example, welfare policies such as old age cash benefits and family cash benefits lower income inequality but reduce economic growth as well. Second, redistributive tax policies lower economic growth without making income distribution more equal.

One of the interesting results is the effects of unemployment benefits and public health expenditures on economic growth and inequality.

TABLE 6.3
Policies, Economic Growth and Income Distribution

	Growth	Inequality
Social Expenditures		
Old age cash benefits	−2056***	−0.463
Family cash benefits	−0.292	−0.513**
Active labour market	−0.419	−1.439
Unemployment benefits	1.625***	−1.648***
Health	1.524**	0.237
Tax		
Income tax	−0.248***	0.087
Sales & VAT	−0.802***	0.311
R-square	0.770	0.495

Note: *** = 99%, ** = 95%.
Source: Kim (2004).

Unemployment benefits turn out to have a positive effect on economic growth and income distribution. It is easy to understand that unemployment benefits reduce income inequality for the following reasons. First, unemployment benefits to some extent reduce income for the unemployed. Second, unemployment benefits make getting a job more attractive to the unemployed. At the same time, an effective unemployment benefits system makes an employer's workforce more flexible as it reduces the resistance of workers in the case of labour adjustment. From these reasons, one may conclude that unemployment benefits promote both economic growth and equal income distribution.

It is not surprising to see that public health expenditures have a positive effect on economic growth. An effective health system enables an economy not only to maintain the quality of its workforce, but enables individuals to increase human capital. The results hint that a country can achieve a virtuous circle of economic growth and equal income distribution with a well-chosen combination of welfare and tax policies.

CONCLUSION

Whether and how much economic growth reduces poverty depends on the magnitudes of the pure growth and the distributional effects. The pure growth effect generally reduces the poverty rate, but if income inequality increases with economic growth, the distributional effect may not be poverty reducing. Thus, if one is trying to reduce poverty, the goal should not be simply economic growth, but inequality-reducing economic growth. The government must select policies that make income distribution more even. If possible, distribution policies should be chosen that stimulate economic growth. Empirical research suggests that unemployment benefits and affordable public education and health services increase both equality and growth. And if one wants to not only reduce poverty, but to protect the environment, one must find environmental policies that hinder growth to the least extent possible. Fortunately, some environmental policies can even speed up growth. As shown in the theoretical model, a tax on environmental pollution should lead people to save more. This should encourage capital accumulation and result in higher economic growth. And, of course, protecting the environment allows growth and poverty reduction to continue for the long term.

Notes

1. For other empirical research supporting the Environmental Kuznets Curve, see Panayotou (1993) and Hilton and Levinson (1998).
2. For a formal presentation and proof, see the appendix in Kim (2009).
3. Benabou (1996) mentioned that "a one standard deviation decrease in inequality raises the annual growth rate of GDP per capita by 0.5 to0.8 percentage points".
4. See Benhabib and Spiegel (1994) and Deininger-Squire (1995).
5. The data sets used come from the WIID (World Income and Inequality Database), PWT (Penn World Table), OECD SOCX (Social Expenditure Database) and OECD RS (Revenue Statistics).

References

Aldelman I. and C. T. Morris. *Economic Growth and Social Equity in Developing Countries*. Stanford, CA: Stanford University Press, 1973.

Alesina, A. and D. Rodrik. "Distributive Politics and Economic Growth" *Quarterly Journal of Economics* 109 (1994): 465–90.

Benabou, Ronald. "Inequality and Growth". *NBER Working Paper* 5648, Working Paper Series, National Bureau of Economic Research, 1996.

Benhabib, J. and M. Spiegel. "The Role of Human Capital in Economic Development: Evidence from Aggregate Cross-Country Data". *Journal of Monetary Economics* 24 (1994): 143–73.

Bovenberg, A. L. and S. Smulders. "Environmental Quality and Pollution Saving Technological Change in a Two-Sector Endogenous Growth Model". *Journal of Public Economics* 57 (1995): 369–91.

Bovenberg, A. L. and S. Smulders. "Transitional Impact of Environmental Policy in an Endogenous Growth Model". *International Economic Review* 37 (1996): 861–93.

Denniger, K. and L. Squire. "*Inequality and Growth: Results from a New Data Set*". World Bank mimeo, 1995.

Denniger, K. and L. Squire. "New Ways of Looking at Old Issues". *Journal of Development Economics* 57 (1998): 259–87.

Fields, G. and G. Jakubson. "New Evidence on the Kuznets Curve". Cornell University, mimeo, 1994.

Gradus, R. and S. Smulders. "The Trade-off Between Environmental Care and Long-term Growth-Pollution in three Prototype Growth Models". *Journal of Economics* 58 (1993): 25–51.

Grossman G. and A. Krueger. "Economic Growth and Environment". *Quarterly Journal of Economics* 112 (1995): 353–77.

Harbaugh, W., A. Levinson, and D. Wilson. "Reexamining the Empirical Evidence for an Environmental Kuznets Curve". *Review of Economics and Statistics* 84 (2002): 541–51.

Hilton, F. and A. Levinson. "Factoring he Environmental Kuznets Curve: Evidence from Automotive Lead Emission". *Journal of Environmental Economics and Management* 35 (1998): 126–41.

Kakwani, N. and E. Pernia. "What is Pro-Poor Growth?". *Asian Development Review* 18, no. 1 (2000).

Kim, Jaehoon. "Economic Inequality, Environmental Protection and Economic Growth". KDI Policy Study Series, 2009–09. Korea Development Institute, 2009.

Kim, Yong-seong. "The Effects of Social Expenditures and Tax Policies on Economic Equity and Efficiency: The Case of the OECD Countries". KDI Policy Study Series, 2002–04. Korea Development Institute, 2004.

Kravis, I. "International Differences in the Distribution of Income". *Review of Economics and Statistics* 42 (1960): 447–75.

Kuznets, S. "Economic Growth and Income Inequality". *American Economic Review* 45 (1955): 1–28.

Ligthart, J. E. and F. van der Ploeg. "Pollution, the Cost of Public Funds and Endogenous Growth". *Economic Letters* 46 (1994): 351–61.

Panayotou, T. "Empirical Tests and Policy Analysis of Environmental Degradation at Different Stages of Economic Development". *Working Paper* WP 238, World Employment Program, Geneva, International Labor Office, pp. 333–354, 1993.

Paukert, F. "Income Distribution at Different Levels of Development: A Survey of Evidence". *International Labour Review* 108 (1973): 97–125.

Persson, T. and G. Tabellini. "Is inequality harmful for growth?". *American Economic Review* 84 (1994): 600–21.

Ravallion, Martin and Shaohua Chen. "Can High-inequality Developing Countries Escape Measuring Pro-Poor Growth". *Economic Letters* 56 (1997): 51–57.

Ravallion, Martin and Shaohua Chen. "Measuring Pro-Poor Growth". *Economic Letters* 78, no. 1 (2003): 93–99.

Shafik, Nemat and Sushenjit Bandyopadhyay. "Economic Growth and Environmental Quality: Time Series and Cross-country Evidence". *World Bank Policy Research Working Paper*, Wps 904. Washington D.C., World Bank, 1992.

Stern, D. and M. Common. "Is there an Environmental Kuznets Curve for Sulfur?". *Journal of Environmental Economics and Management* 41 (2001): 162–78.

Yoo, Gyeongjoon. "Definition and Application of Pro-poor Growth: Effect of Growth and Distribution for Poverty Reduction". *KDI Policy Study Series*, 2008–03. Korea Development Institute, 2008.

III

Pacific Islands

7

CLIMATE CHANGE ADAPTATION AND POVERTY REDUCTION IN SMALL ISLANDS OF THE PACIFIC

Anjeela Jokhan and Murari Lal

Due to their small size, Pacific Island countries are susceptible to the effects of climate change. The Pacific Island countries are likely to suffer in five areas. The first is their coastal protection, including their mangroves, reefs, mudflats, and sea grass beds. The second is their climate regulation, covering seasonal and decadal cycles (e.g., El Niño) and long-term processes such as oceans as heat and carbon sinks. Third is their environmental flows, involving river and floodplain services, livelihoods, soil fertility, and sediment deposition. Fourth is their biodiversity conservation, covering reefs, the deep sea, polar ecosystem, shelf seas, mangroves, floodplains, and ancient lakes. Fifth is the cultural services concerning coastal heritage, identity and spirituality, education and knowledge, aesthetic enjoyment, food, and culture.

Furthermore, the Pacific Island countries rely heavily on imported food. Every Pacific Island country imports most (70–100 per cent) of its food. Increasing food prices are making it more difficult to import food. More and more of Gross Domestic Products (GDP) is devoted to food import. And local food production, both marine and terrestrial, is threatened by the rising temperature of sea water and soil salinization, both of which are caused by climate change, which has become the greatest challenge facing the world since the beginning of the twenty-first century.

In their effort to address these challenges, the Pacific Island countries have embraced sustainable development as a pathway for the future by becoming a party to various international, regional and national agreements. Preparedness is a concern in every small island country in the Pacific. In this essay we show some of the ways Pacific Island countries are adapting to climate change, especially for the poor.

EFFECTS OF CLIMATE CHANGE

Fisheries

The Pacific Island countries rely heavily on the oceans for food (fish, sea shells, sea grass, and others). With a rise in the temperature of sea water, an effect is seen on food supply. Since most populations are living in the coastal areas, this has a major effect on their livelihoods. Less abundance of food, smaller organisms, and the loss of biodiversity are real issues for these people.

Mangroves and Coral Reefs

Coral reefs not only provide protection to the shorelines, but also provide various types of marine food. Coral bleaching is a global phenomenon that seems to be increasing in frequency, scale, and severity. The South Pacific experienced major mass coral bleaching in 2000. From late February to early March 2000, mass bleaching occurred in Fiji. This happened after a prolonged period of temperatures in excess of 30 degrees centigrade (86°F). It coincided with similar coral bleaching being reported across the South Pacific, from Papua New Guinea to Easter Island. A major bleaching occurred subsequently in Fiji in 2002. It mainly affected the north sides of the two main islands, which had escaped bleaching in 2000. Kiribati suffered severe bleaching in 2003 in the Phoenix Islands and in the Gilberts in 2005

(Lovell 2005). An effect of this is being experienced throughout the Pacific Island countries.

Mangroves protect the coastal shorelines, and therefore are crucial to the survival of populations in coastal areas. The effect of the loss of mangroves (both due to the effect of stronger currents and human activity) is the fast-eroding coastal shores. In addition, mangroves provide a haven for many organisms that are food for coastal communities. With the loss of mangroves, the ecosystems are affected in a way that reduces the food supply.

Agriculture

Pacific Island countries are small with small populations and, therefore, there are very few industries. Agriculture is the only industry in which the Pacific Island countries can invest, and even this industry is largely undeveloped. In any case, with the rise in food prices, countries are trying to improve agriculture. However, they are faced with the problem of soil salinization. With sea-level rise and higher waves and stronger winds, water intrusion into the soil is already occurring; and it is likely to occur further (Liz 2007; White and Falkland 2010). That means that people living in the coastal areas face difficulties with agriculture. Tuvalu is a good example of an atoll island that relies on fresh groundwater and rainfall. With the groundwater becoming more saline, the demand for fresh water is increasing, for both human and crop consumption.

There is therefore a need to look for local, salt-tolerant crops that can be farmed for food. Currently, the Secretariat of the Pacific Community and the University of the South Pacific are carrying out research on salt tolerance of the Giant Swamp Taro (*Cyrtospermamerkusii*), a local aroid. Giant Swamp Taro is not only a highly consumed aroid and a local staple root crop, but also holds immense cultural significance for Micronesians, who happen to be one of the most drastically affected group by increased soil salinity (Eid and Huisbergen 1992; Gerald et al. 2007). In terms of aquatic food, an effort is being made to develop aquaculture, but again with soil salinization, this has not become a significant venture. Developing and maintaining aquaculture is expensive, at least initially, and this is one of the deterrents faced by countries.

Sea-level Rise and Coastal Erosion

Many Pacific Island countries are extremely vulnerable to climate-change induced disasters (e.g., large-scale inundation due to sea-level rise and widespread damages from high-intensity tropical cyclones). They could be among the first countries in the world that are forced to relocate people due to accelerated sea-level rise. Most Pacific Island countries settlements are in coastal areas. This is because it is easier to obtain food and transportation there. The sheer smallness of the islands means that most people are affected by sea-level rise and soil salinization. In several cases, the only option people have is to relocate to higher ground inland.

In many other countries with even higher and larger islands, but with a large proportion of the population living in rural areas, the loss of land associated with sea-level rise will be devastating in their coastal areas. In the atolls, where the average height of the landmass is less than five meters, the loss of land or even whole islands will mean catastrophic changes. Therefore, the loss of land is a major concern throughout the Pacific (Veitayaki Manoa, and Resture 2007).

This means that large investments need to be made. But governments have been unwilling to do this, given their many other pressing needs. In Fiji itself, two large towns have a clear need to relocate. Signs of climate change are evident, but relocation is not yet seen as an option for the government because of the resource implications. This problem remains unresolved.

To address climate change effectively, we can combine a variety of development choices, adaptation actions, and adaptation capacities. Because different adaptation strategies are needed for different effects of climate change, understanding the implications of the changing climate at the local level is necessary for effective adaptation. How to choose the adaptation strategies is part of the development process, to ensure sustainability of the system and justice for the people.

POVERTY IN THE PACIFIC ISLANDS

As shown in Table 7.1, the poverty level varies from 22 per cent in Kiribati to 40 per cent in Vanuatu. However, readers are cautioned that the measurement of poverty in the Pacific Island countries is

TABLE 7.1
Poverty Scenarios in Some Pacific Island Countries

Country	Poverty level	Comments
Vanuatu	40%	Largest infrastructure investment is in education. Low in health and agriculture
Palau	25%	
Kiribati	22%	There is variability within the population. Households with female heads and those with elderly heads are often poorer
Solomon Islands	23%	Larger percentage of overall household expenses goes to food. In poorer household about 60%.
Fiji	33%	The poorest 20% of the population would spend about 80% of the income on food

Source: UNDP Reports.

not simple, and numbers presented here may not necessarily present a true picture by standard definition because of the social structures involved. It is not easy to measure the income of a person. People, particularly in the rural areas, live in extended-family communities. They share food and other necessities, and bring in collective income. Therefore, it is not easy to determine poverty in such structures.

In an attempt to reduce poverty, equip the people with knowledge and skills, and work towards a more sustainable future, several national and regional projects are being carried out in the Pacific Island countries. These address issues at the research and higher education levels, short-term training of policy makers and other practitioners, as well as work being done with communities to build their resilience.

CONCLUSION

Climate-change adaptation is critical in the Pacific Island countries. This requires a large investment in capacity building, to enhance their ability to adapt to climate change. The most important issue is food security. They will also have to adapt to conditions with fewer gardens, less pre-cyclone preparation, no surplus of root crops, no storage, delayed post-cyclone replanting, and diminishing wild food stocks. These of course affect population growth, land preservation, food importation, disaster relief, community governance, and social cohesion.

The countries are also losing their traditional knowledge, which will in turn make them more vulnerable to climate change. Formal education no longer emphasizes traditional learning by seeing and experiencing things. There is a breakdown in traditional education and a loss of knowledge and skills. The values are changing, and there are fewer incentives to work. Many cultures actually say that if we plant something every day in the ground, the more food we will have when a natural disaster hits. Also, the countries are losing the tradition of storing food underground. (In the old days, staple food such as breadfruit was stored underground in such a way that it could be eaten several weeks later.) There is a lack of future planning, leading to less production and higher reliance on aid and imports, making the Pacific Island countries very vulnerable to climate change.

Social vulnerability is also a problem. At the national and regional levels, the political and economic systems become the root causes leading to a loss in development directions. The almost complete absence of direction at the national and provincial levels results in confusion in, for example, local markets, institutional capacity, and service provision. At the local level, we can see unsafe conditions, such as dangerous settlement locations, unemployment, and lack of access to information. All these lead to how the people in the countries prepare for and respond to disasters.

Gender dimensions also come into the picture. Men and women are affected differently by climate stress because they have different roles to play in everyday life. Naturally, women are seen to be responsible for food security because they are responsible for the dependants. However, they are normally excluded from information and access to resources.

Therefore, development of the Pacific Island countries should be carried out in a sustainable way. Development should be carried out in a way that will permit continuing improvement in the quality of life, but at a lower intensity of resource use. In this way an undiminished or even enhanced stock of productive assets (manufactured, natural, and social capital) will be preserved for future generations. Climate change is global — but the responses must be local. The hopes of the Pacific Island countries lie in sustainable utilization of natural resources.

References

Eid, E. and C. H. Huisbergen. "Sea level rise and Coastal Zone Management". *Default Hydraulics* (Switzerland), no. 471. 1992.

Gerald, D. M., M. S. Fenster, B. A. Argow, and I. V. Buynevich. *Coastal Impacts due to Sea level rise*, 2007.

Liz, M. "The Tides are Getting Higher and Higher: A Pacific Voice on Climate Change". *Just Change* 10 (2007): 22–23.

Lovell, E. "Coral Bleaching In Fiji and the South Pacific". *PIMRIS Newsletter* 17, no. 4 (2005). PIMRIS Coordination Unit. Marine Studies Programme, University of the South Pacific.

Veitayaki, J., P. Manoa, and A. Resture. *Addressing Climate Change and Sea Level Rise in the Pacific Islands*, 2007.

White, I. and T. Falkland. "Management of Freshwater Lenses on Small Pacific Islands". *Hydrogeology Journal* (2010): 1–20.

8

THE ROLE OF DEVELOPMENT ORGANIZATIONS IN PRO-POOR ADAPTATION TO GLOBAL WARMING IN THE PACIFIC ISLANDS

Paul Bullen

The main subject of this chapter is the what role, if any, development organizations should play in helping the poor in the developing countries of the Pacific Islands adapt to what is commonly called climate change. I first clarify what is meant by *climate change*. I then explain how in the absence of strong governments in these countries, development organizations do and can provide help to the poor in adapting to the changes taking place in their environments. I then explain how these organizations often appropriately use an area approach, one that means excluding some normally targeted people (the poor) and including some normally not-targeted people (the better off). And I try to give the reader a good brief understanding of what the Pacific Islands is, and how the area approach applies to it. I then present two ways the development organizations may succeed in getting better local support for environmental projects than governments have in the past. First, projects that seek to solve long-term problems that local people may not appreciate can be combined with elements that solve more obvious and immediate needs. It will be easier to come up with such projects if global warming is not considered separately from other environmental problems. I present a sketch of the sort of comprehensive classification scheme that would aid such a plan. Second, steps can be taken to make people more aware of the long-term problems, such as sea-level rise. But development organizations should first improve their own intellectual content and to coordinate their activities with each other.

GLOBAL WARMING AND ITS EFFECTS

Anything made of molecules, atoms, and particles emits self-propagating coupled electrical and magnetic waves that move at the speed of light (when in a vacuum). The higher the temperature of a thing, the higher the frequency of its waves and the greater the energy they carry. The spectrum ranges from radio waves, with the lowest frequency and energy, through microwaves, infrared, visible, ultraviolet, and X-rays, to gamma rays, with highest frequency and energy. With an average surface temperature of 288 K, the earth emits a spectrum of wavelengths whose peak is in the infrared area.[1] Before infrared waves from the earth can reach space, they must pass through the atmosphere. Electromagnetic waves interact with matter in a variety of ways. Infrared mostly interacts with the chemical bonds between the atoms of molecules when (1) the bonds vibrate at the same frequency as the waves and (2) the vibrations perturb the electrical field (via a dipole moment). For the latter, there needs to be an asymmetry in the molecular vibration. And with some minor exceptions, that is only possible with molecules that have three or more atoms.[2] Almost all of the atmosphere (99 per cent) consists of molecules made of two identical atoms (oxygen, O_2, and nitrogen, N_2). Such symmetrical molecules make no contact with infrared electromagnetic waves. Just under 1 per cent (0.93) is made up of molecules with only one atom (Argon, Ar). Such molecules do not even have chemical bonds. But the remaining 0.07 per cent of the gases in the atmosphere have molecules with three or more atoms: mainly carbon dioxide (CO_2), methane (CH_4), nitrous oxide (N_2O), and water vapour (H_2O). The vibration frequencies of each of these molecules correspond to one part or another of the infrared area of the spectrum.[3] Such "greenhouse" molecules absorb those wave-lengths and then reradiate them in all directions, including back to the earth. So due to the presence of these trace gases, some energy is kept within the earth system that would otherwise be lost to space.[4]

This mechanism has kept the earth warm enough for life to evolve over millions of years. In the past, the trace gases came mainly from the mantle, via volcanoes and mid-ocean ridges, where new oceanic crust is emerging.[5] At a certain point in history, humans too became a source. For their first 150,000 years or so, they survived by capturing wild animals and fish and by picking wild fruit, berries, and nuts. Then, with the ending of the last 100,000-year-long glacial period and the beginning, 11,700 years ago, of the Holocene, people began staying in one place and farming, possibly prompted by the salutary effect on plants of increasing levels of carbon dioxide.[6] This new source of food and improved nutrition allowed the human population to increase. When the practice of agriculture spread to forested areas, trees had to be cleared. As burning and rotting vegetation emits carbon dioxide, the natural deposit of carbon dioxide in the atmosphere was augmented.[7] Also, there were fewer trees to remove the carbon dioxide during photosynthesis. From about 7,000 years ago, humans started becoming a noticeable source of trace gases in the atmosphere. This effect was strengthened a couple of thousand years later, when people in Southeast Asia started irrigating their rice fields. Wetlands, including such artificial agricultural ones, produce methane.[8] Since the earth had been going through a long-term cooling phase anyway, the human influence mainly offset that cooling, possibly delaying glaciation. Apart from some interruptions when disease caused massive loss of life and the abandonment of farms, the amount of greenhouse gases produced by humans increased only gradually until the late 1700s, when an even more radical change took place.

If the first revolution was agricultural, the second was industrial, a shift in emphasis from farming to manufacturing and services. This was made possible by a transition from an economy based largely on plants and animals to an economy based largely on minerals. Plants grown on land, and animals, had been providing both the raw material and energy needed for manufacturing. Wood was the source of thermal energy. Human and animal muscle (fuelled by plants, and animals fuelled by plants) provided the mechanical energy.[9] In their place came a cheaper energy source, one that was not limited by land: coal for thermal energy and, about a century later, steam engines that burned coal for mechanical energy.[10] The economy could (with the help of clever inventions that made manufacturing more efficient) sustain a rapidly growing population.[11] Surplus populations moved to the cities or wherever manufacturing or mining were centralized. At the same time, the productivity of agriculture expanded greatly, meeting the increasing demand of the urban populations with roughly the same workforce and the same amount of land. The revolution would have been aborted had wood been the only source of energy available. There was just not enough of it and what there was would have been much more expensive than coal. Not only did industrialization allow there to be more people to consume energy (population explosion), but it allowed each new person to use up more energy than in earlier times, both as a producer and as a consumer. Wood burning, coal burning, and later oil burning, generated carbon dioxide at an exponentially increasing rate. Also contributing greenhouse gases were expanding deforestation,[12] more intensive plant and animal agriculture, expanding rice paddies, expanding landfills, and cement production. With time, the transformation that started in England and Scotland spread to Western Europe, the United States, Japan and other parts of the world.

In the rapid increase of greenhouse gases in the atmosphere, carbon dioxide has been responsible for most of the global warming (77 per cent in 2005).[13] Before human deforestation reversed the decline, the concentration of carbon dioxide in the atmosphere had descended to 260 parts per million (ppm).[14] By the Industrial Revolution (1760), it had risen to 280 ppm. In 2013, the number reached 400 ppm.

- About a quarter of the CO_2 in the atmosphere is removed in plant photosynthesis and rock weathering.[15] Extra carbon dioxide encourages growth. It also affects the water cycle: plants don't need to open their stomata as much, making them more efficient in the use of water (so they need less of it). This is a non-radiative, biophysical climate forcing.[16]
- Just under a third is absorbed by surface water. In the past, this was fine; but the heightened concentrations are lowering

ocean pH (hydrogen potency) enough to harm life in the seas, notably that of coral reefs. This process is popularly referred to as acidification.

- Not quite half of the CO_2 emitted into the atmosphere stays there — for a long time —[17] absorbing and scattering infrared electromagnetic radiation. Greenhouse gases heat not just the atmosphere, but also the sea and the land; and they melt ice. As some sort of index, the average global land temperature rose approximately 1.5° C since the beginning of the Industrial Revolution. And the rate of change has been increasing. About 0.9° of the change occurred in the past fifty years.[18] The expected effects of global warming include sea-level rise (due to warmer water's taking up more space and to melted ice), increased humidity and rain (due to greater evaporation and the greater capacity of warmer air to hold water vapour), coral reef degradation (due to warmer water and rising seal levels — adding to the effects of acidification), possibly stronger storms and storm surges (due to warmer water), flooding (due to increased rain, stronger storms, and sea-level rise), coastal erosion (due to sea-level rise and stronger storms), and salinized land and water (due to sea-level rise, flooding, and storms).

I speak of *global warming and its effects* rather than *climate change* because global warming changes more in the environment than just the climate.[19] Climate is average weather; and weather is a condition of the atmosphere. In fact, it is a condition of only part of the atmosphere: the part from the clouds to the ground, and only with respect to certain characteristics of quotidian concern: mainly temperature and rain, but also wind, humidity, and cloudiness. So, of global warming, the warming of the atmosphere could be called climate change, but not the warming of the ocean and land, or the melting of ice. Of the effects of global warming, increased humidity, increased rain, and stronger storms are changes to the climate. But sea-level rise, coral reef degradation, flooding, coastal erosion, and salinized soil and water are not. And for the most part, these are not even the effects of changes to the climate.[20]

The atmosphere, the oceans, the land, the vegetation, and the ice are included in what is called the climate *system* — but only to the extent that they affect the temperature, precipitation, etc. of the atmosphere near the surface. The climate system is not identical with the earth system.[21] The climate system is an explanans for which the climate is the explanandum.[22] And the term is *climate* change, not *climate system* change. There is no reason to so privilege the climate within the environment as to terminologically pretend that all changes brought by global warming are climatic.

Unfortunately, *global warming and its effects* does not include the negative effects that heightened levels of carbon dioxide have on the oceans, namely acidification. And one could not just speak in terms of the harmful effects of too much carbon dioxide because that would exclude the role of methane and other greenhouse gases. And one can't speak of the harmful effects of greenhouse gases because with respect to acidification, carbon dioxide is not acting as a greenhouse gas. There are human causes of change other than greenhouse gases; for example, land use change and aerosol emission. There are natural causes of change that don't involve greenhouse gases, such as volcanic eruptions, cycles in the sun and in the earth's orbit. For considerations such as these, perhaps, and a desire to refer to more than just global warming and its effects (even with acidification added on), some people use *global change, environmental change*, or *global environmental change* rather than *climate change*.[23] These are fine, with the caveat that one wants to add to changes to the climate not just changes to non-climatic aspects of the global environment, but also regional and unchanging elements. So the broadest term would be *environmental problems*, a major source of which is global warming. I will discuss some ways to divide up environmental problems in the section Towards a Comprehensive Classification Scheme.

DEVELOPMENT ORGANIZATIONS

It is generally better for adaptation to global warming and its effects to be carried out by the people who are experiencing them. Nonetheless, most problems cannot be solved by individuals and families on their own. Rather, they must cooperate with the other people, especially the authorities, in their immediate communities. Although a large amount of local control is desirable, some projects are beyond the capacity of the local communities to carry out on their own. For example, in the case of the Pacific Islands, relocation, disaster insurance, early warning systems, fresh water production, improved building codes, and locally managed marine areas involve considerations and resources beyond the village. National governments would normally step in for such larger projects. The nations of Pacific Islands do have some pretty good environmental legislation on the books, including some related to global warming. But these nations do not have the financial resources, institutional capacity, technical knowledge, or leadership needed to implement them, especially outside the capitals on the main islands.[24] And the populace is often reluctant to cooperate since the laws seem irrelevant to their local environments.

Given the large number, small size, and limited resources of most of the developing countries of the Pacific Islands, one might think that the various regional intergovernmental associations would be a force for adaptation and mitigation. But they too have not done much to prepare for global warming.[25] Some of the slack left by governments and regional associations with respect to larger projects could be (and has been) be taken up by development organizations.[26]

Area-based Approach

In tackling the Pacific Islands, the area must be analysed and an area approach used, at least part of the time. In order to achieve the goal of minimizing the number of people below the poverty line, certain organizations limit their attention to countries below an industrialization line. That makes them *development* organizations. The world is first divided into rich and poor countries. And attention is limited to the poor countries, leaving it up to the governments of rich countries to worry about their own poor. One rough edge of the area-based approach is that it excludes some relevant people, such as the poor in the rich counties. If rich countries have poor people, poor countries have rich people. But development organizations sometimes do things in poor countries that help the rich as well as the poor. The other rough edge of the area-based approach is that it sometimes includes irrelevant people. This is quasi-utilitarian since the lines are drawn with a view to overall effectiveness. It is deemed more likely to minimize the number of people under a poverty line than if one acted otherwise.

The area-based approach can be applied with varying degrees of specificity. Special attention may be paid to the poor people within developing countries. This is *pro-poor* development. Policies could be developed that differentially affect (benefit) the poor throughout the country; or, continuing with an area approach, certain regions or villages may be selected because of the prevalence of poverty, but within the region or village, all may be helped, regardless of their position in relation to the poverty line.

There is a geographic species of the area-based approach. In that case, part of what determines the area that is selected is a combination of the prevalence of poverty and a common environmental feature that affects the nature of the poverty in the area. One such scheme distinguishes (flood-affected) wetlands, drylands, uplands, coastlands, and slums. These are "the environments of the poor".[27] Most of the tropical Pacific Islands, especially in Polynesia and Micronesia, is coastland. There may be relevant uplands on the continental, volcanic, and raised limestone islands (but not atolls). Parts of islands that regularly experience river or sea flooding may be wetlands. Some parts of the Pacific Islands are dryland (not humid or rainy, as is common in the tropics), but they are close to unpopulated. I will discuss the situation with respect to slums in the Pacific Islands presently. It is possible for these categories to overlap; for example, it is possible for an area to be a slum, dryland, or wetland, while at the same time a coastland. Coastal areas may have mangrove wetlands. An investigation into such geographical areas and their connection with poverty in the Pacific Islands might be worth making. The category slums suggests a notion of environment that includes the built environment. A case for the coherence of considering built environments together with natural environments needs to be made.

Let us first clarify what the Pacific Islands is and whether a division into poor and rich countries is possible, as well as possible further applications of the area approach.

Continent of Islands

The Pacific Islands comprises that subset of the islands of the Pacific Ocean that was originally colonized by the Papuan and Austronesian peoples, together with the water in which the islands are situated. The darker-skinned Papuans colonized many of the more than 2,400 islands near Australia that are in the area now called Melanesia. The lighter-skinned Austronesians colonized the fewer than 2,400 islands further east, in the area now called Polynesia. They also colonized many of the about 2,400 islands further north, in what is now Micronesia.[28] The islands are today distributed among 13 independent countries, 1 semi-independent country, 10 territories, 3 parts of neighbouring non-Pacific Islands countries, and an infinite assortment of oddities (see Box 8.1, Components of Oceania).[29] Almost all of the Pacific Islands is located between the Tropic of Cancer and the Tropic of Capricorn and has a maritime tropical climate.[30] New Zealand is the exception, being located quite a bit south of the Tropic of Capricorn and having a maritime temperate climate. It is also a settler society, a bridge between the Pacific Islands and the West.

And there is a greater Pacific Islands, created mainly by younger people leaving their villages in search of a better life, or at least work. Some migration ("internal") is within the nations to the cities or towns,[31] or sometimes to the cities or towns of other nations of the tropical Pacific Islands.[32] This trend is part of why the urban population is growing faster than the rural. Now, about one-fifth of Pacific Islanders live in urban areas, about a third if you exclude Papua New Guinea. A few countries have more than half their population classified as urban.[33] But what is called urban in the Pacific Islands is often different from what one might imagine from experiences in other parts of the world. Some urban areas are more like unusually large and crowded villages.[34] A connection, including through family and ethnicity, is often maintained with the villages internal migrants came from.[35] There is also "external" migration to New Zealand, Australia, the United States, and elsewhere.[36] External migrants too keep connected to their families back home — by paying visits and sending letters, money, and products.[37] The families and even economies of many countries depend on remittances from islanders living abroad. Migration in Melanesia is more heavily internal than it is in Micronesia and Polynesia.[38] Together, the islands, rural and urban, and the diaspora form a fairly coherent cultural whole, with overlapping traditions, related languages, and Christianity as the predominant religion.[39]

What happens in the Pacific climate system affects the rest of the world. For example, the El Niño–Southern Oscillation (ENSO) influences rain and drought in Australia, Indonesia, and Brazil; hurricanes in the Atlantic; rain, temperature, and tornadoes in North America; rain and flooding in South America; and snow in Tibet.[40] Unfortunately, the Intergovernmental Panel on Climate Change (IPCC) subsumes the Pacific Islands under "small island states" rather than giving it separate treatment.[41] This despite the fact that the Pacific Islands includes several large islands, one of which (New Guinea) is the second largest in the world, following Greenland.

The Pacific Islands is vast enough, unified enough, and environmentally significant enough to be treated as a continent, with parts of the Pacific Rim as the coast.[42] To encourage seeing the Pacific Islands as a cultural whole, yet covering only part of the Pacific Ocean (not

---

BOX 8.1

Components of Oceania (Pacific Islands)

12 developing members of the United Nations ("least developed" bold; Commonwealth italicized)
  Melanesia (4): *Fiji, Papua New Guinea,* **Solomon Islands,** *Vanuatu*
  Polynesia (3): **Samoa,** *Tonga,* **Tuvalu**
  Micronesia (5): Federated States of Micronesia, **Kiribati,** Marshall Islands, *Nauru,* Palau

1 developed member of the United Nations
  Polynesia: *New Zealand* (Aotearoa) (settler society)

1 developing semi-independent country
  Polynesia: Cook Islands (affiliated with New Zealand)

10 territories
  Melanesia: (1) of *France*: New Caledonia
  Polynesia: (6) of *France*: French Polynesia; Wallis and Futuna; of *New Zealand*: Niue, Tokelau; of the *United Kingdom*: Pitcairn Islands; of *Chile*: Easter Island (Rapa Nui)
  Micronesia: (3) of the *USA*: American Samoa, Guam, Northern Mariana Islands

3 parts of non-Oceanic countries
  Melanesia: (2) of *Australia*: Torres Strait islands; of *Indonesia*: West Papua (Irian Jaya)
  Polynesia: (1) of the *USA*: Hawaii (settler society)

all islands in the Pacific are part of the Pacific Islands), the existing term Oceania could be used. Sometimes this term has been used synonymously with *Pacific Islands*; sometimes it has included Australia. On the recommended use, it would exclude Australia. Australia is a continent in its own right. And if Australia is an island continent, Oceania is a continent of islands.[43]

Since the territories — as opposed to the independent countries — benefit economically from their metropolitan affiliations, development organizations restrict their attention to the independent countries. The thirteen independent countries of the Pacific Islands can be divided into one developed settler society with an indigenous minority (and many immigrants from tropical Polynesia) and twelve developing countries, of which five are "least developed".[44] A development concern with how changes to the climatic and non-climatic aspects of the environment affect the poor can conveniently focus on the *tropical* Pacific Islands (or the tropical Pacific) since that would include all twelve developing independent countries and exclude the one independent country that is non-tropical and developed (New Zealand). The tropical Pacific Islands also includes the developing semi-independent country of the Cook Islands, which some development organizations include within their purview.

As well as being the second largest island in the world, New Guinea is the highest, having even a glacier and snow. Papua New Guinea alone (i.e., excluding West Papua) has more land and people than the rest of the Pacific Islands put together. So for some purposes it may be appropriate to give Papua New Guinea separate treatment.[45] For organizations that treat nearby Timor-Leste (East Timor) as an honorary part of the Pacific Islands, its analysis could sometimes be combined with that of Papua New Guinea, as each shares an island with Indonesia and, together with a few other Melanesian islands, the Monsoon climate.[46] If one were to add the rest of Melanesia to Papua New Guinea, and possibly Timor-Leste, such a grouping would consist predominantly of islands made of continental crust,[47] many of them larger, more biologically diverse, and more blessed with natural resources than the islands of the rest of the Pacific Islands. The remaining tropical countries of Polynesia and Micronesia really would be "small-island states". In fact, they would be *developing tropical Pacific* small-island states.

So what about being pro-poor within the independent developing nations of tropical Oceania? I mentioned earlier that individuals and families must, needs be, cooperate with their communities in responding to environmental problems. This is especially true for the poor. From this, and the passivity of the national governments, it follows that outside aid should generally be provided to villages as wholes (rather than to individuals — or to national governments); it should not involve distinguishing the poor individuals or families from the others within the community.

In any case, identifying poor people within Oceania is hindered by the fact that many islanders live simply in villages (some on small islands far from any towns) and engage in subsistence farming, fishing, or animal husbandry. Some of them would only be considered poor if one were to assume that a person without a television, cell-phone, and indoor plumbing is poor — a reasonable assumption in other places. And their traditional systems of reciprocity and extended family support provide a safety net against destitution.[48]

Although it may sometimes be difficult to know when to apply the term poor to rural life in the islands, it is easier to apply it to those living in urban areas. Many of the urban poor are concentrated in shantytowns, or squatter settlements, that have emerged in, around, or near the cities, usually the capital. In these places, there is limited access to water and toilets, insecure land tenure, and widespread unemployment.[49] This is where internal migrants often end up.

A city is not a community in the way a village is. The slums are not harmoniously integrated into a larger urban community.[50] The rich areas do not take care of the poor areas in the way the better off in villages might take care of hardship in the village. The appropriateness of the focus on slums for pro-poor adaptation to the environment is reinforced by the fact that, in addition to being better able to afford the means of coping, the better off in the cities often live in areas less affected by environmental difficulties.[51]

Once the slums have been selected, it may be better not to differentiate among the residents, even though some there lie above the poverty line. If we can treat shantytowns as local communities (as, in effect, poor people's villages), then an area-based approach could be said to apply on the community level everywhere except the non-slum parts of the cities. They would be treated as though parts of the developed world.

Since it is not possible to help all communities, it must be decided which communities are most appropriate to help. Some will be facing more serious environmental problems than others. This is analogous to dividing countries into developed and developing, and then limiting one's attention to the developing. One of the tasks of the development organizations is to come up with a way of ranking communities (see Educating the Educators below).

There is a way that even the non-slum parts of the city might be included in a pro-poor way. Although I have been assuming no help from governments for the communities of Oceania, the non-slum parts of the city constitute the one place for which it might be worth trying carefully to activate government influence. Authorities may be reluctant to help the poor living in squatter villages since they may view them as illegitimate. Their inclination may be to get rid of them, rather than make them more attractive places to live.[52] But the authorities would not have this reluctance with respect to other parts of the cities. The least the government can be expected to do is take care of the better-off parts of the central city, especially if the seat of government is located there. But some projects that benefit the wealthier areas of the city may benefit squatters incidentally. In this way, what might be a side-effect for the government would be the main goal for the development organizations. In addition, any poor people living in the non-slum parts of the city would quite possibly be benefited.

NO REGRETS: SATISFY EXISTING DEMAND

In order for development organizations to have more success than the governments in getting local support for environmental projects, they can do two things: when possible, choose projects that in part satisfy existing demand; and create new demand through formal and informal education. Let me address no regrets first, and then education.

It will be easier to get local people to support programmes that prepare them for projected long-term changes to the environment if the programmes also serve their immediate needs. These programmes are called no regrets because they provide benefits even if computer-model based projections do not pan out. It is just that they would provide even more benefits if they do — and there are rational grounds to assume they will. Programmes that kill both birds with the same stone can be devised by those whose knowledge of the science is combined with an appreciation of local conditions. They will know whether to advocate one no-regrets policy over another; and since there's no guaranteeing that no regrets actions are always available or optimal, they will know when they have no choice but to advocate a program or policy that is not no-regrets.

Towards a Comprehensive Classification Scheme

One way to increase the likelihood of finding no-regrets courses of action is by considering the response to global warming together with responses to all other sorts of environmental problems.[53] For this, it helps to have a comprehensive classification scheme. There are a number of ways things could be divided up. One initial attempt, which cannot help but be faulty, but which might give an idea, is the following. For humans, their natural environment is both beneficial and problematic (e.g., natural capital vs. natural disasters). It is problematic as it is (hurricanes, droughts, etc.) and because of certain changes to it. The environment sometimes changes all by itself (e.g., sea levels go up and down over history) and sometimes because of human influence. Humans are changing the environment in more reversible ways through water pollution, deforestation, unsustainable practices, changes in land use, and the addition of various kinds of tiny solids or liquids into the atmosphere (aerosols: black carbon, mineral dust, and particulate matter from biomass burning, sulfates, nitrates, ammonium, etc.).[54] And humans are causing more long-term changes (e.g., global warming and acidification of the ocean) through the emission of gases whose molecules have three or more atoms.[55] These changes can be looked at globally and regionally.

Of the effects mentioned, global warming's own environmental effects could be divided into those that are climatic (higher temperatures, increased humidity and rain, and stronger storms) and those that are not climatic (warmer oceans, sea-level rise, salinization, crop failure, and coral reef degradation). The main value of making this distinction is to make clear that *climate change* is a misnomer. Otherwise, the effects of global warming might be more rationally divided in ways that cut across any division between climatic and non-climatic aspects of the environment. But if one did have a reason to focus on changes to the climate (literal climate change) or climate system, one might want to divide influences into forcing agents (things outside the climate system that change the earth's energy "balance", e.g., volcanic eruptions, changes in solar radiation, human deforestation) and feedbacks (things inside the climate system that amplify or dampen the influence of forcings; e.g., human deforestation emitting carbon dioxide, which heats the earth, which increases evaporation, which further heats the earth when the water vapor acts as a greenhouse gas), forcings into radiative (things that affect the energy "budget" by affecting radiation) and non-radiative (in which energy imbalances do not involve radiation at first, e.g., agricultural irrigation leading to increased evapotranspiration), and radiative forcings into direct (affecting the radiative budget right away) and indirect (alteration of a climate component that later leads to a change in the radiative flux).[56] Changes to the environment, human-caused and natural, can be divided up in a variety of ways, depending on the purpose.

In addition to integrating an understanding of global warming and its effects with an understanding of other kinds of environmental problem, the policy response to environmental problems can integrate adaptation and mitigation. For the most part, global warming will not be mitigated in Oceania. The mitigation of that sort of human-caused change to the environment depends mainly on decisions yet to be made by industrializing and industrialized countries (to reduce the emission of greenhouse gases and increase their sinks). But the people of Oceania can perhaps do their part toward reducing global warming, while at the same time mitigating other problems, by limiting the deforestation of large islands, such as New Guinea, the Solomon Islands, and Fiji.[57] And some other local environmental problems can be mitigated by Oceanians. For example, as it is becoming harder for coral reefs to grow, not only because of changing water temperature, pH, salinity, and level, but also because of overfishing and silt runoff from logging, limiting logging and fishing would be a form of mitigation.

Adopting an integrated approach does not mean each programme or policy should address everything at once; it just means that each programme would fit into a comprehensive understanding and plan. Somebody needs to see the big picture. So one wants to approach the situation of environment-related policies and programmes not from the narrow question of, say, How can we adapt to changes to those aspects of the environment that are caused by increased emissions of greenhouse gases by humans? Our concern about changes to (as opposed to normal variations within) ENSO, for example, should not be contingent on whether they can be shown to result from global warming (right now they cannot).[58] It is worth investigating whether global warming is having an influence, but we should be interested in changes to ENSO (and even ENSO without changes) regardless.

Sometimes it is not possible to find a no regrets plan. In that case, and more generally, there is a need for education about global warming and other environmental problems.

EDUCATION: CREATE NEW DEMAND

Most islanders, like most people, are far from fully cognizant of the threat posed by global warming and so are insufficiently motivated to carry out those adaptation projects they are capable of or to support the longer-term policies of others. And some of their ideas about dealing with the problems they *can* see may be mistaken, and can even make things worse, e.g., responding to coastal erosion by building seawalls or removing mangroves. Education can create an awareness of less obvious problems and obviate mistaken responses to the obvious ones.[59]

A good way must be found for communicating with people who live in a region that does not need greenhouses how invisible things emanating from the earth can interact with invisible things in the air in a way that raises temperatures by a only a few degrees but has catastrophic effects. This requires efforts be made to understand the outlook of the islanders, and to insert a clear narrative about what is happening to the environment into that understanding. It also means being ready to counter theologically based fatalism.[60] These are real but surmountable communication challenges.

Texts with a clear narrative must be written and then translated into the local languages. A local language can be on one page and the English on the opposing page, or the two languages could be presented interlinearly. The text should be supported by diagrams and a glossary that explains important terms and translation difficulties. The books could be used secondarily for learning either the local language or English. Such books could be used by trained people visiting villages.

Churches and scouting organizations — or a new "Pacific Corps" — could be enlisted.[61] Informal education could also involve social media, mobile devices, community radio, and motion pictures.[62]

Material and training for courses at high schools could be provided. Scholarships and endowed positions could be financed at the University of the South Pacific for islanders who would like to specialize in environmental or climate or earth science. Education should also extend beyond global warming and its effects to environmental problems in general.

Educating the Educators

If development organizations are going to educate islanders in need of educating about global warming and other environmental challenges, the organizations must better understand global warming themselves and be better able to place it within the context of environmental questions more generally. Development organizations need to see the big picture of the various kinds of environmental problems that poor people in developing countries must adapt to or mitigate. And development organizations should see another kind of big picture. Before starting anything new, they should know what others have already done, are in the process of doing, and are planning to do. By coordinating their projects, development organizations' work would become more efficient and less redundant.

To this end (and others), a central database should be created to allow development organizations to easily find out what is going on. The database should include lists of

- things needing to be done (including research),
- subjects that have been, are being, or are going to be researched,
- programmes and projects,
- organizations,
- publications (comprehensive and constantly updated bibliography of articles, papers, books, and films, findable by subject, key words, title, author, etc.),
- people (experts on how environmental change will affect Oceania; people in each Oceanic country and territory who are

> "climate change" officials or coordinators or former members of climate change adaptation teams; translators of the various languages, etc.),
> - conferences (including the names of the papers and presenters),
> - threatened locations (orderable according to various criteria, including degree of urgency — useful for deciding where to send people for educational activities),
> - all locations (political units, island groups, individual islands, and districts) in Oceania about which there is information, with links to what is available on them, and
> - information about local social structures that affect how education can be carried out.

There should be a centre with a website at which all this information can be read, and from which it can be downloaded. In order to keep the information up-to-date, it should be possible for people around the world to post comments and submit information. The centre would filter and verify these submissions and make additions to the database accordingly. Any such centre should be able to explain why the Australian government's excellent Pacific Climate Change Science website (pacificclimatechangescience.org) is not sufficient (if it is not). If it can, it should see itself as supplementing what is there and on other such sites.

In addition to connecting with and accumulating outside information, the center should itself produce a variety of monographs on basic subjects, such as the area's climate system (including a specification of the respective roles of the Walker circulation and the Hadley cells in creating the Trade Winds; the dynamics of ENSO; and how the Western Warm Pool, the Intertropical Convergence Zone, the South Pacific Convergence Zone, the Asian-Australian monsoon system, and the Maritime Continent overlap and interact), the nature of hurricanes,[63] the situation with coral reefs, the nature of electromagnetic waves and how they interact with gases and aerosols, and the history of the emission of greenhouse gases by humans since the agricultural and industrial revolutions. There is also a need for conceptual clarification. The notion of a forcing need to be carefully laid out. Also, the metaphors of budget and balance (as with energy) need to be unpacked. So likewise, for climate, weather, climate system, earth system, and so on. The centre should also make clear the latest projections for, e.g., how high the sea level will rise at various locations under various scenarios. The information in the monographs and the summaries of projections could perhaps be provided in a way that allows viewers to access it at levels of progressively greater detail. These would not be public relations tracts, bureaucratic "deliverables", or "corporate collateral", but rather documents that attempt to get the analysis and science right. One might think that this is the sort of thing the IPCC already does, but it only reports every several years, and it gives short shrift to the tropical Pacific. Nonetheless, this centre would of course critically assess, make use of, and supplement the IPCC reports.

By being made available on a website subject to public comment, correction, and update, the monographs and reports would be in effect peer reviewed. This intellectual transparency should be part of an alteration of the incentive structure of development organizations in way that discourages the publication of documents that are weak on substance, useless, or worse than useless. There should be improved quality control and a system of intellectual checks and balances.

With time, there would be a reasonable basis for people to depend on this source. One of the purposes of all this information is to allow researchers and writers to have quick access to the state of the art on a subject. So rather than every consultant, employee of an international institution, or other researcher spending hours figuring out what the latest projections are for, say, rain in a certain part of the Pacific, they could reliably base their work on statements made by the center. There should be no need to reinvent the wheel and run the risk of quoting inaccurate, out-of-date, or inconsistent sources. The practice of publishing outdated claims, such as that hurricanes are expected to become more frequent, would be minimized.[64] In publications that use the centre's information, readers should be referred the centre's website to see whether there is more recent information.

Once a development organization itself has a clear understanding of global warming, its effects, and its relationship with other environmental problems, it is in a position to create a narrative suited to the people who need educating, expressed in clear texts translated into the local languages.

CONCLUSION

The Pacific Islands, a subset of the islands in the Pacific, is a reasonably coherent cultural entity that ought to be viewed as a continent. Perhaps using the term Oceania, understood to exclude Australia, would help. The situation with the climate system and environment of this Oceania affects not just the people who live there, but the rest of the world too. In the analysis of global warming and other environmental problems, the Pacific should get separate treatment, and not be an afterthought, subsumed under small island states.

In adapting to and mitigating the various environmental problems, poor people in Oceania have to do so as part of their communities. But there are some problems that are too large for communities to solve on their own. Normally, governments would step in to tackle such problems. But governments, and even regional intergovernmental associations, in the Pacific Islands cannot be counted on to do so. Development organizations have taken up some of the slack.

Development organizations apply an area approach to some extent. They work only in independent developing countries, leaving the metropolitan countries to worry about the poor of the territories. Within those countries, help should normally be provided at the community (rural village and urban slum) level — not at higher (national government) or lower (individual or family) levels. This means leaving the better off parts of the cities to the governments to take care of and not differentiating rich and poor within the communities. The communities should be ranked in order of need, which means some communities will not be helped. It would be worth looking into to what extent adding a geographical element to the area approach would be good, that is to say, considering the environmental context of poverty: Is it affected by being not just in an urban slum, but also by being in coastland, wetland, dryland, or upland — the so-called "environments of the poor"? If so, then everyone within that relatively poor area may be helped, even though some of the people are not poor. This way of doing things is justified on utilitarian grounds. It is deemed most likely to minimize the number of people below a poverty line. It is chosen because and when it is likely to bring better results than restricting aid to individuals and families below the poverty line.

Because people in local communities are often unaware of scientific claims about global warming, it will be easier to get their support if adaption projects also served their more obvious needs. And the chances of coming up with such "no regrets" projects increase if the response to global warming is considered together with the responses to all other kinds of environmental problem. For that, a comprehensive classification scheme should be developed. But there is no guarantee that a no-regrets path will always be available or that serious trade-offs can be avoided. Support can also be generated by educating people about what is happening to the environment.

The educators themselves must first be educated, about the relevant science and history and about the worldviews and social structures of the islanders. Information should be critically acquired, organized, centralized, and made available on a website to all who provide environment-related aid to the Pacific Islands. It should be possible for people from around the world to point out errors and make submissions to that site. Rationalizing the production of information can also make it easier for development organizations to determine which communities are most in need of help and to coordinate their projects.

On the foundation of a solid understanding of the science, a narrative must be produced that can be understood within worldview and languages of the islanders; and means must be devised for communicating that narrative within their social structures. For the presentation of this narrative, churches, scouting organizations, and schools could be enlisted. And possibly, a volunteer Pacific Corps could be created. It would be good to invest in and cultivate indigenous specialists in environmental problems, through scholarships and endowed chairs.[65]

Notes

This chapter was written for the Asian Development Bank under the supervision of Armin Bauer. It is part of a larger project of elucidating the connections between poverty, the environment, and global warming in the developing member countries of ADB's Pacific region. Use was made of the unpublished study produced for ADB by Mohinudin Alamgir, "Climate Change Adaptation and Poverty Reduction in the Pacific Islands" (2011). The opinions expressed are mine, and not necessarily those of ADB.

For their help, I would like to thank Aris Ananta (Institute of Southeast Asian Studies), Armin Bauer (Asian Development Bank), Mark Bullen (Commonwealth of Learning), Michelle Keown (University of Edinburgh), Marika Nabou (United Parcel Service), Patrick Nunn (University of New England, Australia), Pascal Paschos (Northwestern University, USA), Jay Roop (AusAID), and Julianne Walsh (University of Hawai'i at Mānoa). Please report errors or send comments to pbullen@uchicago.edu.

1. As the sun's average surface temperatures is higher (5,778 K), the peak of the spectrum of wavelengths it emits is located in a higher frequency and energy part of the electromagnetic spectrum, mainly the visible and ultraviolet.
2. Archer (2012), part I (or the lectures at forecast.uchicago.edu/lectures. html); Chaisson and McMillan (2005), pp. 94–95; Randall (2012), p. 34; Vallis (2012), p. viii; Daniel J. Jacob, *Introduction to Atmospheric Chemistry* (Princeton University Press, 1999), Ch. 7.
3. See Bender (2013), p. 8 for a diagram.
4. Chaisson and McMillan (2005), p. 71.
5. Bender (2013), pp. ix, 21, 27, 55–60, 69; Archer (2009), pp. 83–85, 87; Archer (2010), p. 108.
6. Bender (2013), p. 290; Archer (2009), pp. 65–66. For a plausible, fuller account of the transition from foraging to farming and its relation to changes in the climate, see Ch. 2 of Ian Morris, *Why the West Rules — For Now* (Farrar, Straus and Giroux, 2010).
7. Ruddiman (2010), pp. 89–90, 93–94.
8. Schimel (2013), pp. 138–41; Archer (2010), pp. 151–55; Ruddiman (2010), pp. 79ff, 90–93. Ruddiman changes the time from 8,000 BP to 7,000 BP in the afterword because of what the more recent ice core taken from near Dome C on Antarctica indicated, by contrast with the ice core drilled earlier 560 km away at the Vostok station (p. 201; see also pp. 196, 198, 202, 204, 205, 207, 208). Archer (2009), pp. 153–54 assesses Ruddiman's hypothesis, but this was before the 2010 edition of Ruddiman's book came out with an afterword. See Maslin's more recent (2013, p. 142) assessment of "the wonderful Ruddiman early anthropocene hypothesis", which includes this: "it has been tested again and again, and no one has yet been able to disprove it". For what may be an implicit view, see Bender (2013), p. 264.
9. Raw materials included such things as wool, hides, flax, tallow, hair, bone, bark, wood, cotton, and silk (Wrigley 2010, p. 66; see also pp. 30, 85, 86, 87, 245). Gregory Clark and David Jacks, "Coal and the Industrial Revolution, 1700–1869", *European Review of Economic History* 11, no. 1 (April 2007): 39–72; p. 27 of the free version; McMichael (1993), pp. 96–98, 134–135; Wrigley (2010), pp. 17, 175, 234; Chadwick D. Oliver, Melih Boydak, and Roger Sedio, "Deforestation", in Cuff and Goudie, eds. (2009), p. 162.

10. And raw materials shifted to minerals too, e.g., bricks made from clay (baked with coal) replaced wood in the construction industry; and glass for windows, pottery pipes for drainage, and an expanded use of iron (Wrigley 2010, p. 190; see also pp. 96, 98, 100, 174; McMichael 1993, pp. 96–97).

11. Wrigley (2010), pp. 152–53. See Gregory Clark, *A Farewell to Alms* (Princeton University Press, 2008), part I (pp. 19–192).

12. Ruddiman (2010), p. 88; Archer (2010), pp. 106, 116–17; Schimel (2013), pp. 121–26.

13. Methane: 15%; nitrous oxide: 7% HFCs, etc: 1% (World Resources Institute).

14. Ruddiman (2010), p. 86.

15. David Archer and Stefan Rahmstorf, *The Climate Crisis* (Cambridge University Press, 2010), p. 100. I've seen slightly different numbers elsewhere.

16. Bender (2013), pp. 62–63; Schimel (2013), pp. 20–21, 61–63. Archer (2009), p. 82; Archer (2010), pp. 119–20; National Research Council of the National Academies (2005), pp. 96–97; William R. Cotton and Roger A. Pielke, Jr., *Human Impacts on Weather and Climate*, 2nd ed. (Cambridge University Press, 2007), pp. 238–39; Roger Pielke, Sr., "Overlooked Issues in the U.S. National Climate and IPCC Assessments", *Climatic Change* 52 (1–2), p. 1.

17. Archer (2009 and 2010).

18. "Summary of Findings" on Berkeley Earth website <berkeleyearth.org/summary-of-findings>.

19. By "environment" I mean *natural* environment. The environment includes the climate. The Merriam-Webster Unabridged (Third International) Dictionary gives one definition of environment as "the surrounding conditions, influences, or forces that influence or modify: such as the whole complex of **climatic**, edaphic [soil-related], and biotic factors that act upon an organism or an ecological community and ultimately determine its form and survival". Note that one element of the environment is the climate, or at least certain "climatic factors". Similarly: "By an *environment*, geographers mean the sum total of conditions that surround (literally, environ) a person at any one point on the earth's surface. For early people these conditions were largely natural and included such elements as the local **climate**, terrain, vegetation, and soils" (Peter H. Haggett, *Geography* [Prentice Hall, 2001], p. 16). This definition allows for expansion to include to the built environment.

20. Sea-level rise is the result of directly heated water and the melting of ice from several causes, including a change to the climate (warmer air), but also including non-climatic changes: warmer water, albedo changes, and direct solar heat. Coral reef degradation is the result of the warming

ocean (a non-climatic part of global warming) and rising sea levels. It is also the result of acidification, not caused by global warming, but in any case non-climatic. Flooding is partially the result of a climate change: more rain (including from storms), but partially because of non-climatic sea-level rise. Coastal erosion is the result of storms (climatic), but also sea-level rise (non-climatic). Salinized soil and water is the result of sea-level rise and flooding (non-climatic, although some of the flooding is due to rain, which is climatic).

21. Schimel (2013), p. 8; see Andrew Goudie, "Earth System Science", in Cuff and Goudie, eds. (2009), p. 193.

22. "Earth's climate system includes all the realms of the planet that interact to produce the seasonal march of temperature, wind, and precipitation" (Bender 2013, p. 1). Oddly, the entire edifice of climate science is built on the foundation of the practical human desire to know whether to take an umbrella to work (etc.). However, for scientific purposes it may be that a new definition of *climate* is necessary, one that is less dependent on the meaning of *weather*. This tension may be why scientists, when trying to explain things to others, occasionally conflate climate and climate system — and forget why the word climate is in the term climate system (e.g., National Research Council of the National Academies 2005, p. 12; Maslin 2013, p. 11; Bender 2013, p. viii; Andrew P. Ingersoll, *Planetary Climates* [Princeton University Press, 2013], p. 1). One could take what is loosely called the climate system and treat it as a whole in which the explanation of weather is simply one useful byproduct. The atmosphere would not necessarily have a privileged position. If so, what has hitherto been called the climate system should perhaps be called something else. And the analytic benefit of demarcating this system within the earth system should be explained.

23. See, e.g., *The National Global Change Research Plan 2012–2021* (2012), the subtitle of McMichael (1993): *Global Environmental Change and the Health of the Species*, the subtitle of Anderson, Goudie, and Parker, *Global Environments Through the Quaternary* (2013): *Exploring Environmental Change*, and the title of Cuff and Goudie, eds. (2009): *Oxford Companion to Global Change*. The introduction to the latter has a useful discussion of terminology. See also its entry, "Global Change History" by William B. Meyer (pp. 294–96).

24. Nunn (2009), p. 225. "National policy has little or no influence on most decisions undertaken with reference to the environment in rural parts of the Pacific Islands. In fact, there is very little evidence that such decisions pay attention to science or other sources of insights concerning climate change" (Patrick D., Nunn coordinator, "Understanding Environmental Decision-Making in the Rural Pacific Islands", Final Report submitted to

APN CAPABLE Project: CBA2007-03NSY [Suva, Fiji: Asia-Pacific Network for Global Change Research, 2008], p. 3). On "state fragility" in the Pacific Islands, see Volker Boege, "Australian Approaches to State Fragility in the South Pacific Region", Paper presented at the 49th Annual ISA Convention, San Francisco, 26–29 March 2008. "As of 2010, Kiribati, Marshall Islands, Federated States of Micronesia, Nauru, Palau, Papua New Guinea, Solomon Islands, Timor-Leste, and Tuvalu — are formally classified by ADB as fragile states due to their low country performance assessments" (ADB 2012, p. 2). See a footnote below for more on this. "Villagers receive little government development aid or services. They feel alienated from the government, [although several villages visited in Fiji and Solomon Islands] were close to a main road and also to the seat of government]. Villagers find it difficult to bring their problems to the attention of the authorities. When they do, the response is generally not satisfactory" (Mohinudin Alamgir, "Strategies for Pro-Poor Adaptation to Climate Change in Small Island Pacific Communities: Case Studies of Fiji and Solomon Islands". Unpublished Draft Final Report. Manila: Asian Development Bank, October 2011, pp. 177ff/241ff, pagination for the edited and unedited versions). "From an administrative perspective, the remoteness and geographic dispersal [of the Pacific Islands] makes governance and the provision of public goods more difficult and costly. At the same time, the cost for tax enforcement increases" (Paul Holden, Malcolm Bale, and Sarah Holden, *Swimming Against the Tide* [ADB, 2004], p. 34).

25. "The role of intra-regional advisory bodies [such as the South Pacific Regional Environment Programme and the South Pacific Applied Geoscience Commission] is determined by their member countries, but it could be argued that this role should extend to advising member countries about the non-sustainability of the paths currently being pursued by governments with respect to the environments of the Pacific Island countries, particularly with reference to their exploitation for short term economic gain. To date, the writer is not aware of any of these bodies having made such a statement in unequivocal terms" (Nunn 2009, p. 216).

26. See David G. Victor, "Nongovernmental Organizations", in Cuff and Goudie, eds. (2009), pp. 460–62.

27. For more on this subject, see Armin Bauer, "The Environments of Poverty" (ADB, 2008) and the ADB web page, "Environments of the Poor".

28. The numbers are taken from E. H. Bryan, Jr., "Discussion", in Fosberg, ed. (1963), p. 38.

29. Ten of the independent countries are members of the Commonwealth of Nations. It would be worth looking into to what extent Oceania, from the viewpoint of legal systems, can also be divided into a Common Law sphere

(British, American, New Zealander, and Australian influence) and a Civil Law sphere (French influence, mainly; but possibly also German, Dutch, Portuguese, and Japanese).

30. Tom L. McKnight, *Oceania* (Prentice Hall, 1995), p. 148; William L. Thomas, Jr., "The Variety of Physical Environments Among Pacific Islands", in Fosberg, ed. (1963), p. 28; Jack Williams, *The AMS Weather Book* (University of Chicago Press/American Meteorological Society, 2009), p. 235.

31. The political entities of Oceania frequently have a main island and a multitude of secondary islands, some of which are quite far from the main island and each other ("outer islands"). The main islands tend to be bigger and more populous, urban, modern, and politically central. "Most Pacific Island countries have only one major urban centre (Papua New Guinea and Fiji are the exceptions) and most of many countries' critical infrastructure is in these urban localities" (Barnett and Campbell 2010, p. 14). The Marshall Islands also has more than one urban area.

32. "Even by the mid-1980s, over 37 per cent of ethnic Polynesians were living outside their home countries, and in countries such as Niue, the Cook Islands, and Tokelau, the number of expatriates currently far exceed those remaining at home" (Michelle Keown, *Pacific Island Writing* [Oxford University Press, 2007], p. 187).

33. "While a small island such as Nauru is defined as being 100% urbanized, in reality, only parts of the coastal perimeter are urbanized in the traditional sense of the term" (ADB 2012, p. 4).

34. "Modern-day Pacific urban areas have developed around clusters of traditional villages in which traditional village life became intermixed with both planned and unplanned urban development. The traditional villages located within the now-modern Pacific urban areas remain territorial enclaves that operate under traditional rules of governance. As a result, their status and rights have been preserved under current land use planning and governance arrangements. With the acceleration in rural–urban migration beginning in the 1960s, a new type of village has emerged and blossomed — the squatter settlement — which over time has become a nearly universal phenomenon in Pacific urban areas.... Many of these settlements are in fact rural villages within a modernized urban setting that exhibit the physical, social, and cultural characteristics of traditional rural villages, including their ethnic and kinship composition. In such settlements, identity and association with rural place-of-origin and kin are paramount. Subsistence living and mixed levels of commercial activity are an inherent part of life in such settlements... Settlements of this type are now a permanent feature of the Pacific urban landscape. During the coming decade, 'village cities'

will likely emerge as the dominant urban form in many Pacific urban locales" (ADB 2012, pp. 4–5).

35. "In Port Moresby, for example, these settlements have been described as 'cosmopolitan networks of tribal groupings or anarchical subcultures, which have been defined by ethnicity and regionalism within an urban context'" (ADB 2012, p. 5).

36. Fischer (2002), p. 265.

37. "Today the huge phenomenon of circular migration is creating a new kind of cultural formation: a determinate community without entity, extending transculturally and often transnationally from a rural centre in the so-called Third World to 'homes abroad' in the metropolis, the whole united by the toing and froing of goods, ideas and people on the move.... The structural complementarity of the indigenous homeland and the metropolitan 'homes abroad,' their interdependence as sources of cultural value and means of social reproduction. Symbolically focused on the homeland, whence its members derive their identity and their destiny, the 'translocal' community is strategically dependent on its urban context on the basis of their relationships at home. Kinship, community and tribal affiliations acquire new functions, and perhaps new forms, in the relationship among migrants: they organize the movements of people and resources, the care of homeland dependents, the provision of urban housing and employment" (Marshall Sahlins, "On the Anthropology of Modernity, or, Some Triumphs of Culture over Despondency Theory", in *Culture and Sustainable Development in the Pacific*, edited by Anthony Hooper [Asia Pacific Press, 2000], pp. 53–55).

38. "Micronesia has the highest per capita net emigration rates in the world" (Pacific Institute of Public Policy [Port Vila, Vanuatu], "The Micronesia Exodus", *Discussion Paper* 16, December: 1). "Auckland has the highest Polynesian population of any city in the world — fully half the people are dusky islanders" (Paul Theroux, *The Happy Isles of Oceania* [Mariner, 2006 (1992)], p. 20). "At the time of the 2006 census, there were 265,974 people of Pacific ethnicity living in New Zealand — 6.4% of the New Zealand population. Not all of them are immigrants: indeed, six out of ten were born in New Zealand. Nevertheless, the impact of a liberal citizenship regime is revealed by the fact that there are fourteen times as many Niueans, six times as many Tokelauans and three times as many Cook Islanders in New Zealand than in their home islands. Australia has been indirectly affected by these policies because New Zealand citizens also have a right of access to Australia under long-standing Trans-Tasman travel arrangements, thus facilitating step-wise migration. The United States has also facilitated migration between its affiliated Pacific Islands and the mainland" (Brian Opeskin and Therese MacDermott, "Resources, Population and Migration

in the Pacific: Connecting Islands and Rim", *Asia Pacific Viewpoint* 50, no. 3 (December 2009): 365–66).

39. Because of the many Indians in Fiji, the population is only 58 per cent Christian, while 34 per cent is Hindu and 7 per cent Muslim.

40. "The most coherent, widespread interannual variations in global climate are tied, through teleconnections, to tropical variability associated with the El Niño–Southern Oscillation (ENSO)" (Katherine E. Dayem, David C. Noone, and Peter Molnar, "Tropical Western Pacific Warm Pool and Maritime Continent Precipitation Rates and their Contrasting Relationships with the Walker Circulation", *Journal of Geophysical Research* 112 [2007], p. 1). See also Vallis (2012), pp. 141, 144; Maslin (2009), p. 95; Maslin (2013), pp. 38–40; Luoa, Jing-Jia, Wataru Sasakia, and Yukio Masumoto, "Indian Ocean Warming Modulates Pacific Climate Change", *PNAS Early Edition*, 9 October 2012: 1, 4; K-M Lau and S. Yang, "Walker Circulation", in *Encyclopedia of Atmospheric Sciences* (Academic Press, 2003), p. 2505; Zhiwei Wu et al., "Modulation of the Tibetan Plateau Snow Cover on the ENSO Teleconnection: From the East Asian Summer Monsoon Perspective", *Journal of Climate* 25, no. 7 (April 2012): 2481–89; Shang-Ping Xie in David Biello, "Is the Pacific Ocean Responsible for a Pause in Global Warming?" *Scientific American* website, 28 August 2013.

41. IPCC 2007 has a chapter titled Australia and New Zealand. The tropical Pacific Islands are covered in a chapter titled Small Island States, which also includes islands from the Indian Ocean and the Atlantic, especially the Caribbean. IPCC SREX 2012 has a chapter titled Oceania, which includes only New Zealand and Australia, but refers the reader to the section Small Island States for the rest of what it calls Oceania — that rest being the tropical part of the Pacific Islands. Better would be a section titled Australia and New Zealand (as in 2007) and another titled Tropical Pacific. However, the boundaries of an environmental analysis need not follow political or cultural boundaries. It may make better natural-geographic sense to include the Maritime Continent together with the tropical Pacific, for example.

42. "By 2010 around 500,000 people born in Pacific island countries — roughly equivalent to the total population of Micronesia — were living in towns and cities on the Pacific Rim, mainly in Auckland, Wellington, Sydney, Brisbane, Honolulu, Los Angeles, San Francisco and Vancouver" (Richard Bedford and Graeme Hugo/Labor and Immigration Research Centre, *Population Movement in the Pacific* [Wellington: Department of Labour 2012], p. 24.

43. "Continent of islands" echoes Epili Hau'ofa's "sea of islands" (Waddell, Naidu, and Hau'ofa, eds., *A New Oceania: Rediscovering Our Sea of Islands* [1993]). At least one other person has already referred to the Oceania as a continent: "As a whole the islands in the Pacific Region are called Oceania,

the tenth continent on Earth. Inherent to their remoteness and because
of the wide variety of island types, the Pacific Islands have developed
unique social, biological, and geological characteristics" (Anthony A. P.
Koppers, "Pacific Region", in *Encyclopedia of Islands*, ed. Rosemary G.
Gillespie and David A. Clague [University of California Press, 2009], p.
702). However, since his entry includes Vancouver Island, the Galapagos
Islands, and the Kurile Islands, it's not clear what the referents of *Pacific
Region*, *Oceania*, or *Pacific Islands* are. In any case, he does not seem to
be including Australia. Asia, Europe, and the Maritime Continent are not
literal geographic continents either. Under this scheme, "the Asia-Pacific
region" would comprise two quasi-continents, with Pacific = Pacific Islands
= Oceania. It would not refer to the Pacific Ocean and everything in it.
So "the Pacific" would not include, e.g., the Philippines. Determining the
meaning of *continent* requires some effort. Problems arise when a notion
taken from one sphere (e.g., geography and climate) is used in another
sphere (e.g., culture and history).

44. For what this means, see the website of the UN Office of the High
Representative for the Least Developed Countries, Landlocked Countries
and Small Island Developing States. Timor-Leste (introduced below) is a
Least Developed Country too. In ADB (2012), p. 2's list of fragile states
given in an earlier footnote, the only two countries not on that list, Samoa
and Vanuatu, are Least Developed countries. Putting aside Timor-Leste,
that means eleven of the twelve developing countries of Oceania are either
fragile or least developed. And three are both. The only country that is
neither fragile nor least developed is the Kingdom of Tonga.

45. "Papua New Guinea is so large compared to the other countries and
territories it could be considered a distinct biophysical area" (Johann D.
Bell, Johanna E. Johnson, and Alistair J. Hobday, eds., *Vulnerability of Tropical
Pacific Fisheries and Aquaculture to Climate Change* [Noumea, New Caledonia:
Secretariat of the Pacific Community, 2011], p. 5). On West Papua as part of
the Pacific Islands, see Johnny Blades, "Mood for Self-determination Grows
Among Small Pacific Nations: West Papuan Efforts to Put Self-determination
on the International Stage Gain Momentum", *The Guardian*, 23 July 2013.

46. Timor-Leste does have some Austronesian blood, and Christianity is the
predominant religion (97 per cent of the total population is Catholic, 2 per
cent Protestant).

47. The crust of the earth divides into two types, made with chemically
distinct rocks. "Ocean crust is thinner and denser than continental crust,
so it floats lower than continental crust does. The waters of the ocean
simply fill in the deep parts, and so it mostly covers the oceanic type of
crust" (Archer 2009, p. 86). Continental crust frequently extends beyond

the exposed area of a continent to a continental shelf. Islands rising from this submerged continental crust are called continental islands. In Oceania, Melanesia has most of the continental islands. New Zealand (part of Polynesia) consists of continental islands too, but from a submerged continent rather than a continental shelf. The islands further out than the shelf, in the ocean basis, are called oceanic islands, being made of oceanic crust. Barnet and Campbell (2010), p. 22 summarizes this view when it says, "A fairly basic distinction is made between the oceanic islands, which are found east of the andesite line (which runs along the boundary between the oceanic and continental plates in the western Pacific and is part of the 'ring of fire') and the 'continental' type islands that lie to its west" (22). But it then adds, "Nunn (1994) prefers to use the terms 'intra-plate islands' and 'plate boundary islands' respectively, which tend to be more indicative of the their respective geological origins" (22). And it proceeds to use "plate boundary" interchangeably with "continental", and "intra-plate" interchangeably with "oceanic". But Nunn's distinction is made *after* he has put aside continental islands. The title of his 1994 book is *Oceanic Islands* (Blackwell), and his division is *within* the genus of oceanic islands. So plate-boundary and intra-plate islands are both oceanic. (Nunn then subdivides each type; see a summary in table 1.1 p. 10.) Also, Nunn does not "prefer" his terminology. His terminology is adopted for the sake of a classification made on specialized, "genetic", grounds. It is not meant to replace the older classification system or terminology. A less serious problem is that table 2.2 on pages 25 and 26 gives the impression that the heading Intra-plate (Oceanic) Islands is meant to apply only to the first-listed species of oceanic island, the one immediately below it (volcanic high islands), while the authors clearly (to those who take the time to figure it out) intend for it to apply also to the two other kinds of oceanic island, which appear on the following page: atolls and raised limestone islands. Barnett and Campbell are (unfortunately) trying to communicate that everything below "Intra-plate (Oceanic) islands" (all three oceanic subtypes) comes under that heading. Both these confusions (the misinterpretation and the misleading representation of the misinterpretation in the table) unfortunately made their way into IPCC SREX 2012 (p. 263). The report mistakenly claims to be following J. R. Campbell, "Traditional Disaster Reduction in Pacific Island Communities", *GNS Science Report* 38 (Institute of Geological and Nuclear Sciences, 2006), which does not in fact have this problem. IPCC SREX 2012's table at p. 263 solidifies the (unintentionally) misleadingly chart at Barnett and Campbell 2010, p. 23. Unfortunately, once one finally arrives at a correct interpretation of these tables, one is still left with a misinterpretation of the plate-boundary/intra-plate distinction itself — not to mention an incoherent typology. IPCC SREX 2012 is also marred by a complete lack of awareness of ABM/CSIRO 2011 and by the categorizing of the tropical Pacific as "small-island states".

48. Partha Dasgupta, *An Inquiry into Well-Being and Destitution* (Clarendon, 1993), pp. 137, 189, 208–12, 215, 295–96, 322, 352, 542–43, 545; see also his *Human Well-Being and the Natural Environment* (Oxford University Press, 2004), pp. 51, 113–14, 194, 203; and his *Economics* (Oxford University Press, 2007), pp. 30, 34, 39, 105, 150.

49. "The spread of unemployment and underemployment ... has caused a dramatic rise in malnutrition, begging, child labor, and security issues; and a general decline in the ... fabric of Pacific urban areas. In fact, according to official statistics, urban poverty is now more widespread than is rural poverty in Cook Islands, Kiribati, the Federated States of Micronesia, Samoa, Solomon Islands, Tonga, Tuvalu, and Vanuatu, a statistic underscored by the sprawling squatter settlements that now house an estimated 800,000 to 1 million Pacific urban residents. This problem of inadequate housing, coupled with land tenure issues, is particularly acute in the Melanesian capitals of Honiara, Port Moresby, Port Vila, and Suva, where 15%–50% of the urban population now lives in squatter settlements" (ADB 2012, p. 2). "For many urban dwellers, under-employment, unemployment and, increasingly, poverty are elements of their lives. Squatter settlements have emerged in many Pacific Island towns and cities where much of the land is held in communal ownership of the original clan families. The buildings in these areas often lack the qualities of traditional dwellings that are resistant to tropical cyclones. People who live in this peri-urban areas often have poor access to sanitation infrastructure and clean water, and so typically have higher rates of water-borne diseases. The quality of infrastructure in these areas is constrained by uncertain land tenure: households and public authorities are reluctant to invest in areas liable to be reclaimed by their customary owners. Because urban growth has failed to successfully adapt to land tenure arrangement across the region, but also because of the cost of urban development and the lack of capacity in urban design and management, urban areas in PICs [Pacific Island Countries] have a chequered history with respect to effective urban planning. Accordingly, the infrastructure and people in urban areas in PICs are vulnerable to natural hazards" (Barnett and Campbell 2010, p. 39). "Increasing urbanization is leading to the growth of squatter areas, to youth unemployment, and to increasing social dislocation for many families living in poor and overcrowded conditions and the irrelevance of traditional systems of land tenure and labor to the new demands of society" (Abbott and Pollard 2004,

p. xi). "Although in aggregate urban areas tend to be better served [with respect to water], there are many squatter settlements where the urban poor tend to be concentrated that have no access to safe water" (Abbott and Pollard 2004, p. 45).

50. "While urbanization has exposed some Pacific Island people to poverty, most outer island communities … still enjoy relatively secure, if relatively basic, livelihoods" (Barnett and Campbell 2010, p. 157).

51. "It is the urban poor living away from their customary lands and in hazard-exposed areas that are often the most affected by storms. In this sense, adaptation to climate change is about practices to bring about sustainability, such as implementing effective systems for sanitation and waste disposal, improving access to health care, the adaptive management of resources, and small-scale income generation schemes for the most vulnerable communities" (Barnett and Campbell 2010, p. 48).

52. "The urban growth which has characterized particularly the past generation in Pacific Islands defies many fledgling nations to provide the necessary infrastructure and social services. Authorities who then conscientiously address and resolve problems of water supplies, waste disposal, health, employment and rising crime as more and more shanty towns spring up alongside the Pacific's expanding coastline metropolises, experience that the resulting improved quality of urban life there only draws even more migrants, further depopulating the rural countrysides and entire islands…. Not all of Pacific Islands struggles with urbanization. Around 70 per cent of Polynesians are still rural dwellers" (Fischer 2002, p. 268).

53. "Overcoming climate exceptionalism can only occur when climate change is understood as being one of a number of issues to be addressed under the general rubric of sustainable development…. Activities to mitigate greenhouse gas emissions and to facilitate adaptation cannot be treated as special stand-alone issues requiring distinct policy frameworks and institutions" (Barnett and Campbell 2010, pp. 180–81).

54. Pielke, Jr. (2010), p. 17 and environs.

55. Not all environmental changes are for the worse, even human-caused changes. But I am speaking now within the division of problematic environmental changes. In practice, beneficial changes should be considered together with harmful changes.

56. I am here trying to follow National Research Council of the National Academies 2005 (see, e.g., pp. 1–10, 12–22, 47–48, 78, 85–87, 92–97, 147). But I am not sure the distinctions are fully coherent, at least as they have worded them. For one thing, they defined a climate forcing as an energy imbalance. But if a forcing necessarily involves an imbalance, it would

have to be the causing of the imbalance, not the imbalance itself. Starting at the earth's current globally averaged surface temperature of 288 K, a 1 K increase would cause about a 7 per cent increase in the saturation vapour pressure. But a 3 K increase would lead to a 25 per cent increase (a non-linear, exponential function is involved). Given the "tendency for the relative humidity of air to remain constant as the climate changes", this means a 1 per cent increase in temperature (which is what a 3 K increase would be, if you started at 288 K) could lead to a 25 per cent increase in rainfall in particular thunderstorms (Randall 2012, pp. 178–81; note that the reference to Figure 3.3 should be to Figure 3.4, on p. 77; see also pp. 12–13, 76, 146–47).

57. "Deforestation in the tropics will play a significant role in the CO_2 increase" (Ruddiman 2010, p. 173). "Modern rates [of tree cutting] are very high because of rapid clearance of tropical rain forests in South America and Asia. By comparison, the estimated annual clearance rate just two centuries ago was almost ten times smaller than today" (Ruddiman 2010, p. 88).

58. "The impacts of global warming on ENSO amplitude and frequency are unclear" (ABM/CRISO 2011 1:146; see also pp. 7, 163, 179, 215). "There is also considerable debate about whether ENSO has been affected by global warming.... Most computer models of ENSO are inconclusive; some have found an increase while others have found no change" (Maslin 2009, 94; see Maslin 2013, pp. 41–42, where the position is repeated, but expanded on a bit).

59. "Governments are best placed within the Pacific Islands to undertake such programs of community outreach, but few do systematically, at least in the field of environmental decision-making. To date, the NGOs have been most effective in advising communities on how to best respond to the challenges of environmental management, including climate change. Some of the best examples are found in forestry, where NGOs, which do not profit from logging, are often able to advise communities of their choices before they allow their forests to be logged. Another example comes from mangrove replanting as a solution to shoreline erosion; NGO personnel are able to invest more time in advising on sustainable solutions than governments, which tend to favor short-term, hard-fix solutions like seawalls. NGOs are perceived differently from governments by local-area communities; they are often able to spend more time engaging the community and often bring in volunteers for prolonged attachments, thereby displaying the kind of commitment that governments cannot afford. Further, NGOs often come with some funding attached, which is a powerful incentive for communities to listen to their message and act on it. Finally, NGOs often exhibit the kind of long-term interest in projects within particular communities that

governments are generally unable to do" (Nunn 2009, pp. 220–21).

60. Statements only make sense to a person within a network of already-held relevant beliefs and against a background of certain non-propositional capacities. See John R. Searle on "the Background" and the "Network", introduced in his 1983 book *Intentionality* (especially chapter 5) and developed in his later works.

61. Barnet and Campbell (2010), p. 183.

62. Although new educational documentaries should be made, there are some excellent existing movies that could be donated to the villages, e.g., the documentary *There Once Was An Island* (2011); and Michael Powell's *The Edge of the World* (1937), inspired by a true story of the residents of a small, isolated Scottish island who had to be relocated. See also the Australian government's animated cartoon, "The Pacific Adventures of the Climate Crab". An interesting challenge is to consider what sort of "background" or "network" of beliefs is required to understand something even as simple as this video (see discussion of Searle above).

63. The practice of a single speaker referring the same phenomenon by different names depending on where it occurs (e.g., Ruddiman 2010, p. 181) should be discouraged. As it is now, you have newscasters reporting that there was a typhoon in the Philippines, a cyclone in the South Pacific, and a hurricane in the Caribbean. As a result, most people do not realize that hurricane = typhoon = (tropical) cyclone. For an English-speaking audience in the Pacific or the United States, *hurricane* should be adopted and *typhoon* and *cyclone* (etc.) dropped. "Hurricane" is commonly used in indigenous Pacific Island literature (e.g., novels by Albert Wendt and Sia Figiel). Perhaps for scientific purposes *tropical cyclone* could be used as a technical term when there is an implicit or explicit contrast with non-tropical cyclones or anti-cyclones.

64. IPCC SREX (2012), p. 163; see also pp. 169, 185; Morris A. Bender et al, "Modeled Impact of Anthropogenic Warming on the Frequency of Intense Atlantic Hurricanes", *Science* 327 (5964) 22 January 2010: 454–58, 454; ABM/ CSIRO 2011, 1:203. See also IPCC SREX (2012), p. 169; Pielke, Jr. (2010), p. 172; Kerry A. Emanuel, "Extreme Events" (p. 254) and Andrew S. Goudie, "Tropical Cyclones in a Warming World" (pp. 594–96), both in Cuff and Goudie, eds. (2009).

65. For more practical suggestions about adaptation to "climate change" in the Pacific Islands, see the recent essays by Patrick Nunn, such as "Climate Change and Pacific Island Countries" (United Nations Development Programme, forthcoming); "The End of the Pacific? Effects of Sea Level Rise on Pacific Island Livelihoods", *Singapore Journal of Tropical Geography* 34, no. 2 (July 2013): 143–71; "Understanding and Adapting to Sea-Level Rise", in *Global*

Environmental Issues, 2nd ed., ed. Frances Harris (Wiley-Blackwell, 2012), pp. 87–104; and (with W. Aalbersberg, S. Lata, and M. Gwilliam), "Beyond the Core: Community Governance for Climate-Change Adaptation in Peripheral Parts of Pacific Island Countries", *Regional Environmental Change* 13, no. 2 (April 2013).

References

ABM/CSIRO. *Climate Change in the Pacific*. Vol. 1: *Regional Overview*; Vol. 2: *Country Reports*. Canberra: Australian Bureau of Meteorology, Commonwealth Scientific and Industrial Research Organisation, 2011. Available at <cawcr. gov.au/projects/PCCSP/publications1.html>.

Abbott, David, and Steve Pollard. *Hardship and Poverty in the Pacific*. Manila: Asian Development Bank, Pacific Area Department, 2004.

ADB. *The State of Pacific Towns and Cities*. Manila: Asian Development Bank, 2012.

Archer, David. *The Long Thaw*. Princeton, N.J.: Princeton University Press, 2009.

———. *The Global Carbon Cycle*. Princeton, N.J.: Princeton University Press, 2010.

———. *Global Warming*, 2nd ed. Hoboken, N.J.: Wiley, 2012.

Barnett, Jon, and John Campbell. *Climate Change and Small Island States*. London: Earthscan, 2010.

Bender, Michael L. *Paleoclimate*. Princeton, N.J.: Princeton University Press, 2013.

Chaisson, Eric, and Steve McMillon. *Astronomy Today*. 5th ed. Upper Saddle River, N.J.: Prentice Hall, 2005.

Cuff, David, and Andrew Goudie, eds. *The Oxford Companion to Global Change*. Oxford: Oxford University Press, 2009.

Fischer, Steven Roger. *A History of the Pacific Islands*. New York: Palgrave, 2002.

Fosberg, F. R., ed. *Man's Place in the Island Ecosystem*. Honolulu: Bishop Museum Press, 1963.

IPCC. *Climate Change 2007: Impacts, Adaptation and Vulnerability*. Contribution of Working Group II to the Fourth Assessment Report of the Intergovernmental Panel on Climate Change. Cambridge: Cambridge University Press, 2007.

IPCC SREX. *Managing the Risks of Extreme Events and Disasters to Advance Climate Change Adaptation*. A Special Report of Working Groups I and II of the Intergovernmental Panel on Climate Change. Cambridge: Cambridge University Press, 2012.

Maslin, Mark. *Global Warming*. 2nd ed. Oxford: Oxford University Press,

2009.

————. *Climate.* Oxford: Oxford University Press, 2013.

McMichael, Anthony J. *Planetary Overload.* Cambridge University Press, 1993.

National Research Council of the National Academies. *Radiative Forcing of Climate Change.* Washington, D.C.: National Academies Press, 2005. Available at <nap.edu/catalog.php?record_id=11175>.

Nunn, Patrick D. "Responding to the Challenges of Climate Change in the Pacific Islands: Management and Technological Imperatives". *Climate Research* 40 (10 December 2009): 211–31.

Pielke, Jr., Roger. *The Climate Fix.* New York: Basic Books, 2010.

Randall, David. *Atmosphere, Clouds, and Climate.* Princeton, N.J.: Princeton University Press, 2012.

Ruddiman, William F. *Plows, Plagues, and Petroleum.* Princeton, N.J.: Princeton University Press, 2010.

Schimel, David. *Climate and Ecosystems.* Princeton, N.J.: Princeton University Press, 2013.

Vallis, Geoffrey K. *Climate and the Oceans.* Princeton, N.J.: Princeton University Press, 2012.

Wrigley, E. A. *Energy and the English Industrial Revolution.* Cambridge: Cambridge University Press, 2010.

IV

Mainland Southeast Asia (Cambodia, Thailand, Vietnam)

9

POVERTY AND THE ENVIRONMENT IN RURAL CAMBODIA

Tong Kimsun and Sry Bopharath

In Cambodia, the poor depend largely on natural resources for their livelihoods. This is particularly true for the rural poor. Hence, decline in the quality and accessibility of natural resources due to climate change is likely to affect them more seriously than the non-poor. Specifically, the poor become more vulnerable because they are less able to adapt to environmental change. Despite the fragility of Cambodian politics in the 1990s, the economy grew at a remarkable 7.2 per cent (average). After political stability returned in 1999, the rate rose even higher — to an average of 9.3 per cent for 2000–08. This resulted in an increase in per capita income and a decline in poverty. According to the latest World Bank Poverty Assessment report, the poverty headcount in Cambodia declined from 47 per cent in 1993/94 to 30 per cent in 2007. During the same period, school enrolment, housing, and access to safe drinking water, electricity, and sanitation also improved (MOP 2006; World Bank 2009).

Despite this impressive performance, poverty rate was not uniform across the country. Poverty rates are higher in rural areas than in urban areas in all geographical zones (MOP 2006). Of the country's five geographical zones, Plateau and Mountains is the poorest, with a poverty rate of 52 per cent in 2004, followed by Tonle Sap (42 per cent), Plains (32 per cent), Coastal regions (27 per cent), and Phnom Penh (4.6 per cent). Since the Tonle Sap zone, has so many poor, and contains 30 per cent of Cambodia's population (MOP 2009), it has become of special concern to policy makers and other national and international stakeholders. The Participatory Poverty Assessment of the Tonle Sap region conducted by the Cambodian Development Resource Institute (2007) reveals that the poor there have benefited less from Cambodia's rapid economic growth than the non-poor. The poor of this zone are still heavily dependent on land- and water-based natural resources for their livelihoods. Several years of drought and flood, along with poor soils and a lack of water-management capacity, have eroded farming capacity. This in turn has pushed a large number of the poor to emigrate. The report also shows that the poor lack access to basic public services, such as safe drinking water, education, and health services.

It is widely noted that the frequency and severity of droughts, floods, hurricanes, tropical storms, landslides, earthquakes, volcanic eruption, and El Niño episodes during 1980–99 seem to have increased globally (IADB 2000). The same general trend has been observed as major challenges in Cambodia. The incidence of flooding in the 2000s has increased sharply compared to the late 1990s (MRC 2009). Such shocks are often considered to be a cause of poverty, but there have been few empirical studies of their effects on household welfare in Cambodia. Analysis has not been possible due to a lack of household survey data that integrates local environment variables. In this essay, we attempt to fill the gap by using the 2007 CSES data and environmental indicators (drought, flood, and soil erosion) to correlate poverty and the environment. We investigate how the loss of forestry income has contributed to poverty, how the government's mitigation and adaptation programmes play the dual role of providing both immediate and effective relief to households affected by crisis, and how rural households respond to environmental change with ex-ante and ex-post risk coping strategies.

DATA AND METHODOLOGY

The analysis in this study uses the Cambodia Social Economic Survey (CSES) 2007, collected by the National Institute of Statistics. That survey provides a wide range of detailed information about households, such as their food and non-food consumption, durable assets, livestock, household farm production, non-timber forest collection, other non-agricultural production, wage work, and remittances. The CSES 2007 environmental income sources data is not as precise as that collected by Cavendish (1999).[1] To a lesser extent, CSES 2007 captures forestry and hunting income from sawing logs, firewood, wood for charcoal, rattan, bamboo, palm leaves, and palm juice, root crops, fruit, vegetables, herbs, honey, wild animals, and birds. This enables us to measure the environmental resources for rural households income.[2] Following Cavendish (1999), we examine how the exclusion of environmental income increases poverty. In addition to the household information, the National Institute of Statistics collected village information, related to natural disasters. Therefore, we should be able to directly examine, to some extent, the connection between poverty and environment.

In order to figure out what general strategies households have for coping with risk, and what their limitations might be for handling environmental change, we adopted qualitative methods: focus group discussions and in-depth interviews. Given our budget and time limitations, we carefully selected one commune in a rural area, in Pursat province, that had been hit by natural disaster. It had been hit by severe drought for three years in a row (2008–10).[3]

STATISTICAL ANALYSIS

Environmental income

Table 9.1 presents per capita income from five sources: livestock, forestry and hunting (hereafter "environmental income"), non-agricultural, wage, and others. On average, per capita environmental income accounts for 200 riels — equivalent to 7 per cent of total income. Rural households in Plateau and Mountains areas rely on environmental income the most (16.7 per cent), followed by those in the Tonle Sap (7.8 per cent), Plains (5.6 per cent) and Coastal regions (3.9 per cent) areas. Though the proportions of these environmental resources are

TABLE 9.1
Rural Per Capita Income by Aggregated Income Sources
(in riels)

	Plains	Tonle Sap	Coast	Plateau and Mountains	Total
Livestock	709.71	517.07	590.27	606.12	636.88
Forestry and hunting ("environmental")	161.17	219.89	134.19	408.60	200.18
Non-agricultural	672.56	844.45	1970.23	484.84	760.51
Wage	996.99	911.97	504.36	748.41	928.87
Others	344.47	315.54	195.33	192.79	316.01
Total	2884.90	2808.92	3394.38	2440.76	2842.45
Sample Size	1259	689	90	190	2228

Source: Authors' calculation from CSES 2007.

small, it is possible that there is a substantial gap between the estimated environmental income and actual income. However, because it is not easy to get a reliable data on income, most poverty studies use per capita consumption as the welfare indicator.

To address this issue, we must first set the income poverty line, to shed some light on the effect of the exclusion of environmental income on poverty. Neither the Cambodian government nor relevant international organizations (particularly the World Bank which often engages in poverty studies) attempt to determine the poverty line using income data that cover environmental income.

Given the consumption poverty line, we re-estimate the poverty headcount ratio in rural areas by geographical zone. To have a consistent poverty rate estimated from consumption data, we note that four cut-off lines can be used: (a) 29.0 percentile of income for Plains, (b) 39.6 for Tonle Sap, (c) 28.5 for Coastal regions, and (d) 32.8 for Plateau and Mountains. As a result, we count a household as poor if its per capita income is less than 29, 40, 29, and 33 percentile of income distribution for those residing in Plains, Tonle Sap, Coastal regions, and Plateau and Mountains, respectively.

Table 9.2 shows the poverty rate computed from an income measure that includes environmental income and an income measure

TABLE 9.2
Rural Poverty Estimates for Differing Measures of Income
(per cent)

	Income (including environmental)			Income (excluding environmental)			Poverty differences		
	Headcount	Poverty gap	Poverty severity	Headcount	Poverty gap	Poverty severity	Headcount	Poverty gap	Poverty severity
Plains	30.21	14.10	8.55	33.88	19.45	13.69	12.15	37.94	60.12
Tonle Sap	42.44	22.10	14.77	47.60	28.42	20.63	12.16	28.60	39.68
Coast	32.80	15.89	9.51	36.55	20.54	13.64	11.43	29.26	43.43
Plateau and Mountains	33.34	11.53	6.65	48.06	21.93	14.70	44.15	90.20	121.05
Total	34.88	16.58	10.46	40.43	22.84	16.15	15.91	37.76	54.40

Source: Authors' calculation from CSES 2007.

that excludes environmental income. On average, in 2007, the poverty rate increases by 16 per cent if rural households are unable to access forestry and hunting at all. Of these, the most affected region is Plateau and Mountains, where the poverty headcount edges up by 44.2 per cent, followed by Tonle Sap 12.2 per cent, Plains 12.2 per cent, and Coastal regions 11.4 per cent. The poverty gap and poverty severity increase at a larger degree of 37.7 per cent and 54.4 per cent, respectively, if environmental income is excluded from income measurement. In line with the poverty headcount, households in the Plateau and Mountains region are likely to suffer the most. However, Tonle Sap, which appears to be the second largest affected region in terms of headcount ratio,[4] becomes the least affected region in the cases of the poverty gap and poverty severity. This may indicate that the moderately poor and/or the poorest of the poor in the Tonle Sap region are less reliant on environmental resources.

Natural Disasters and Poverty

CSES 2007 shows that 62 per cent of villages have experienced natural disaster (drought, flood, crop failure, fire, and others) in the past five years. Of these villages, 82.6 per cent were rural. In the Plateau and Mountains region, the incidence of natural disaster reaches 94 per cent, followed by Tonle Sap at 85 per cent, Plains at 81 per cent, and Coastal regions at 50 per cent (Table 9.3). The frequency of drought in rural areas increased from 11.4 per cent in 2001 to 34.2 per cent in 2005. In contrast, the flood numbers show a declining trend over the same period, decreasing from 14.6 per cent to 7.3 per cent. Plain and Mountains is more likely to be affected by drought, while floods seem to occur more often in the Tonle Sap than other regions.

Using CSES 2007, the World Bank (2009) reports that the poverty headcount ratio using total poverty line for Cambodia is 30.1 per cent, of which 34.7 per cent lives in rural areas. In line with the World Bank, we then re-estimate rural poverty rate by breaking it into four regions and various types of natural disaster (Table 9.4). We see that the poverty headcount in villages in all regions except Plateau

TABLE 9.3
Incidence of Natural Disasters

		Rural				
	Full Sample	Plains	Tonle Sap	Coastal regions	Plateau and Mountains	Total
Natural Disaster in the past 5 years	0.63	0.82	0.85	0.50	0.94	0.83
Drought 2005	0.23	0.34	0.32	0.25	0.44	0.34
Drought 2004	0.22	0.27	0.41	0.00	0.39	0.32
Drought 2003	0.21	0.30	0.29	0.13	0.28	0.29
Drought 2002	0.11	0.14	0.13	0.13	0.11	0.14
Drought 2001	0.08	0.10	0.13	0.00	0.17	0.11
Flood 2005	0.09	0.05	0.12	0.00	0.11	0.07
Flood 2004	0.07	0.08	0.10	0.13	0.11	0.09
Flood 2003	0.08	0.09	0.13	0.00	0.06	0.10
Flood 2002	0.08	0.13	0.09	0.13	0.06	0.11
Flood 2001	0.10	0.18	0.09	0.38	0.06	0.15
Sample Size	356	125	68	8	18	219

Source: Authors' calculation from CSES 2007.

TABLE 9.4
Rural Poverty Headcount Index by Region and Natural Disaster
(per cent)

		Plains	Tonle Sap	Coast	Plateau and Mountains	Total
Disaster (2001–2005)	No	29.43	27.93	32.09	56.60	31.11
	Yes	30.16	44.22	32.49	32.56	35.50
Drought (2001–2005)	No	29.45	31.91	32.09	55.60	31.86
	Yes	30.30	45.57	32.49	31.78	35.88
Flood (2001–2005)	No	31.30	39.05	29.33	39.89	34.68
	Yes	26.70	45.75	37.59	16.36	34.73
Total		30.02	42.21	32.28	34.64	34.70

Note: Poverty rate is estimated by consumption approach.
Source: Authors' calculation from CSES 2007.

and Mountains during 2001–05 is higher in villages hit by drought. Meanwhile, flooded villages in the Tonle Sap and Coastal regions had much higher poverty rates than the flooded villages in two other regions. These descriptive statistics provide preliminary evidence on the connection between environmental change (drought and flood) and poverty for the whole country — though here it does not holds for all regions. This suggests that investigations that take into account other factors are necessary.

To address this concern, we use the probit regression technique to assess the effect of the environment (in the form of drought, flood, and land erosion) on poverty, as the dependent variable. Droughts and floods are measured at the village level, while land erosion (land productivity) is measured at household level. Furthermore, we also attempt to capture the spatial effects of safe water and sanitation on poverty. The control variables are household size, a set of household head characteristics (sex, age, marital status, race, and education), and regional dummies. The dependent variable takes the value of 0 and 1 for non-poor and poor households, respectively.

Table 9.5 reports descriptive statistics on both explanatory and explained variables. It indicates that the poverty headcount in rural

TABLE 9.5
Descriptive Statistics of Dependent Variable and Independent Variables

Variables	Obs.	Mean	Std. Dev.	Min	Max
Poor (1=Yes)	2228	0.35	0.48	0	1.0
Natural disaster 2001–2005 (1=Yes)	2228	0.82	0.39	0	1.0
Drought 2001–2005 (1=Yes)	2228	0.71	0.46	0	1.0
Flood 2001–2005 (1=Yes)	2228	0.32	0.47	0	1.0
Paddy productivity (tones/ha)	1514	2.20	1.32	0	6.9
Safe drinking water (1=Yes)	2226	0.47	0.50	0	1.0
Having toilet (1=Yes)	2228	0.22	0.42	0	1.0
Cultivated/fallow ratio	1797	0.33	4.61	0	166.7
Household size	2228	5.57	2.02	1	13.0
HHH gender (1=Male)	2228	0.83	0.38	0	1.0
HHH age	2228	44.88	12.84	16	91.0
HHH marital status (1=Yes)	2228	0.83	0.37	0	1.0
HHH race (1=Khmer)	2228	0.98	0.13	0	1.0
HHH education (Years)	2228	4.25	3.32	0	17.0

Note: * HHH: Household head.
Source: Authors' calculation from CSES 2007.

area accounts for 34.7 per cent. Approximately 81.7 per cent of the total households may have experienced natural disaster during the period of 2001–05, of which 70.5 per cent were affected by drought and only 32 per cent by flood. However, this figure may be largely overestimated as drought and/or flood would probably affect only a certain proportion of households, given the village's size.

Of 2,228 households, 46.6 per cent have access to safe drinking water (in this analysis a household is said to have access to safe drinking water when its drinking water is piped to the dwelling during both the dry and wet seasons, it is extracted from a tube/piped/protected well, or it is purchased from a tanker truck/vendor.[5]) Only 22.4 per cent of rural households have a toilet (the proxy for sanitation) in and around the house.[6] As suggested by Pieri (1995), we use paddy productivity to capture the effect of land degradation/soil fertility on

TABLE 9.6
Results of the Probit Regression Analysis

Variables	Marginal effects						
	Model 1	Model 2	Model 3	Model 4	Model 5	Model 6	Model 7
Natural disaster 2001–2005 (1=Yes)	0.038						
Drought 2001–2005 (1=Yes)		0.057***		0.063***			
Flood 2001–2005 (1=Yes)			−0.035*	−0.043**			
Paddy productivity					−0.031***		
Safe drinking water (1=Yes)						0.035*	
Having toilet (1=Yes)							−0.210***
Household size	0.075***	0.075***	0.075***	0.076***	0.081***	0.074***	0.076***
HHH gender (1=Male)	0.036	0.035	0.039	0.038	0.034	0.039	0.028
HHH age	−0.015***	−0.015***	−0.015***	−0.015***	−0.016***	−0.015***	−0.014***
HHH age squared	0.0001***	0.0001***	0.0001***	0.0001***	0.0001**	0.0001***	0.0001***
HHH marital status (1=Yes)	−0.090*	−0.090*	−0.095**	−0.094**	−0.096	−0.093**	−0.090**
HHH race (1=Khmer)	−0.121	−0.111	−0.130	−0.118	−0.124	−0.117	−0.111
HHH education (years)	−0.022***	−0.022***	−0.022***	−0.022***	−0.021***	−0.022***	−0.015***
Plains dummy	−0.047	−0.041	−0.049	−0.039	0.003	−0.062	−0.048
Tonle Sap dummy	0.037	0.041	0.041	0.048	0.080*	0.030	0.053
Coastal regions dummy	0.006	0.011	0.006	0.019	0.001	0.009	−0.025
Number of Observations	2228	2228	2228	2228	1514	2226	2228
LR Chi2	275.17	280.09	276.61	285.18	197.22	275.43	355.88
Prob>Chi2	0.0000	0.0000	0.0000	0.0000	0.0000	0.0000	0.0000
Log-likelihood	−1210.99	−1208.53	−1210.77	−1206.49	−862.5	−1210.17	−1170.64
Pseudo R-squared	0.1020	0.1038	0.1022	0.1054	0.1026	0.1022	0.1319

Source: Authors' calculation from CSES 2007.

poverty.[7] It should be noted that these indicators (safe water, sanitation, and paddy productivity) are quite broad and sometimes hide the real meaning of safe water, sanitation, and land degradation. In addition, water- and sanitation-related diseases, such as diarrhoea, depend on behavioural practices, for example, hand washing. Interpretation should be made carefully since these indicators could represent different stresses.

Our regression results (Table 9.6) show that the coefficient of the drought dummy is positive and statistically significant at 1 per cent level, which suggests that drought is likely to increase the likelihood of being poor in rural Cambodia — holding other factors constant. The coefficient of paddy productivity is negative and statistically significant at 1 per cent level, implying that an increase in paddy productivity (soil fertility) would reduce rural poverty rate. In other words, poverty rate is likely to increase due to soil fertility loss. Similarly, the coefficient of the toilet dummy is negative and statistically significant at 1 per cent level, indicating that sanitation has played a crucial role in poverty reduction in Cambodia. Unexpectedly, the dummy variable for safe drinking water is positive, and that for flood is negative. Both coefficients are statistically significant at 10 per cent level. This may be partially due to the definition of safe drinking water, which does not reflect its quality. Since flood is commonly viewed as a source of profit rather than a disaster — because it usually contributes to biodiversity, fish abundance, and soil fertility (MRC 2006) — floods (at a certain level) would reduce the rural poverty rate in Cambodia.

MITIGATING AND ADAPTING TO CLIMATE CHANGE

In order to better understand the ways villagers adapted to drought, we conducted a focus group (six to eight people) in each of three villages in Pursat Province. It was our impression that the villagers did not have effective strategies. They responded to drought by selling durable assets, adding household members (including children) into the labour force, and migrating. We also found out that some villagers were using a new type of rice seed as a way of adapting to extreme weather; and some were relying on common property resources, such as vine to weave mats, to compensate for the loss of income because of the drought. Nevertheless, it has been widely noted (e.g., Fafchamps and Gavian 1997; Morduch 1999) that these informal mechanisms for adapting with risk become ineffective during a common shock (economic crisis or natural disaster).

Government agencies can also protect households from natural disasters. The Cambodian government has undertaken numerous activities to tackle climate change, some of which are in line with the United Nations Framework Convention on Climate Change (adopted in 1992) and the Kyoto Protocol (in force as of 2005).[8] More precisely, the government has considered renewable energy, improved cooking stoves, energy-efficient building codes, tax relief for renewable energy and mass transit, reforestation, forest protection, intermittent irrigation, organic matter management, direct seeding and zero tillage as mitigation options for climate change. In this regard, the Angkor Bio Cogen Rice Husk Power Project (ABC) is designed to use rice husks to generate electricity for the Ankor Kasekam Roongroeung rice mill. The project will displace the use of diesel oil for power generation and lead to an estimated carbon emission reduction of 45,815 tonnes (CO_2) per year. In order to mitigate the effects of the droughts and floods that occurred in the early 2000s, the government improved the irrigation systems, the water supply, and sanitation; established Farmer Water User Communities; constructed water culverts, dams, pumping facilities, water gates, and canals; and rehabilitated roads and bridges (MOE 2005). More recently, the Cambodian National Adaptation Programme of Action for Climate Change (NAPA) has been developed to provide a framework to guide the coordination and implementation of adaptation initiatives (MOE 2006).[9]

CONCLUSIONS

In this essay, we have examined how poverty can be caused by the loss of "environmental" income from forestry and hunting due to environmental events, such as flood, drought and land erosion. Our study differs from that of Dasgupta et al. (2005) who investigated the poverty-environment connection at the provincial and district level. We use the 2007 household socio-economic survey data set. The main feature of our study is the use of local area environmental variables in a standard household survey.

From the study, we find that the poverty rate would increase by an average of 16 per cent if rural households were unable to engage in forestry and hunting. The poverty headcount ratio in Tonle Sap would edge up by 12 per cent. Drought would increase the poverty rate by 6 per cent, but, unexpectedly, flood would decrease it by 4 per cent. The unexpected effect of flood on poverty is largely because floods are commonly viewed as a source of profit, rather than a disaster. As reported in MRC (2006), flood often contributes to the wealth of biodiversity, and abundance of fish as well as soil fertility in Cambodia. We also find that a 1 per cent increase in land erosion (land productivity as proxy) would raise the poverty rate by 3 per cent. This statistical result confirms the common sense belief that more drought and soil infertility are associated with higher poverty rates.

The review of current household and government mitigation and adaptation strategies is very useful for setting priorities for public programmes and formal social safety nets. Since group-based informal risk mitigating and adapting strategies become less effective during natural disasters, households may be pressured to rely on self-insurance strategy that are costly and inefficient, such as selling land or other assets, taking loans in cash or in kind, working longer, migrating, taking children out of school, and increasing the exploitation of natural resources. This suggests that public actions that prevent the deterioration of household welfare, particularly children's nutritional status, and maintain access to health services for poor and vulnerable households deserve top priority.

Notes

The authors would like to thank Ms Pon Dorina for her excellent fieldwork assistance.

1. Cavendish (1999) was initially intended to quantify environmental income including a wide range of consumption goods (wild fruit, vegetables and animals; mats, pottery and wild medicine), input goods (firewood, leaf litter, and thatching grass), output goods (wild fruit, vegetables and animal sales; firewood, construction wood, thatch grass, carpentry, and pottery sales), and durable goods and stock (furniture, firewood store and fencing wood).
2. The household income is divided by household size in order to adjust for inter-household differences.

3. Pursat is the fourth largest province in Cambodia and is located in the western part of the country. The eastern part of the province is part of the Tonle Sap Lake and the surrounding basin area. The selected villages for this paper's case study are implicitly considered to be part of the floodplain of the lake.

4. It should be noted that the difference between the gaps in headcount in Tonle Sap and the third largest, Plain, is only 0.01 percentage point.

5. Ideally, safe drinking water should reflect a quality of water that can be consumed or used without risk of immediate or long-term harm. Despite this fact, Feldman et al. (2007) note that very few data have been collected on the chemical quality of the nationwide drinking water sources and specifically, the capacity to assess chemical quality is extremely limited in Cambodia.

6. Shyamsundar (2002) emphasizes that sanitation, water and indoor air pollution related diseases are the most important for developing countries. Various studies (Akbar and Lvovsky 2000; Bosch et al. 2001) suggest that environmental factors have a negative significant effect on the health of the poor through inadequate sanitation, water and indoor air pollution. However, water and air pollution are also caused by development that lacks environmental safeguards.

7. Soil fertility is a common and important form of environmental loss in many developing countries (Shyamsundar 2002). Pieri et al. (1995) suggest that soil quality can be observed indirectly through crop yields or directly by measuring soil changes. Change in crop yields over time is a highly significant indicator of soil fertility loss. Soil fertility loss and land degradation could increase rural poverty headcount, infant mortality rate, rural-urban migration and female headed households, and decrease food production.

8. For example, the government has established the Cambodian Interim Designated National Authority (DNA), the Cambodia Climate Change Office (CCCO), the National Climate Change Committee (NCCC), and implemented several capacity-building activities such as the Clean Development Mechanism (CDM) project, the Integrated Capacity Strengthening for CDM project, and the Asia EU Dialogue on the CDM project.

9. Cambodia's NAPA has identified priority projects to address the effects of climate change in key sectors such as agriculture, water resources, coastal zone and human health.

References

Akbar, S. and K. Lvovsky. "Indoor Air Pollution: Energy and Health for the Poor". *ESMAP Newsletter* No. 1, World Bank, Washington, D.C., 2000.

Binswanger and Rosenzweig. "Behavioral and Material Determinants of Production Relations in Agriculture". *Journal of Development Studies* (April 1986): 503–39

Bosch, C., K. Hommann, G. M. Rubio, C. Sadoff, and L. Travers. *Water, Sanitation and Poverty chapter, Poverty Reduction Strategy Papers' Source Book*. Washington, D.C.: World Bank, 2001.

Brown O., and A. Crawford. *Assessing the Security Implication of Climate Change for West Africa*. Winnipeg, Canada: IISD, 2008.

Cambodia Development Resource Institute. *We are Living with Worry all the Time: A Participatory Poverty Assessment of the Tonle Sap*. Phnom Penh: CDRI, 2007.

Cavendish, W. "Poverty, Inequality and Environmental Resources: Quantitative Analysis of Rural Households". *Working Paper Series*, 99–9, Centre for the Studies of African Economies, University of Oxford, 1999.

Dasgupta S., U. Deichmann, C. Meisner, and D. Wheeler. "Where is the Poverty-Environment Nexus? Evidence from Cambodia, Lao PDR, and Vietnam". *World Development* 33, no. 4 (2005): 617–38.

Fafchamps, M. and S Gavian. "The Determinants of Livestock Prices in Niger". *Journal of African Economics* 6 (1997): 255–95.

Feldman, Peter R., Jan-Willem Rosenboom, Mao Saray, Peng Navuth, Chea Samnag and Steven Iddings. "Assessment of the Chemical Quality of Drinking Water in Cambodia". *Journal of Water and Health* 5, no. 1 (2007): 101–16.

Inter-American Development Bank. *Social Protection for Equity and Growth*. Washington, D.C.: IADB, 2000.

Mekong River Commission (MRC). "Annual Mekong Flood Report 2005". Vientiane, 2006.

———. "Annual Mekong Flood Report 2008". Vientiane, 2009.

Ministry of Environment. "Analysis of Policies to Address Climate Change Impacts in Cambodia". Phnom Penh, 2005.

Ministry of Planning. "A Poverty Profile of Cambodia. Phnom Penh, 2006.

———. *General Population Census of Cambodia 2008 (National Report on Final Census Result)*. Phnom Penh: National Institute of Statistics, 2009.

Morduch, J. "Between the State and the Market: Can Informal Insurance Patch the Safety Net?". *The World Bank Research Observer* 14, no. 2 (1999): 187–207.

Pieri, C., J. Dumanski, A. Hamblin, and A. Young. "Land Quality Indicators". *World Bank Discussion Paper* No. 315, World Bank, Washington, D.C. 1995.

Shyamsundar, P. "Poverty-Environment Indicators". *Environmental Economics Series*, Paper No. 84, World Bank, Washington, D.C., 2002.

Tong, K. *How Did Cambodian Rural Households Cope with Shocks from Food and Oil Price Increase?* Phnom Penh: CDRI, 2009.

World Bank. "Poverty Profile and Trend in Cambodia: Findings from the 2007 Cambodia Socio-Economic Survey (CSES), East Asia and Pacific Region". Washington, D.C., 2009.

10

CONSERVATION AGRICULTURE IN CAMBODIA
A Triple-Win Option

Stephane Boulakia, Pen Vuth, Sann Vathana, Stephane Chabierski, and Olivier Gilard

The Mekong River runs through or along Myanmar, Laos, Thailand, Cambodia, and Vietnam. In these "Mekong countries", agriculture provides a livelihood for a larger proportion of the population than the proportion of GDP derived from agriculture. Agriculture also functions as a safety net for the cities: many workers return to the country to work on farms when there is a rise in unemployment. But the degradation of the environment (soil fertility, erosion, increased population density) and climate change threaten the agriculture sector's ability to play these two roles. Plans must be implemented to keep the agriculture sector sustainable and competitive. Such plans must be adapted to the fact that farmers are financially fragile. Most of their revenue is absorbed by day-to-day expenses, and their investment capacity is low. Also, population growth has saturated the available cultivable lands. As the capacity of urban areas to accommodate rural migration has in most cases reached its limit, crop cultivation is being extended to less fertile areas, often with slopes where erosion happens. Such areas are typically in the peripheral region of Cambodia, the hilly areas of Sayaboury in Laos, and the highlands of Vietnam. As more and more marginal land is being cropped, the sustainability of this activity decreases and the rate of rural poverty increases. Within the Mekong countries rural poverty usually is higher than the national average, and it is higher than rural poverty elsewhere in Asia.

The Mekong countries agriculture is based on irrigated rice, but this system has reached its limits. For rain-fed agriculture, even on sloppy areas, direct sowing (or seeding) mulch-based cropping (DMC), also known as "no tillage" systems, is a better choice. This method was originally developed for tropical upland agriculture in central-west regions of Brazil. For some years, the Agence Française de Développement (AFD) funded research and development projects based on DMC. These projects were implemented with the technical and scientific support of the Centre de Coopération Internationale en Recherche Agronomique pour le Développement (CIRAD) in Cambodia, Laos, and Vietnam. Direct sowing based on mulch is capable of providing three benefits to rain-fed agriculture:

- DMC can mitigate climate change by increasing organic matter in the soil. This allows the soil to store more CO_2. The soil becomes a sinkhole. DMC is also able to allow farmers to *adapt* to climate change by making crops more resilient to rain pattern climate hazard. There is less erosion, less evaporation, and better repartition of water in the soil.
- DMC can make agriculture more productive by maintaining and even increasing the long-term fertility of the soil. In some cases, lost fertility can be recovered in a way that requires less use of chemicals than other methods.
- DMC can reduce poverty by decreasing the need for fertilizers and chemicals. This makes the process more affordable for smallholders.

Initial results from both controlled experimentation and the network of farms are highly promising. At the field level, gross profit margins quickly reached US$500–US$600 per hectare after one to two years of DMC practice, even when starting from severely degraded soil conditions, and increased to US$800–US$900 per hectare after four to five years. Under the same conditions, traditional plow-based systems can get similar gross profit margins when implemented in years without major climate incident on soil that is still good, but their performance rapidly decreases on degraded soil and gross profit margins become negative when prices are low. Direct sowing mulch-based cropping (DMC), with totally covered and protected soil and diversified crops rotations (as opposed to dominant mono-cropping patterns), leads to more resilient production systems. Climatic variations can be managed and the negative impact of economic crisis on people's income can be reduced through introducing more climate resilient crop species at the farm level, such as maize and soybean, as they obtain quite stable prices year-round. Increasing the amount of fresh organic matter on soil surfaces (via crop residues and cover crops) leads to a positive balance for organic matter (humification rate is higher than the mineralization rate) and soil carbon sequestration (up to 2 tons/ha/year in Brazil) (Sá et al. 2004; Séguy et al. 2003; Séguy et al. 2008). These systems are affordable for poor farmers as they reduce the need for inputs. Soil fertility is maintained mainly by the cover crop.

The French development bank (AFD) funded the piloting of such adaptation crops for more than ten years in Cambodia, Laos, and Vietnam. The results are encouraging. CIRAD provided technical assistance and scientific support to national partners to ease the South to South transfer from Brazil. Local partners, usually depending on the ministry in charge of agriculture, handle the projects. Farmers are local partners of the experiment so as to ensure that the technical proposals fit real constraints. A network at the regional level is currently under development to share the experiences between partners. These initiatives are gathered into the Conservation Agriculture Network for South East Asia (CANSEA). The network shares experiences at a regional level and accumulates agronomic, economic, and physical data, such as CO_2 concentration in the soil, at a broader and more significant scale, taking into account the diverse situations. The accumulated data demonstrate the relevance of such no tillage system: reduction of erosion in northern part of Vietnam, carbon storage in uplands of Laos, economic development of maize or cassava commodity in

Cambodia. In the rest of this essay, we will focus on the agricultural problem in Cambodia.[1]

CAMBODIAN AGRICULTURE

The Cambodia case is illustrative of the capacity of DMC to fundamentally modify the usual agriculture-versus-environment conflict by reconciling these two concerns and providing opportunities for a more sustainable economic development. Historically, the central plains of Cambodia have been the most cultivated part of the country. Farmers there mainly used climate-sensitive rain-fed lowland rice production systems. But this part of the country has become overcrowded. Opening up to the market, rather than just relying on subsistence farming, and new modes of consumption in the sub-region are also provoking a rethinking of farming systems, especially in agricultural regions recently created on the "upland" of the country's periphery. The land of Cambodia's central plain along the Mekong River and its tributaries is saturated, while the peripheral areas originally covered by forests are almost empty. The cities have limited opportunities for new jobs, so their capacity to accommodate population growth is limited. Consequently there is a migration from the central plains to the peripheral upland. This can be observed when analysing the statistical data of the previous census. Agriculture is the main activity of these migrants, usually mono-cropping. Unfortunately, the soil is not very fertile and in the first few years following the forest clearance, fertility dropped drastically. This leads to an increase in poverty and new migration, causing more forest clearance.

Cambodian agriculture must answer two related questions:

- how to secure and intensify rice production in the central region. About 70 per cent of the active population (sixteen years and older) in the central region is involved in rice production. Eighty per cent of Cambodian poverty is located in the central region.[2]
- how to develop efficient family-based commercial agriculture on the vast land reserve of the peripheral areas while protecting their natural resources.

One response to these two questions could be an adaptation strategy which is based on DMC. The Project for the Development of

Agriculture in Cambodia (PADAC), which started in 2008, demonstrated the viability of DMC in Cambodia by diversifying crops in a way that was able to maintain the soil fertility on a long-term basis. Moreover, as seen during the 2010 cropping season, the plots under DMC have suffered far less from the late arrival of the rainy season. The economic survey of farmers involved in the project demonstrates the possible margin available for farmers with such a method: US$800–US$900 per hectare and per year, which is of the same magnitude as traditional cropping, but with a better resiliency (to meteorological hazard), price of commodities (due to diversification) and sustainability. A standard family could easily manage up to 6 hectares. That would provide a comfortable income by comparison with the urban standard. The proposed systems are based on maize, cassava, and soybean, which are needed in increasing quantities by the livestock feed industry. Proposed cover-crops are the grass species *Brachiara* and the legume species *Stylosanthes* and *Crotalaria*. Using them would make it possible to have pastures that better integrate livestock in the cropping systems. Secondary crops that are adapted to drought could be introduced, for example, millet and sorghum,

Another response could be country-level spatial planning[3] that aims for an equilibrium between natural forests' biodiversity, productive forests, and agricultural zones. The infrastructure development that is already partly identified in ADB's Greater Mekong Subregion initiative will facilitate the structuring of this territorial planning and improve livelihood conditions in the rural areas as soon as land access is secured and technical support is provided. The improvement of livelihood in rural areas will reduce people's motivation to live in urban areas. The economic efficiency of this development could be improved by complementing the large economic concessions with help for smallholders.

These proposals suggest there is room to expand to 5 million hectares of land useable for productive and sustainable agriculture. They also suggest that up to 2 million jobs could be created and US$5.6 billion per year of revenues could be generated (part of which could be dedicated to poor households). In the case of Cambodia, this pilot phase would pave the path for a strategy of territorial planning in the less densely populated peripheral areas. That would allow a sustainable equilibrium to be created between natural conservation forests, productive forests, and agricultural development.

SMALLHOLDER AGRICULTURE AND COUNTRY DEVELOPMENT

In Cambodia, the traditional family farm is mainly based on rain-fed lowland rice cropping, taking place in the Mekong's Tonle Sap system of lakes and rivers in the central region. This type of cultivation combines the country's two main agro-ecosystems: the strict rain-fed areas on upper and sandy terraces (1.05 million ha) and the lower hydromorphic plains that are reached by river floods during the second half of the rice cycle (0.55 million ha). To simplify the cultivation process, the two agro-ecosystems alternate between photosensitive-rice–crop growing during the rainy season and common grazing during the dry- and early-rainy seasons. Two other types of rice cultivation occur on the lowest of the lands along the Tonle Sap. Since these very low areas are deeply flooded, they permit only floating rice cultivation in rainy season (0.1 million ha) and counter season rice cropping patterns before and/or after floods. All of these agro-ecosystems of growing rice are rain-fed.

Two and half million families share 2.2 million hectares of land. In the predominantly rain-fed rice-based production methods, both land and labour have low productivity. These methods are largely determined by the needs of climatic risk management under conditions of no or limited water control. The combination of global land limitation and traditional practices based on an extensive management of labor leads to underemployment in the farms and pushes families to look for complementary incomes in off-farm activities. The shortage of job opportunities in the countryside not only causes seasonal migrations toward cities and fishing zones, but also other important migration streams: Between 2003 and 2007, 1.62 million people (12 per cent of the total population) changed residential province. Among these migration streams, 0.52 million moved to the province of Phnom Penh; 0.26 million moved from the province of Phnom Penh; thus showing the dominance of movement from and to Phnom Penh, the capital of Cambodia. The remaining 0.84 million move from and to other provinces. These migrations, mostly triggered by possibility of (illegal) land access, increases the pressure on natural resources. After claiming forested areas, the new migrants implement methods of cropping that are mainly oriented to upland cash crops (e.g., maize and cassava).

Upland cultivation based on annual cash crops has soared in recent years. Officially about 350,000 hectares of land were developed between 2002 and 2009, with more than 50,000 hectares per year being developed since 2006 (MAFF 2010). This new type of spontaneous agricultural development of land arose first in the western regions (Pailin and West Battambang) at the turn of the 2000s without any incentives from the government. This resulted from a combination of specific historic factors (more important land share per family linked to the fact that these areas were the last Khmer Rouge strongholds) and strong Thai market solicitations. More recently, spontaneous pioneers reclaimed upland areas for cash crops in the sparsely populated northern periphery of Cambodia.

Unfortunately, the cropping methods being employed are mostly based on disk plowing and mono-cropping through either corn or cassava without fertilizer. These methods rapidly degrade the soil via erosion, organic matter mineralization, and nutrient impoverishment. For instance, in Pailin, corn yields decreased from 7–8 t/ha just after the land reclaimation in early 2000s to less than 3 t/ha now. There was a loss to cultivation of 10 to 15 per cent of the surface within less than ten years, according to the provincial department of agriculture.

DEVELOPING PRODUCTION BASINS OF SUSTAINABLE UPLAND AGRICULTURE

The lack of land access rights, lack of efficient and sustainable cropping practices, and lack of affordable credit sources largely prevent the migrants from using fixed, profitable, and environment-friendly production methods. Current (2004–2012) research and development experiments carried out by the Ministry of Forest and Fisheries (MAFF) with the support of CIRAD are starting to demonstrate on a pilot scale[4] that the strong but destructive spontaneous farming efforts could be channelied into efficient, pro-poor, and green farming methods. The pilot project progressively highlights the requested attendant measures to be initiated for farmers support in the process of adoption. This support involves technical training and easier access to factors of production, such as credit, certain inputs (seeds of cover crops), certain machinery (planters, sprayers, rollers). The ways explored by the current research and development experiment relies on contract farming between farmer groups that adopt DMC and national or regional agro-industries that produce raw agricultural products (corn, cassava, soybean, etc.) in the studied regions.

Such a pilot action aims to demonstrate the possibility of smallholders' upland agriculture development. It also prepares the operational basis for a larger scale project carried out in close connection with private sector. That project would have a four-year *pre-development phase* of supporting the adoption of DMC on about 4,000 hectares. The new areas would be centred on the areas that were originally piloted. There should be progressive densification of DMC adoption among farmers at a local scale. This would increase the share of land and the number of farms managed on the sustainable basis allowed by DMC. This should allow the gradual integration of measures related to landscape and collective natural resources management (tracks to reach fields, river protection, hedges, and corridors of biodiversity). The development process would move from a farmer approach to a spatial approach.

A final public support might be necessary through a relay project (development phase), targeting 10,000 hectares of extension within five years. It would aim to reach a situation where the adoption and extension of DMC can take place in one or two districts without public support on the focus zone. This last phase will give birth to a production basin of agricultural commodities and should be coupled with state incentives to boost the commitment of the private sector, e.g., infrastructure development (road, energy), platform for industries, security funds for banks that provide credit to farmers' organizations, the allocation of small-to-medium land economic concessions (<1,500 hectares) for companies wishing to act as nucleus estates[5] in technology transfer to farmers.

The proposed sequence of three phases (research-development, pre-development, development) would overlap in time in order to be implemented in ten years. The three phases will set the basis for the creation of a sustainable production basin on 50–100,000 hectares. They would be predominantly run by small (<5 hectares) and medium (<15 hectares) landholders in close coordination with the preservation of the natural capital at farms, local and small regions levels. Using a growth cost assumption based on the research and development experience of the Cambodian Ministry of Forest and Fisheries (MAFF), we calculate that it would cost about US$35–US$40 million to support an extension to 15,000 hectares in a project of ten years' duration. That would be less than US$2,500 per hectare. And a total profit would be generated at field level of about US$10 million per year. The gross profit margins would be US$650–US$700 per hectare per year, from added value of the local agro-industries.

FIVE MILLION UPLAND HECTARES FOR SMALLHOLDER CONSERVATION AGRICULTURE

Cambodia has 3.5 million hectares of officially protected area. It has also several million hectares of reserved land with agricultural potential. According to MAFF data, on twelve central and northern provinces comprising 12.2 million hectares (two-thirds of the national territory), 1.28 million hectares of forest were converted to non-forest cover between 1996 and 2006, and another 0.24 million hectares were converted between 2006 and 2009. Based on this, it can be assumed that forest (including rubber and cashew plantations) still covers 7.71 million hectares, crops occupy about 1.78 million hectares (1.30 million hectares of rice, 0.43 million hectares of annual upland, 0.05 million hectares of tree crops). Thus 2.52 million hectares can be considered underused (cropless) non-forest areas.

Part of this huge national asset could be gradually allocated to smallholder agricultural development. Such an agrarian policy might be the best adapted to climate change. This policy has three purposes. First is to fight poverty and rural underemployment. Second is to develop the nation in a way that strikes a better balance between the booming cities and the countryside. Third is to allow the rise of an agro-industrial sector that is connected to the national and regional demand. The latter would provide a new outlet for the local and international investors.

This new agricultural development, centred on small and medium farmers should be based primarily on annual crops. Annual crops have a lower implementation cost, no immature period, and highly flexible and diverse cropping systems (mixing grain, tubers, and livestock).

If agriculture is going to be oriented in this way, it must be based on a strong promotion of DMC, which is the only method available that allows strictly upland and wet tropical soil to be managed in a sustainable way. The sequence of three relay projects described above can be the tactics to implement this strategy. At both the national and local scales, this development should be closely coordinated with a reinforcement of the conservation plan for natural resources: buffer zones, river protection, and a network of primary and secondary corridors of biodiversity between protected areas.

The implementation of a twenty-year plan with a goal of 5 million hectares of upland cultivation (with land allocated mainly to small- and medium-holders) could result in 1.86 million new jobs. It could also generate US$5.6 billion per year–US$3.8 billion per year would be on farms and US$1.8 billion per year would be in agro-industry and services. The total implementing cost would be US$5.35 billion, shared between public investment (US$1.76 billion) and private sector (US$3.59 billion).

CONCLUSION

While Cambodian agriculture has not undergone a major transformations for centuries, it must do so now. Cambodia demonstrates the capacity of DMC systems to reduce the conflict between agriculture and the environment and thereby make economic development more sustainable (Lal et al. 2007). Each country is unique, and so it is not possible to mechanically apply the Cambodian scheme to, say, Laos, Vietnam, or China. But adaptive research using the same conceptual framework can produce a similar solution to local problems. There is still a large potential for developing better agriculture that will both respect the local environment and provide economic opportunities for the poor. AFD, as the donor, and CIRAD as the research institute, built the basis of this edifice, which remains fragile and in need of complementary support.

Notes

1. We present results achieved through the research-development Project to Support Agricultural Development in Cambodia (PADAC), implemented by

the Ministry of Forest and Fisheries of Cambodia (MAFF) with the scientific and technical assistance of CIRAD, using funds granted by AFD.

2. Poor people account for 25.8 per cent of the Cambodia's population (US$1.25/day in 2007) and up to 57.8 per cent of the population with a US$2/day threshold (World Bank database). Due to a large share of rural population (78 per cent of the total population), poverty is dominantly located in countryside and linked to small land area per household (estimate of 25 per cent of landless farmers and 25 per cent supplementary with less than 0.5 ha/household).

3. In France, the concept of "territory" is based on the specificities (environment, culture, economy, etc.) of a small region called "territory" which is used as the basis of some spatial planning and country development measures. These views underlined the concepts developed here.

4. 700 ha of extension in 2012, 350 ha in 2010.

5. Nucleus farming is based on an industrial nucleus with smallholders all around providing raw material to the industrial partner. It has been efficiently developed for perennial crops — rubber — in Africa for instance.

References

Lal, R.; R. F. Follett, B. A. Stewart, and J. M. Kimble. "Soil carbon sequestration to mitigate climate change and advance food security". *Soil Science* 172, no. 12 (2007): 943–56.

MAFF. "The Annual Report for Agriculture Forestry and Fisheries 2009–2010". 2010.

Sá, J. C. M., C. C. Cerri, M. C. Piccolo, B. E. Feigl, J. Buckner, A. Fornari, M. F. M. Sá, L. Séguy, S. Bouzinac, S. P. Venkze-Filho, V. Paulleti, and M. S. Neto. "O plantio direto como base do sistema de produção visando o seqüestro do carbono". In *Revista Plantio Direto Ano XIV n° 84 Novembro/Dezembro 2004*, pp. 45–61.

Séguy L., S. Bouzinac, E. Scopel E., and M. F. S Ribeiro. "New concepts for sustainable management of cultivated soils through direct seeding mulch based cropping systems: The CIRAD experience, partnership and networks. Producing in harmony with nature". II World Congress on Sustainable Agriculture proceedings, Iguaçu, Brazil, 10–15 August 2003.

Séguy L., Bouzinac S. et partenaires brésiliens. "La symphonie inachevée du semis direct dans le Brésil central: le système dominant dit de «semi-direct». Limites et dégâts, eco-solutions et perspectives: la nature au service de l'agriculture durable". <http://agroecologie.cirad.fr>. 2008.

World Bank database <http://data.worldbank.org/country?display=default>.

11

VOICES OF THE POOR ON CLIMATE CHANGE IN THAILAND AND VIETNAM

Hermann Waibel, Songporne Tongruksawattana, and Marc Voelker

The poverty headcount ratios of the emerging market economies of Thailand and Vietnam have declined impressively (World Bank 2008). However, the rural areas are still much poorer than their urban counterparts (Healy and Jitsuchon 2007). Furthermore, the environments in which the poor live make them more dependent on agricultural and natural resources. Hence, climate change is especially affecting the rural poor (Millennium Ecosystem Assessment 2005; Ngyuen 2010). But little is known about how the poor perceive climate change or how it affects their livelihood. In general, vulnerability to poverty remains a major problem in emerging market economies such as Thailand and Vietnam, especially in the low-potential and poorer geographical areas, where infrastructure is weak and insurance and credit markets are often missing. For example, it was found in Thailand that agriculture in low-potential areas is often performed by the elderly, as part-time farmers who adjust their farm organization in response to the outmigration of younger household members (Gödecke and Waibel 2011). Such farmers are probably less inclined to adopt the sort of new agricultural technology that could reduce the negative effects of climate change.

In this essay we analyse the perceptions of the members of rural households in Vietnam and Thailand as expressed in a comprehensive set of panel data collected in 2007 and 2008 from some 4,400 households. We look at how rural households, especially the poor and vulnerable among them, experienced economic, environmental, and idiosyncratic and covariate shocks.[1] We raise three questions that bear on the planning and implementation of interventions aimed at mitigating the negative consequences of climate change:

- How seriously do rural households take climate-related risks compared to other shocks endured in the recent past?
- How much of an effort do poor and vulnerable rural households make to reduce the impact of climate-related risks?
- Do poor people experience or perceive climate-related risk differently than the non-poor and do they act differently in coping with it?

METHODOLOGY AND DATA

To investigate the perceptions of rural households on climate change, three regression models were developed. The first aims to establish connections between someone who had experienced shocks in the past and their present perception of risk coming from future changes to the climate. A Tobit regression model was developed to estimate the households' perception of risk as the dependent variable and climate-related shocks on households' risk perception as the independent variables. The model also incorporates other socio-demographic factors as independent variables. The distribution of the dependent variable is both positively skewed and censored as about 12 per cent of households did not perceive any climate-related risk. To control for skewness a rank-preserving log-transformation of the dependent variable with censoring is undertaken by using a Tobit model. The Tobit model takes the following form:

$$R_i^* = \lambda S_i^c + \phi X_i^y + \gamma P_p \qquad (1),$$

where R_i^* is a latent variable which is equal to the observable variable R_i whenever the latent variable is above zero. i indexes household and R_i is an ordinal risk score which indicates the magnitude of climate risk which a household expects to happen in the future. In the household questionnaire respondents were asked to quantify both the expected frequency of each climate shock type which they expected to happen in a 5-year future reference period and the expected severity of each of these events. The expected severity was stated separately in terms of income and asset loss, and by using an ordinal scale from 0 (no effect) to 3 (high severity). The risk score is computed by summing up all events expected by a household and by adding up the severity score for income and assets multiplied by the expected frequency of the event. The sum of the risk scores of all expected climate shocks of a household is then R_i. Furthermore, S_i^c is a vector of dummy variables that indicate whether or not a household was affected by climate shock incidents from 2002 to 2008 and X_i^y is a vector of socio-demographic characteristics of the interview respondent. P_p is a vector of dummy variables introduced to capture the effect of provinces. The parameters λ, ϕ and γ are to be estimated.

The second model is a standard probit model and aims to identify the factors that induce households to apply climate-related *ex-ante* risk-mitigation action.[2] The third model estimates the likelihood of households taking up a specific type of *ex-ante* risk management strategy. For Vietnam a bi-variate probit model is used because of the dominance of two types of strategies, namely collective action and investment activities. In Thailand a multivariate probit model is used since coping strategies are more varied.

The data used in this analysis were collected in a long-term DFG research project of four German universities on "Impact of Shocks on the Vulnerability to Poverty: Consequences for Development of Emerging Southeast Asian Economies".[3] Focusing on rural households in northeastern Thailand and central Vietnam, a comprehensive survey among some 4,400 rural households in six peripheral provinces was conducted in 2007, and the same households were followed up in 2008. Sampling of households followed a three-stage random sampling procedure (Hardeweg, Klasen, and Waibel 2012). In Thailand, in the first stage within the province subdistricts were chosen with a probability proportional to size. In Vietnam, stratification within the provinces was applied by three agro-ecological zones with disproportional sample allocation in order to ensure sufficient sample size in the less densely populated highland areas.

The provinces covered by the survey are Buriram, Nakhon Phanom, and Ubon Ratchathani in Thailand, and Dak Lak, Ha Tinh, and Thua Thien Hue in Vietnam. Provinces were selected to include peripheral areas in the poorest parts of Thailand and provinces representing various levels of economic development of the central coast and central highland regions of Vietnam. All of them are located in rural and peripheral areas (bordering Laos and/or Cambodia). This choice is motivated by the stylized fact derived from earlier studies on vulnerability that people in rural and geographically remote regions are more vulnerable to poverty than people in urban and central regions.

In Thailand, the selected provinces belong to the northeastern Isan region, which is still the "poverty pocket" of Thailand. Nakhon Phanom is located 700 kilometres northeast of Bangkok. Most of its population of 720,000 lives in rural environments. Farther south is Ubon Ratchathani, bordering Laos and Cambodia, with a population of 1.7 million. While still dominated by agriculture, the economy of this province is rapidly diversifying, with significant infrastructure development. The third Thai province is Buriram (1.5 million inhabitants), which hosts a sizeable Khmer-speaking minority. The structure of agricultural production is similar in all three provinces, with rice as the dominant crop (over 80 per cent of agricultural land), followed by cassava. Perennial crops like rubber have recently become more important.

In Vietnam the provinces belong to the central highlands. Ha Tinh and Thua Thien Hue have a coastline with the South China Sea and extend to the Laotian border, while Dak Lak is landlocked and borders Cambodia to the west. Dak Lak (1.9 million inhabitants) is a major producer of coffee. Ha Tinh (1.2 million inhabitants) mainly produces rice, while Hue (1 million inhabitants) shows a high degree of diversification with tourism, fishing, rice, and forestry as the main sources of income.

The survey instrument followed the general living standard survey type. It contains questions on retrospective information (2002–08) in which households reported their subjective assessments of shocks and their assessments of risks in the next five years. Also included were questions about the implications of shocks and risks for income and asset loss, the coping actions adopted, and the cost and scope of such preventive measures. Shocks and risks were divided into four major categories, namely socio-demographic, economic, biological, and climate-related events. Climate shocks/risks were further specified into six types: drought, flood, heavy rainfall, ice rain, storms, and erosion. There were two sets of questions asked of the respondents. The first set was on the type of shocks experienced during the past seven years and their frequency and severity. The second set of questions was aimed at the respondents' judgements of risk (the likelihood that shocks would happen in the future), with the same qualifications as for shocks, type of risk, expected frequency, and expected severity.

RESULTS

The household survey revealed shock experiences and the risk expectations of the rural households. For both shocks and risks, three variables were defined: (1) percent of households reporting an event, (2) the average frequency of the event (for those households who had experienced any shock), and (3) the severity of the event (if the event was experienced). The shock experience shows the relative abundance and importance of the various types of shocks and in particular the relative importance of climate-related shocks. The households' future expectations of risky events are assumed to reveal their perceptions about possible changes in the factors that have caused these shocks. Hence, for climate-related events the difference between shocks and risks can provide some indication of climate change as perceived by the rural population. Furthermore, the comparison between past experience and future expectations for biological, socio-demographic, and economic events can indicate some trends in ecological, social, and economic conditions, albeit based on subjective information from the rural population.

As a first result, shock experience and risk expectation for poor and non-poor households for the two countries are presented as an overview in Table 11.1. In Vietnam over 80 per cent of the poor households had experienced at least one shock. This was clearly higher than for the non-poor households. In Thailand this figure is just over 50 per cent with only a small difference between poor and non-poor. Quite the same can be said for the average number of shocks experienced per household. In relative terms, it is higher in Vietnam than in Thailand, with no poverty effect in the latter country. It is interesting, however, that the perceived risks are much higher than the shocks experienced, which indicates some change in the underlying structure of the events. Again, the difference is bigger among the poor, and this is also the case in Thailand. Taking the average number of shocks, for example (Table 11.1), risks for households in Thailand were four times higher than what they had experienced in the past. In Vietnam perceived risks were six times higher than shocks experienced. For this parameter there is little difference between poor and non-poor households, i.e., the latter are also rather pessimistic about the future. The consistency of these results of the two groups lends some support to the notion that results based on subjective information are valid for the environments where these people live.

In Figure 11.1, shock experience and risk expectation for the same type of event measured by the per cent of households reporting is compared for poor and non-poor households in Thailand. It is shown that over 50 per cent of the non-poor households reported experience with weather-related shocks, which is the highest among the four shock categories. However, only slightly lower are socio-demographic

TABLE 11.1
Climate-related Shock Experience (2002–08) and the Risk Expectations (2008) of Poor and Non-poor Households in Thailand and Vietnam

	Vietnam		Thailand	
	% of HH	Frequency	% of HH	Frequency
Poor (< US$2 PPP)				
Shocks	81.5	1.4	54.3	0.8
Risks	89.7	8.5	72.1	4.3
Non-Poor (> US$2 PPP)				
Shocks	65.2	1.0	52.0	0.8
Risks	86.4	6.2	71.2	4.0

Source: DFG survey.

shocks, which include illness and loss of family members. A striking difference can be observed between experience and expectations. Overall, a much higher share of households in Thailand expect much worse in the future than what they had experienced in the past. The largest difference is for economic shocks where more than twice the shares of households that have experienced such shocks expect them in the future. This difference may indicate the general uncertainty in connection with the global financial and the food price crisis in 2008. Climate-related shocks are expected by over 70 per cent, and socio-demographic shocks by almost 90 per cent of the households, which is also a strong increase compared to past experience. The increase in the share of households that expect climate-related risks in the future compared to a lower share who experienced past shocks could be taken as an indicator that rural households in Thailand are aware of climate change. Generally, the difference between poor and non-poor households in Thailand is small. This may be related to the

FIGURE 11.1
Shock Experience (2002–08) and Risk Perception (2008) — Vietnam

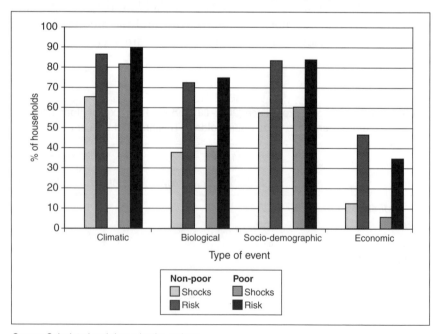

Source: Calculated and drawn by the authors.

fact that the headcount ratio has also declined in rural areas, although vulnerability to poverty may remain high.

The dominance of climate-related shocks is much more apparent in Vietnam with a visible poverty difference (see Figure 11.1). Weather-related shocks rank highest with over 80 per cent of the poor and 65 per cent of the non-poor households reporting. This is a good reflection of the high exposure to weather conditions in Vietnam, which is stronger than in Thailand. The even higher share of households that expect such events in the future, is again more pronounced for poor households (almost 90 per cent). The fact that people have high risk expectations compared to what they have actually experienced during the past suggests that they perceive that climate change is taking place although they may not understand the phenomenon as such. Economic shocks are higher for non-poor households, which make sense as they are more integrated in product, labour, and other factor

FIGURE 11.2
Shock Experience (2002–08) and Risk Perception (2008) — Thailand

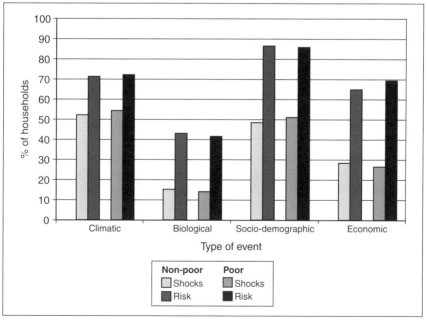

Source: Calculated and drawn by the authors.

markets than the poor. Remarkably, while only around 10 per cent of the households reported economic shocks in the past, around 35 per cent of the poor and almost 50 per cent of the non-poor see there to be a risk of economic shock in the future. This may well reflect the general uncertainty arising from the global financial and economic crisis in 2008.

For rural households, events related to climate change can result in lost income and assets and increased expenditures. For households just above the poverty line that depend on agriculture as their main source of livelihood, weather shocks such as flood and drought can mean descent into poverty. Over 50 per cent of poor households and about 40 per cent of non-poor households reported monetary losses from climate-related shocks.[4] In this situation, income losses exceeded the combination of asset losses and adjustment expenses. The majority of the households lost or spent money in relation to flooding events, especially the poor. But non-poor households that experienced floods spent on average about 30 per cent more than did poor households. Drought and cold weather were reported next as climate-related events with financial consequences. The average time in months that poor and non-poor households needed to recover from a climate shock was always reported as more than half a year.

While on average the monetary effect of climate shocks in Thailand was about the same as in Vietnam, the proportion of households that reported monetary losses or additional expenditures was lower than in Vietnam. On the other hand, the monetary effect is stronger in poor households. Income and asset losses or expenditures are primarily incurred for drought followed by flood. Recovery time from shocks for poor households in Thailand was a month longer than for poor households in Vietnam.

To test the validity of the risk perceptions, a regression model has been developed that tries to establish causality between a set of household and respondent characteristics and the risk scores calculated from the respondents expectations of frequency and the severity of future risks. Regression results provide some indication of the validity of the subjective assessments which form the basis of this analysis. Household and respondent characteristics, location factors, and the shock experiences of the households are included as independent variables of the equation. The hypothesis that poor people are more affected by climate change has been tested by means of a dummy variable that divides the respondents into those below and above the US$2 poverty line. Overall, the hypothesis of the models is that past shock experiences, in addition to other factors, could explain risk expectations using the 2008 database. The models were estimated for the two countries separately.

In both countries, the poverty variable is significant. It suggests that the poor are more exposed to climate risks because they live in more

TABLE 11.2
Tobit Regression of Weather Risk Perception Against Socio-Demographic Characteristics

	Vietnam		Thailand	
Tobit weather risk perception	Coef.	t-value	Coef.	t-value
Respondent characteristics				
Household below poverty line (1=Yes)	0.18	2.52**	0.17	1.96*
Agricultural occupation (1=Yes)	0.59	5.63***	0.86	7.75***
Member in socio-political organization (1=Yes)	0.01	0.12	−0.06	−0.48
Age (Years)	0.04	2.76***	−0.01	−0.30
Age squared (Years)	0.00	−3.00***	0.00	0.23
Ethnicity (1=Kinh)	−0.11	−0.92	0.09	0.35
Education (Years)	0.00	−0.04	0.02	0.17
Gender (1=Male)	−0.04	−0.67	−0.12	−1.35
Province dummies				
Buriram (TH)/Ha Tinh (VN) (1=Yes)	−0.42	−3.11***	1.11	9.86***
Nakhon Panom (TH)/Dak Lak (VN) (1=Yes)	−1.27	−9.50***	0.22	1.13
Climate shock incidents 2002–2008				
Climate shocks of high severity (1=Yes)	0.58	7.87***	1.07	11.78***
Climate shocks of medium severity (1=Yes)	0.13	1.63	0.76	7.79***
Constant	1.69	4.45***	0.23	0.28
P > F (joint significance)	0.00		0.00	
n	2146		2116	

Note: *P<0.1, **P<0.05, ***P<0.01
Source: Authors' own calculation.

vulnerable areas or they are more pessimistic about the future than the non-poor. The variable *agricultural occupation* is highly significant, which suggests that agricultural households live in areas where climate factors are more important. The coefficients for the provinces of Dak Lak and Ha Tinh are negative. This is plausible because Thua Thien Hue province is a coastal province located in the central part of Vietnam and thus most exposed to storms coming from the South China Sea, while the two other provinces are less exposed. Location variables for Thailand confirm the results from Vietnam, i.e. that households located in more vulnerable environments expect more climate-related shocks in the future. Membership in socio-political organizations and ethnicity are not significant. Hence, contradictory to common assumptions, we do not find any difference for ethnic minorities in their subjective assessment of the future as compared to the Kinh majority. Weather shock experience of high severity, and in the case of Thailand also of medium severity, are significant, confirming the assumed strong relationship between shocks and perceptions of risk. See Table 11.2.

In Table 11.3, the results are presented from the use of the adoption model to explain climate-related risk-management strategies used by the households in the two countries. The dependent variable is the probability that a rural household in 2008 has adopted any measure suitable to lessen the effect of climate-related events, such as flood, drought, or storm. As explanatory variables, the usual location and village characteristics, as well as household and farm characteristics, have been included. The variable of interest is the climate-risk score derived from the household's subjective assessment of aggregate climate risk for the near future. The explanatory variables vary slightly between Thailand and Vietnam so as to reflect country-specific situations. For example, in Thailand an aggregate measure of wealth was included, while in Vietnam tangible assets and land were separated. In Vietnam land values are less reliable as a result of the government-influenced land market. Furthermore, to portray the widespread use of off-farm wage and non-farm self-employment in Thailand, the variable "engagement in agriculture" was included. The main message of the model is that in both countries climate risk perception significantly influences the households' decision to adopt climate-related risk management measures. The model also shows some consistency with the previous one. For example, households in

TABLE 11.3
Standard Probit Regression of Household Use of Ex-Ante Weather Risk
Management Strategies in 2008

Probit: Ex-ante climate risk mitigation (1=Yes)	Thailand		Vietnam	
	Coef.	dF/dx	Coef.	dF/dx
Household characteristics 2007/2008				
Household below poverty line (1=Yes)	−0.125	−0.031	0.021	0.005
Maximum education (Years)	0.016	0.004	0.002	0.001
Wealth per capita (PPP$)	0.000	0.000	–	–
Tangible assets value (PPP$)			0.000	0.000
Number of household members	−0.008	−0.002	0.038	0.008
Average monthly per capita income (PPP$)	−0.000*	−0.000	−0.000	−0.000
Ethnicity of household head (1=Kinh)			0.462*	0.084
Engagement in off-farm employment (Number of months)	0.000	0.000	−0.009*	−0.002
Farm size (ha)			0.792	0.174
Age of household head (Years)	−0.023	−0.006	0.009	0.002
Age of household head squared (Years)	0.000	0.000	−0.000	−0.000
Engagement in agriculture (%)	0.143	0.036	–	–
Climate risk score	0.005**	0.001	0.004*	0.001
Village/province characteristics				
Off-farm employment as main option (1=Yes)			−0.142	−0.031
Time to district town (minutes)	−0.000	−0.000	0.001	0.000
Time to marktet (minutes)	−0.006	−0.001	−0.004	−0.001
Ha Tinh (VN) / Buriram (TH) (1=Yes)	−0.097	−0.024	0.079	0.018
Dak Lak (VN) / Nakhon Panom (TH) (1=Yes)	0.312**	0.086	−2.336***	−0.428
Constant	−0.226		−0.928	
P > F (Wald test)	0.000		0.000	
n	1555		1476	

Note: *P<0.1, **P<0.05, ***P<0.01. dF/dx indicates the marginal effect of a one-unit change in the
  explanatory variable on the probability to use any ex-ante climate risk management strategies.
Source: Authors' own calculation.

the province of Dak Lak, in Vietnam, which is less prone to climate-change factors, have a lower probability of adopting *ex-ante* risk management measures. Similarly, in Thailand the province of Nakon Phanom, bordering Laos alongside the Mekong River, the probability of adopting risk-management measures is higher. In Thailand richer households tend to do less in adopting risk-management measures, and in Vietnam if a household belongs to ethnic Kinh majority it is more likely to adopt them. This may be due to the generally poor access of ethnic minority groups to knowledge and resources. Also, engagement in off-farm wage- or non-farm self-employment in Vietnam lowers the likelihood that households will undertake *ex-ante* climate risk management, which is consistent with the findings of Phung and Waibel (2010).

To refine the findings on the adoption of climate-related risk management strategies, a third model was developed. It aims to assess the likelihood of adopting various practices. In Table 11.4 results are shown for Vietnam.[5] In the bi-variate probit model the dependent variables were (a) collective actions and (b) individual investments. The statistical quality of the model is weaker than for the two previous ones. The main conclusion is that climate risk perceptions make a difference for the decision of households to participate in collective actions related to climate-related problems. This suggests an awareness of climate change and some preparedness of rural village households to undertake collective action at village level to build infrastructure such as dikes and irrigation canals or take reforestation measures in order to reduce vulnerability to climate risks. Results for the location variable found in the previous models are consistent. For example, the coefficients for the Dak Lak province dummy are negative. Results for individual investment activities, which include improving homestead security, do not confirm the significance of the climate experience variable. This suggests that, individual investment for *ex-ante* weather risk management variables are driven by factors other than those in the collective action equation. However, the location variables show the expected signs and are significant, including the dummy variable for Ha Tinh, a province which is much exposed to weather risks. It must be noted that interpretations of this model must not be overstated as the empirical basis for the investment activities is one year, namely, 2008. Longer term data would show clearer results.

TABLE 11.4
Bivariate Probit Regressions for Two Ex-Ante Weather Risk
Management Strategies in Vietnam

(n=1476)	Collective action		Investment activity	
	Coef.	dF/dx	Coef.	dF/dx
Household characteristics 2007/2008				
Household below poverty line (1=Yes)	−0,00104	−0,0001	−0,0904	−0,0001
Education (Years)	0,001351	0,0001	0,01812	0,0000
Tangible assets value (PPP$)	0,000369***	0,0000	−0,0002*	0,0000
Number of household members	0,054351	0,0034	−0,0353	0,0000
Average monthly per capita income (PPP$)	−0,00086	−0,0001	−0,0023	0,0000
Off-farm employment (Months)	−0,00948	−0,0006	0,00241	0,0000
Age of household head (Years)	−0,00592	−0,0004	0,01203	0,0000
Age of household head squared (Years)	3,26E	−050,0000	−0,0002	0,0000
Land size (ha)	−2,71994	−0,1713	2,1966**	0,0030
Ethnicity of household head (1=Kinh)	0,298643	0,0154	0,47076	0,0004
Weather risk score	0,010245***	0,0006	−0,0012	0,0000
Village/province characteristics				
Off-farm employment = main option (1=Yes)	−0,39725	−0,0239	0,21956	0,0003
Time to district town (minutes)	−0,00122	−0,0001	0,00361	0,0000
Time to marktet (minutes)	0,005487	0,0003	−0,0009	0,0000
Ha Tinh dummy (1=Yes)	0,190242	0,0125	0,46861***	0,0008
Dak Lak dummy (1=Yes)	−1,5047***	−0,0903	−6,0304***	−0,1639
Constant	−1,77908**		−1,8098***	

$P > F$ (Wald test) = 0.0000
Rho (_) = −0.2641639***

Note: *P<0,1, **P<0,05, ***P<0,01
Source: Authors' own calculation.

IMPLICATIONS FOR DEVELOPMENT ORGANIZATIONS

Here are some main points and corresponding recommendations from this study. First, weather-related shocks were the most prevalent type experienced by rural households in six provinces of northeast Thailand and the central highlands of Vietnam. Rural people from these areas are knowledgeable about the role of climate for their livelihoods. Development agencies could make more intensive use of this experience and knowledge. The "voices of the poor" can be helpful in developing solutions that are fine-tuned to local conditions and can thus increase the overall effectiveness of interventions. Information on subjective probabilities of weather events can provide a basis for a more broad-based participation of the target group in project design and planning. Therefore, climate change related experience and perceptions should become a standard module in baseline surveys and monitoring and evaluation systems for development projects.

Second, people who experienced climate-related shocks in the past expect the future to be much worse. This suggests that people have noticed that climate change is taking place. The implication of such perceptions for development interventions is that incentive structures must be designed so they will guide rural people well in their adaptation and investment decisions. While future scenarios must be taken into account, people's fear needs to be taken seriously as it influences their behavior. But it should not be the sole guide to climate change related investment decisions.

Third, the poor perceive the future as riskier than the non-poor do because they tend to live in riskier environments and have experienced disaster. Climate change, therefore, brings the prospect of cementing current "poverty pockets". Development organizations should therefore build in an explicit pro-poor focus to their climate change related investment and interventions.

Fourth, for those households that undertake coping measures, their perceptions play an important role. This suggests that for projects that deal with climate change, locally tested measures should be considered in the design and planning of such projects. The notion that measures to tackle the consequences of climate change should be externally developed is challenged by this study.

Fifth, the knowledge of a rural household about its natural environment can provide a good basis for designing publicly supported collective actions aimed at responding to the effects of climate change in rural areas. So can the coping actions that rural households have already implemented. We show that risk perception is a significant factor in the participation in village- or community-based collective actions (in Vietnam). However, the opposite was found for individual investment decisions. This underlines the need for policies that remove barriers to rural households carrying out their own measures and that stimulate the investments necessary to cope more effectively with the consequences of climate change.

Notes

1. Covariate shocks (e.g., flooding, drought) are those that can possibly affect all households in a community or area while idiosyncratic shocks (e.g., illness, unemployment) typically take place at the household level.
2. For details on the modeling procedure, see Tongkruksawattana et al. (2010).
3. The project number is DFG FOR 756.
4. For details on monetary losses from climate related shocks, see Tongkruksawattana et al. (2010).
5. For Thailand a multivariate model was used (see Tongkruksawattana et al. 2010). Results are not presented here due to space limitations

References

Gödecke, T. and H. Waibel. "Rural–Urban Transformation and Village Economy in Emerging Market Economies During Economic Crisis: Empirical Evidence from Thailand". *Cambridge Journal of Regions, Economy and Society* 4, no. 2 (2011): 205–19.

Hardeweg, B., S. Klasen and H. Waibel. "Establishing a Database for Vulnerability Assessment. In *Vulnerability to Poverty: Theory, Measurement, and Determinants*, edited by Stephan Klasen and Hermann Waibel. New York: PalgraveMacmillan, 2012.

Healy, A. J. and S. Jitsuchon. "Finding the Poor in Thailand". *Journal of Asian Economics* 18 (2007): 739–59.

Millennium Ecosystem Assessment. *Ecosystems and Human Well-Being: General Synthesis*. Washington, D.C.: Island Press, 2005.

Ngyuen Tuong, L. "Climate change and climate variability in Viet Nam". The Netherlands climate assistance programme, 2010 <http://www.nlcap.net/countries/Viet Nam/>.

Phung D. T. and H. Waibel. "Diversification in Land and Labor Allocation in Response to Shocks among Small-Scale Farmers in Central Vietnam". *Schriften der Gesellschaft für Wirtschafts- und Sozialwissenschaften des Landbaues* e.V., Bd. 45 (2010): 91–111.

Tongruksawattana, S., M. Völker, B. Hardeweg, and H. Waibel. "Climate Risk Perception and Ex-Ante Mitigation Strategies of rural households in Thailand and Viet Nam". Contributed paper accepted for oral presentation at 117th European Association of Agricultural Economists (EAAE) Seminar, Hohenheim, 25–27 November 2010 <https://eaae-fsc.uni-hohenheim.de/>.

Tongruksawattana, S., V. Junge, J. Revilla Diez, E. Schmidt, and H. Waibel. "Ex-post Coping Strategies of Rural Households in Thailand and Vietnam". In *Vulnerability to Poverty: Theory, Measurement, and Determinants*, edited by Stephan Klasen and Hermann Waibel. New York: PalgraveMacmillan, 2012.

World Bank. "Taking Stock: An Update on Vietnam's Recent Economic Developments". World Bank Report to the Annual Consultative Group Meeting from Hanoi, Vietnam, 4–5 December 2008.

12

POOR THAI FARMERS' ADAPTATION TO CLIMATE CHANGE

Somchai Jitsuchon

The temperature in Asia increased at a rate of 0.1–0.3 degrees Celsius per decade from 1951 to 2000, while sea level rose and rainfall increased but with greater variation.[1] Changes in weather resulting from climate change come in various forms: heat waves, droughts, floods and cyclones. These become more often and more intense, and interfere with human activities, including economic activities. Over the period 1990–2100, there could be a decline of up to 50 per cent in rice yield in Indonesia, Vietnam, the Philippines, and Thailand.[2] Agriculture is therefore among the most affected sectors. Agriculture is also a major cause of climate change. For example, the emission of methane (CH_4) from rice fields contributes to greenhouse gas. Agriculture therefore should be managed in a way that both mitigates and adapts to climate change. Adaption is especially important for poor farmers who lack the resources needed to properly deal with the problems of climate change.

CLIMATE CHANGE AND AGRICULTURE

Changes in temperature, rainfall, and CO_2 release are all critical to agricultural activities. Pests and diseases are also likely to change and therefore alter food productivity. Geographic changes to land affect their suitability for cultivating staple crops.[3] Other negative effects include the reduction in the quantity of water and the loss of land due to rise in sea level. Climate change will most likely be experienced differently from one area to another. Some areas may benefit from increased temperature, especially those areas that currently have limited potential due to cold weather. Atmospheric CO_2 may also speed up growth process of some plants. Rain-fed crops declined in South and Southeast Asia.[4] Crop yields might increase by 20 per cent in East Asia and Southeast Asia.[5] In Thailand, the effects on yields can be either positive or negative, depending on the CO_2 regime.[6] Given the mixed findings, even if global effects were small or moderate, regional effects could be large and devastating — at least for some parts, such as Southeast Asia, which is among the most vulnerable places due to its high forestation and strong dependence on agriculture.[7]

For farmers, climate change mean more weather variation. There is more rain in some areas and during some periods, and less in others. As a result, some farmers gain and some lose. Likewise, the rise of temperature can make some plants grow faster. But it is the increased variation that causes concern for farmers. More unpredictable weather makes farm planning difficult, and adjusting to the changes costly. Droughts are more frequent and uncertain. Thicker clouds from heightened evaporation obstruct sunlight and interfere with crop growth. Overall, global warming and climate change add more challenges to farmers trying to maintain their traditional way of cultivation.

How climate change affects agriculture depends on various factors, including adaptive capacity. Adaptive capacity is in turn affected by the social and economic situation of the particular population. Poor and low-income farmers are vulnerable because they depend on nature in their agricultural activities and are already at risk to food loss and hunger. Small shocks can cause their lives severe hardship.

CLIMATE CHANGE AND AGRICULTURE IN THAILAND

Thailand is located in the southeastern part of Asia, and so is vulnerable to climate change. Thailand's experience of climate change is much like that of most other countries in the region.[8] For example, temperature increased between 1 and 1.8 degrees Celsius between 1900 and 2010.[9] As recently as this year, many provinces in Thailand reported new temperature highs since records started being kept (see Table 12.1). Droughts occur more often, and cyclones are becoming more difficult to predict.

Although Thailand does not suffer from hazards as much as the Philippines, Indonesia, and northern Vietnam,[10] some parts do suffer. Besides, being subject to hazards is not the only cause of vulnerability to climate change. For example, Thailand's southern region and Bangkok and surrounding areas are subject to higher hazards than other parts of the country.[11] But when measured by overall vulnerability, which is a function of exposure, sensitivity, and adaptive capacity,[12] other parts such as the western, the north, and the northeast regions are also highly vulnerable to climate change. This may imply a high sensitivity or low adaptive capacity, or both, of those regions. A doubling of CO_2

TABLE 12.1
Rises of Temperature in Thailand

Provinces	New High 2010		Previous High		
	Degree	Degree	Year	Difference
Mae HongSon	43.3	43.0	1991	0.3
Nan	42.5	41.7	1983	0.8
Lam Pang	43.1	42.9	2007	0.2
Sukothai	42.6	41.6	2003	1.0
Tak	41.0	40.9	2004	0.1
Pichit	40.7	39.3	2001	1.4
Buriram	41.7	40.8	2007	0.9
Kanchanaburi	43.0	42.0	1998	1.0
Songkhla	37.5	37.3	1998, 2004	0.2

Source: Weather Center, Thailand

would result in (a) a decline of the tropical forest areas in most of
the country outside the south, and (b) an increase of very dry tropical
forests in the north and the northeast regions. The general weather is
clearly becoming more unpredictable. Seasons are not as regular as in
the past. Summers are longer. Southeast monsoons are more severe
with heavier and irregular rains, that is, heavy rains alternate with
long spells of no rain. Floods are more severe and frequent in some
parts, such as in the south. In 2010 and 2011, Thailand witnessed
ones of the most severe floods in a quarter of century. The prospect
is not bright either. The average yearly amount of rainfall over the
next sixty years could be 20 per cent more than the average yearly
rainfall of the previous 100 years. Increased weather variability alters

TABLE 12.2
Changes in Rainfall Patterns According to Rice Farmers
in Yasothorn Province in 2008

	April	May–June	July–September	October	November
Activities	Prepare soil	Plant seedlings	Transplant seedlings	Seedlings allowed to flower and grow	Harvest rice
Normal climate	No or hardly any rain	Rain starts	Rain continues	Rain continues but intensity decreasing	No rain
Climate now	Rain starts	Little or no rain	Rain comes at the end of August, heavy in September	Rain continues	Rain continues even heavier, stops at the end of November
Effects		Drought	Drought		Water logging
Effects on crops			Seedlings wilt, difficult to transplant		Quality of grains affected by high moisture and absence of dry and colder weather

Source: Supaporn Anuchiracheeva and Tul Pinkaew (2009).

biodiversity, which might cause the extinction of some animals and plants.

For agriculture, the increase in weather variation is the major cause of concern. This is true for rice farmers, as the usual farming patterns are no longer applicable. An altered rainfall pattern affects the crop cultivation cycle (see Table 12.2).[13] Rain that came too soon at the beginning of the cycle make soil preparation difficult, while planting is delayed due to the smaller-than-normal subsequent rainfalls. At harvesting time, too much rain now causes water logging and moisturized grains.

ADAPTATION TO CLIMATE CHANGE BY THAI FARMERS

A small project was conducted by Oxfam International in one of Thailand's poorest provinces, Yasothorn in the northeast region of the country, where most agricultural activities are tied to weather. Rain-fed rice farming is the most prevalent occupation among the province's farmers, as most of the areas are outside large-scale irrigation area. Yasothorn has had its share of difficult experiences with climate change. Weather changes are shown in Table 12.2 above. In the past few years, rainfall became more unpredictable and often during harvesting seasons rain did not fall as much as it used to. There was also an increasing risk that depressions from the South China Sea would come less often to Thailand falling from an average of once a year to about once every three years. Actually, these depressions are important, as they provide rainfalls needed by the agriculture in Thailand, especially in the northeast region.

In 2007, Yasothorn experienced one of the longest drought seasons in decades. The drought spell lasted from June to late August. And as mentioned earlier that the delay of rainfall is likely to repeat itself more often in the future, this will affect rice farmers, who represent around 90 per cent of the province's total population. As most farmers grow jasmine rice, which is light-sensitive and thus requires a fixed timetable of cultivation, plantation, and harvesting, the climate change has taken a high toll on the lives of the province's farmers.

As part of an effort to help the Yasothorn farmers adapt to and mitigate the effects of climate change, Oxfam International and some partners set up a pilot project in 2008–09 that focused on organic agriculture as a safeguard for the farmers. Fifty-seven organic farming households, with a total of 285 beneficiaries (57 of them female), joined the project. The project's activities consisted of providing information about climate change, making loans for water management (pond, underground water, water distribution system, and pump), promoting crop diversification (vegetables, fruit trees). Farmers were encouraged to share experiences.[14] A post-project evaluation revealed that the participating farmers were satisfied with the project outcomes, as food became more secure; rice yield was not as low as they feared at the beginning of the year, and water management mitigated the effects of the drought. In an interview, one of the participating farmers mentioned the importance of crop diversification as a risk-management tool.

In spite of this Oxfam initiative and its favourable outcomes, the adaptive measures in this project were limited in scope. Except for the loan for water management which requires an external subsidy, most of the measures adopted by the farmers were somewhat traditional. For example, crop diversification has long been adopted by farmers in many areas and locations.

The questions we have are then, to what extent can farmers, especially the poorer ones, adapt to climate change on their own, and what type and amount of external help is needed? Farmers in four villages of Sisaket, another poor Thai province in the northeast, had limited capability to counter the adverse effects of climate change, especially when the change was extreme.[15] The farmers were understandably more able to cope with milder climate change, and sometimes even benefit from it by adjusting their input process in rice cultivation. This coping potential was, however, more limited for poor farmers.

One striking element of the Oxfam project mentioned earlier is that all the participating farmers grew organic rice. I will discuss how organic agriculture can provide a better and more sustainable response to climate change later. It is one way to avoid climate change effects.[16] There are plenty of other adaptation and mitigation practices around the world.

Farmers should use scientific data on the effects of climate change as much as they can in their attempts to adapt. They should combine it with their own knowledge derived from a long history of combating climate uncertainty. Information and experience sharing among farmers can help screen and speed up adjustment measures.

RECENT DEVELOPMENTS IN CLIMATE-SENSITIVE AGRICULTURAL PRACTICES

Organic Agriculture

Organic agriculture by itself can mitigate climate change, as the production process involves less emission of greenhouse gas than conventional, non-organic agriculture. Using less chemical inputs reduces carbon content in soil.[17] Organic agriculture also provides better adaptation to climate change. For example, organic rice is usually stronger and more resilient to climate variation than non-organic rice. The spread of aphids and weevils, which are sometimes associated with climate change, is also less likely with organic agriculture. In marginal lands, organic agriculture farming is usually more profitable, as the benefits from using chemical fertilizers and pesticides can fall short of cost of purchasing them. Climate-related poverty is thus less prevalent among organic farmers.

Community-based Adaptation

Communities can spread agricultural practices that are more adaptive to climate change by sharing information and experiences. Other related functions are also possible, especially post-climate change assistances. In many cases, communities can act as an effective conduit to channel social safety net assistance from the central and local governments. Some can even mobilize their own resources to mitigate the effects. Some communities can also manage public assets or common resources (such as fish stocks). As climate change may cause damage to common assets as well, this capability should be useful. However, there seems to be a limit to communities' ability to deal with extreme climate changes because most communities have not had experience with adjustments needed on the large scale that is needed.[18]

Insurance Against Climate Change

There is a growing interest in employing financial innovation, most notable insurance schemes, to help the farmers to mitigate the adverse effects of climate change (financial instruments enhance farmers' capability to mitigate the effects of climate change). Weather insurance is a prime example of such efforts. Since farmers are usually able to cope with mild climate change, but not with the extreme kind, the suitable insurance schemes insure against catastrophic losses.[19] Some initial attempts in this area have also been implemented in Thailand.[20] In the long run weather insurance should replace the crop-price guarantee scheme currently in place. This will be a good move, as insurance is more market-based and more effective in dealing with climate change risks, and also a better targeting measure for the poor farmers.

Bioenergy

One recent development is bio-energy crops. As most long-term forecasts have fossil-based energy as high priced, it is envisioned that the production of bio-energy crops will expand and become more popular among farmers. It is still not clear what the net effects of these crops are in terms of greenhouse gases. Citing studies in Indonesia, ADB (2009) finds that bioelectricity can reduce CO_2 emission by 50–185 ton carbon-equivalent per hectare. Thailand has a strong potential in this area, given its well-developed agricultural sector. However, a recent study in Thailand (JGSEE 2010) reveals that that some of these crops might produce net positive greenhouse gases.

Payment for Environmental Service

One novel idea for mitigating climate change is to give incentives to farmers and non-farmers to adopt, or refrain, from activities that are more, or less, environmental friendly. For example, payments are made to farmers who adopt agro-ecological practices that increase the resilience of the ecological system. Moreover, the schemes could be sustainable by themselves, as the World Bank (2008) shows in the case of Nicaragua, that although many farmers stopped the practices they were paid for once the payments stopped, some resumed when they recognized the long-term benefit of the practices.

Protecting the Poorest

Since poor families are more vulnerable to climate change, they require special treatment. A guarantee of food sufficiency, either through cash or in-kind transfers from the governments, or with help from communities, should be implemented. More generally, a more complete, perhaps universal, welfare system is required in order to make sure that the poorest are not left out of the safety net. The above developments should be considered in addition to usual advice on policy measures, such as tax policy, better land and farm management, regulatory measures, and international cooperation.

Role of the Private Sector

Perhaps the most promising area of public private partnership is in weather insurance schemes. Most schemes involve the private sector as the final and sometimes intermediate insurers. Governments can use tax money to buy crop insurance contracts, which can be designed as option contracts triggered by climate-related indicators, such as rainfall. Alternatively, a completely market-based scheme can be developed, where individual farmers purchase the insurance contract themselves.[21]

Another recent development that can be fit into the climate change context is the social enterprise, which is getting more attention in Thailand. It is viewed as having the potential for being a means to mitigate the environmental effects of economic activities that is both sustainable and effective. Social enterprises are *sustainable* because they run on profit, or at least no-loss, basis. And as private entities, they are *effective*, as they are able to avoid much of the red tape faced by public agencies. Many social enterprises already focus on improving the environment; so steering them toward climate change mitigation and adaptation should not be difficult.

CONCLUSION

Thailand shares Southeast Asia's high vulnerability to climate change. A rise in temperature and heightened variation in rainfall is resulting in more frequent and prolonged droughts, as well as floods. Bangkok and its surrounding areas and Southern Thailand are particularly at risk of suffering from hazards, but other regions are also vulnerable to climate change as they host the country's poorer population, especially those involved in agriculture. Thai farmers have a limited adaptive capacity: they can adapt to mild, but not extreme, climate changes. Without major adjustments or external help, the livelihood of poor farmers is at risk. Organic agriculture provides a better choice than conventional farming practices for both mitigation and adaptation. Other means should also be encouraged, including community-based adaptation, weather insurance, bio-energy, and market-based payment incentives for environmental services.

Notes

1. A recent ADB study (Asian Development Bank 2009) says that in Asia interventions are needed sooner rather later, as temperature was found to increase at a speed of 0.1–0.3 degrees Celsius per decade during 1951–2000, while rainfall increased and the sea level rose.
2. The ADB report (2009) forecasts a decline of up to 50 per cent on average in rice yield in Indonesia,Vietnam, Philippines, and Thailand by the year 2100, compared to 1990.
3. Grasty (1999).
4. C. Rosenzweig et al. (2001).
5. Cruz et al. (2008).
6. Parry et al. (2004).
7. ADB (2009).
8. There are plenty of studies pointing out that Thailand's experience of climate change is much like that of most other countries in the region.
9. ADB (2009).
10. To get a better view of how climate change affects Thailand, a comparison with other countries in the region would be useful. Yusuf and Herminia (2009) have constructed a hazard index map (a combination of climate-related hazards, such as tropical cyclones, floods, landslides, droughts, and sea level rise) for Southeast Asia. According to their map, Thailand does not suffer from hazards as much as the Philippines, Indonesia, and northern Vietnam.

11. Yusuf and Herminia (2009)
12. The aforementioned hazard index map only refers to exposure. Yusuf and Herminia use the Intergovernmental Panel on Climate Change's definitions of these three factors to construct another map that displays climate change vulnerability in Southeast Asia.
13. Oxfam International (2009) surveyed farmers in Yasothorn province of Thailand and showed that an altered rainfall pattern affected the crop cultivation cycle.
14. Despite their smaller numbers, female participants were actively involved in the project.
15. A study by Townsend Felkner and Tazhibayera (2009) offers an answer to the first question. The study combines an economic model with a biophysical model of rice cultivation and allows for a stochastic realization of a weather generator. They calibrated the integrated model into two climate change scenarios (mild and severe) against the no-climate benchmark. Farmers in the model were allowed to adopt a mitigation strategy. The model used a panel data of four villages in Sisaket, another poor Thai province, in the northeast. The primary finding was farmers had limited capability to counter the adverse effects of climate change, especially when the change was extreme.
16. On migration, the recent World Bank's World Development Report (World Bank 2010) acknowledges this.
17. A study by the Soil Association (2009) found that although organic agricultural activities tend to emit less greenhouse gases per planted areas, the emission may not be less per yield (see, e.g., Flessa et al. 2002)
18. The World Bank (2010) calls for "scaling up" community-based success to wider uses.
19. See, for example, the Caribbean Catastrophe Risk Insurance Facility (World Bank, 2010, Box 2.10).
20. The World Bank launched weather insurance scheme a few years back. It is received warmly by the government and policy makers.
21. Chantarat et al. (2007) provide a theoretical background on the conditions under which such schemes can exist.

References

Anuchiracheeva, Supaporn and Tul Pinkaew. "Oxfam Disaster Risk Reduction and Climate Change Adaptation Resources: Case Study Jasmine Rice in the Weeping Plain: Adapting Rice Farming to Climate Change in Northeast Thailand". Oxfam GB, 2009.

Asian Development Bank. *The Economics of Climate Change in Southeast Asia: A Regional Review*. Manila: Asian Development Bank, 2009.

Buddhina Nuntavorakarn and Decharut Sukkumnoed. "How Sustainable Agriculture Provide the Solutions to Low Carbon and Low Risk Society". Paper presented during the Franco-Thai Seminar on "Fostering Economic Growth through Low Carbon Initiatives in Thailand". 25–26 February 2010, Chulalongkorn University, Bangkok, Thailand.

Chantarat S., Christopher B. Barrett, Andrew G. Mude, and Calum G. Turvey. "Using weather index insurance to improve drought response for famine prevention". *American Journal of Agricultural Economics*. (December 2007).

Cruz, Rex Victor, Hideo Harasawa, Murari Lal, Shaohong Wu, Yurij Anokhin, Batima Punsalmaa, Yasushi Honda, Mostafa Jafari, Congxian Li, and Nguyen Huu Ninh. "Asia". In *Climate Change 2007: Impacts, Adaptation and Vulnerability*. Contribution of Working Group II to the Fourth Assessment Report of the Intergovernmental Panel on Climate Change, edited by M. L. Parry, O. F. Canziani, J.P. Palutikof, P. J. van der Linden and C. E. Hanson, pp. 469–506. Cambridge: Cambridge University Press, 2008.

Flessa, H, R. Ruser, P. Dörsch, T. Kampb, M. A. Jimenez, J. C. Munch, and F. Beese. "Integrated evaluation of greenhouse gas emissions (CO2, CH4,N2O) from two farming systems in southern Germany". *Agriculture, Ecosystems and Environment* 91 (2002): 175–89.

Grasty, Shelly. "Agriculture and Climate Change". *TDRI Quarterly Review* 14 (2 June 1999): 12–16.

JGSEE. "Biomass Supply Chain Production Cost". A presentation material at BEFS Thailand Technical Consultation, 11 March 2010. Joint Graduate School of Energy and Environment.

Oxfam International. "People-Centred Resilience Working with vulnerable farmers towards climate change adaptation and food security". Oxfam Briefing Paper, November 2009.

———. "Sustainable Agriculture, the Hope for Cooler World" (in Thai). 2010*a*.

———. "Adaptation to Climate Change for Food Security". Video presentation, 2010*b*.

Parry, M., C. Rosenzweig, A. Iglesias, M. Livermore, and G. Fischer. "Effects of Climate Change on Global Food Production under SRES Emissions and Socio-Economic Scenarios". *Global Environmental Change* 14, no. 1 (2004): 53–67.

Rosenzweig, C., A. Iglesias, X. B. Yang, P. R. Epstein, and E. Chivian. "Climate Change and Extreme Weather Events". *Global Change & Human Health* 2, no. 2 (2001): 90.

Sucharit Koontakakulvong. "Impacts of Climate Change on Hydology and Agriculture". Paper presented at Climate Thailand Conference, August 2010 (in Thai).

Townsend, R, John Felkner, and KamilyaTazhibayeva. "Impacts of Climate Change on Rice Production in Thailand". *American Economic Review: Papers & Proceedings 2009* (99) 2 (2000): 205–10.

Yusuf, Arief Anshory, and Herminia A. Francisco. "Climate Change Vulnerability Mapping for Southeast Asia". Economy and Environment Program for Southeast Asia, 2009.

World Bank. *World Development Report 2008: Agriculture for Development.* Washington, D.C.: World Bank, 2008.

———. *World Development Report 2010: Development and Climate Change.* Washington, D.C.: World Bank, 2010.

V

Archipelagic Southeast Asia
(Indonesia, Malaysia, Philippines)

13

THE POLITICAL ECONOMY OF ENVIRONMENTAL POLICY IN INDONESIA

Arianto A. Patunru

In Indonesia, there is widespread awareness of climate change and environmental problems, at least in academia, policy-making, civil society organizations, and NGOs. However, the ways climate change and the environment affect poverty are not so well understood. Indonesia, like many other countries, is preoccupied with achieving economic growth in a business-as-usual manner. The government emphasizes social protection rather than reducing vulnerabilities and improving livelihoods of the poor through a green economy. In this essay, we review the current discussion on the economics of environmental protection in Indonesia, especially with regards to climate change, and propose ways to fill in certain gaps between discourse and policy. We also discuss the poverty situation of Indonesia and highlight its relationship with the environment. Finally, we discuss the policy possibility of using the environment-climate connection as a way to accelerate poverty reduction. In particular, we argue that policies that take into account climate change and its effect on poverty should be applied at three different levels: micro, macro (national), and global (international).

THE ENVIRONMENT — POVERTY CONNECTION IN INDONESIA

Poverty in Indonesia has been decreasing (Figure 13.1), although there were a few spikes following the Asian Financial Crisis in 1997/98 and the rice and fuel price increases in 2005. As of February 2010, the poverty headcount index in Indonesia is around 13.3 per cent.[1] (Figure 13.1 depicts GDP growth rates and the open unemployment rates during 1998 to 2010.) The Asian Financial Crisis hit the country severely, resulting in a 13 per cent contraction. Slowly the country recovered, reaching its pre-crisis level in 2007, after ten years. The recent global financial crisis turned out to be far less damaging. In fact, Indonesia (along with China and India) was quite resilient, with a growth rate

FIGURE 13.1
Growth, Poverty, and Unemployment, 1998–2010 (%)

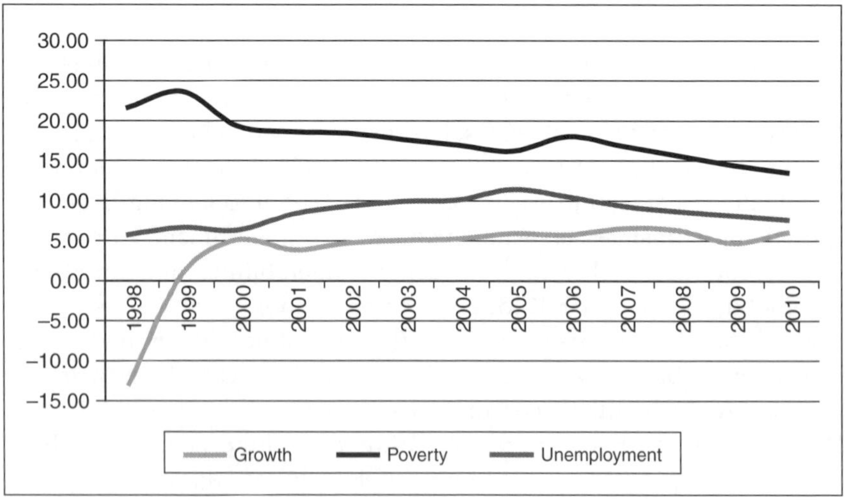

Note: 2010 growth is GoI's estimate.
Source: BPS (various years), GOI (various years).

of 4.5 per cent in 2009, while most countries in the world experienced a contraction or near-zero growth.

Unemployment rate dynamics, on the other hand, reflect the four phases of the labour market in Indonesia, namely "growing rapidly" (1990–97, not shown on the figure), "crashing and coping" (1997–99), "jobless growth" (1999–2003), and "job recovery" (2003–08) (World Bank 2010). According to this view, in the aftermath of the Asian financial crisis, agriculture and non-formal sectors served as buffers by absorbing the labour force. Then the capacity of the two sectors diminished. So the accompanying growth did not result in sizeable job creation. Next, real wages started to fall and stagnate, which induced job creation.[2]

The connections between economic growth, unemployment, and poverty are reasonably well researched in the literature. Environment, on the other hand, is not — at least not in its relationship with poverty and employment. But to assess the connection, one needs to see poverty's broader context (for example, Indonesia's poverty in comparison with other countries) and its important features. Then the situation of poverty should be juxtaposed with the situation of environment.

Indonesia's Poverty in Comparison

Table 13.1 shows Indonesia's poverty and inequality in comparison with a number of Asian countries. China and India are the most populous and most rapidly developing countries. The other countries are nearer Indonesia's, i.e. Southeast Asian countries.

Using the US$2 per day threshold, more than half of Indonesia's population is still poor. It is ahead of India, Lao PDR, and Cambodia, but behind China and the other countries. The two measures of inequality show a rather mixed picture. However, Indonesia's inequality is still relatively high. It is comparable to that of Vietnam; but Indonesia has a worse poverty rate.

In the ADB report (2010), China, Malaysia, Thailand, and Vietnam are recognized as "early achievers" in meeting the Millennium Development Goals (MDG) target of US$1.25/day, while Cambodia is "on track," and India, the Philippines, and Laos are those with "slow progress". As for Indonesia, the ADB report makes no assessment, due to insufficient data, but it asserts that in 2007, 29.4 per cent of

TABLE 13.1
Poverty and Inequality: Indonesia in Comparison with other Countries

Country	% Population below $2 (PPP)/day	Income Ratio of Highest 20% to Lowest 20%	Gini Coefficient
China	35.7 (2005)	8.3 (2005)	0.415 (2005)
India	75.6 (2005)	5.6 (2005)	0.368 (2005)
Indonesia	54.6 (2005)	6.2 (2007)	0.376 (2007)
Lao PDR	76.9 (2002)	4.9 (2002)	0.326 (2002)
Cambodia	57.8 (2007)	8.1 (2007)	0.442 (2007)
Malaysia	7.8 (2004)	7.0 (2004)	0.379 (2004)
Philippines	45.0 (2006)	9.0 (2006)	0.440 (2006)
Thailand	11.5 (2004)	8.1 (2004)	0.425 (2004)
Vietnam	48.4 (2006)	6.4 (2006)	0.378 (2006)

Source: ADB (2010).

Indonesians were still living on less than US$1.25/day. This suggests it will be difficult to reach the MDG target by 2015.

While the MDG target might be missed, Indonesia has also missed its own national poverty-reduction target. The medium-term plan (Rencana Pembanguan Jangka Menengah, or RPJM) 2005–09 aimed for poverty reduction from 18.2 per cent in 2002 to 8.2 per cent in 2009. In fact, the poverty headcount rate was still high, at 14.2 per cent, in 2009. This was primarily due to a rather steep increase in poverty in 2006, after a slow-but-steady decrease since 2002. In 2005 the poverty headcount index was 16 per cent, but it increased to 17.8 per cent in 2006, due mostly to a 33 per cent increase in rice price, and to a lesser extent an increase in fuel price in October 2005 (World Bank 2006a).

Features of Indonesian Poverty

Poverty in Indonesia has three salient features.[3] First, it is something a large number of Indonesians are vulnerable to falling into. That is, those scattered just above the poverty line are many, and are very sensitive to the change in the line. As a result, mobility of the poor to join the near-poor (or vice-verse) is high. A recent study by Suryahadi et al. (2010) confirms this. The study finds that in 47 per cent of the poor in

2008 stayed poor in 2009, and 53 per cent graduated to near-poor and non-poor. But 49 per cent of the poor in 2009 were not poor in 2008. A social safety net was first set up in 1998. Even though the poverty rate has gone down, from 23.4 per cent in 1999 to 13.3 per cent in 2010, the number of vulnerable (near-poor) people more than doubled.

Second, non-income poverty is more serious than income poverty. This includes high malnutrition rates, poor maternal health, weak education outcomes, and low access to water and sanitation. Table 13.2 shows some of the "monetary poverty" measures along with the "non-monetary" or non-income measures of poverty incidence. With the exception of unhygienic floor, all the non-income poverty measurements are worse than the monetary poverty. It is also important

TABLE 13.2
Poverty Profiles 1976–2009

Indicators	Definition	Rural (%)	Urban (%)	Gap (% point)
Lack of sanitation (toilet)	Percentage of population living in house without proper toilet	50.42	15.05	35.37
Low education of the head of household (HHH)	Percentage of population living in household in which HHH do not finish 9-year basic education	83.65	50.47	33.18
Lack of access to clean water	Percentage of population living in household without proper access to clean and protected source of drinking water	56.53	30.55	25.98
Low education of youth	Percentage of population living in household in which youth (18–24 years) do not finish 9-year basic education	40.70	15.97	24.73
Unhygienic floor	Percentage of population living in earth-floor housing	15.79	5.03	10.76
Monetary Poverty	Percentage of population below official poverty line	17.35	10.72	6.63

Source: Suryahadi et al. (2010).

to note that non-income poverty is more prevalent in rural areas. As the table shows, gaps in non-income poverty between rural and urban areas are far wider than that in income (or monetary) poverty. The implication for policy is obvious: poverty eradication should mainly take place in rural areas, taking into account especially non-income poverty.

Third, there are considerable regional disparities in Indonesia. Poverty incidence is far higher in eastern Indonesia; however, most of the poor live in western Indonesia. For example, as shown in Table 13.3, in 2009 poverty rate in Java/Bali was 13.7 per cent (down from 15.7 per cent in 2004) while that in the remote Papua 37.1 per cent (down from 38.7 per cent in 2004). But Java/Bali is home to 57 per cent of Indonesia's poor, while Papua has only 3 per cent.

Environmental Degradation

Indonesia is one of the biggest emitters of CO_2 in the world, even though per capita CO_2 emission is below countries like China, Malaysia, and Thailand (Table 13.4a). In terms of deforestation, Indonesia along with Malaysia and the Philippines have worrying rates (Table 13.4a and Table 13.4b). This is of concern especially because forests are central

TABLE 13.3
Regional Poverty 2009

	Rural	Urban	Total	Per Capita Income: Rural	Per Capita Income: Urban
Sumatra	15.0	12.2	13.9	357	558
Java-Bali	17.7	10.6	13.7	294	543
Nusa Tenggara	22.4	24.6	23.0	253	405
Kalimantan	9.1	5.1	7.5	376	697
Sulawesi	18.3	6.7	14.8	275	570
Maluku	25.9	7.5	20.9	313	591
Papua	46.3	5.9	37.1	315	707
Indonesia	18.9	10.7	14.1	311	550

Note: Per capita income in Rp '000 (2008 prices).
Source: BPS (2009), Resosudarmo and Yusuf (2009).

to the livelihood of 10 million of the poorest 36 million Indonesians (World Bank 2006*b*). At the same time China, India, and Vietnam show net reforestation rather than deforestation during 2000–07. Limited

TABLE 13.4a
Environment: Indonesia's Deforestation and CO_2 Emission

Country	Forest coverage (% of land, 1990)	Forest coverage (% of land, 2005)	CO_2 emission (thousand metric tons, 1990)	CO_2 emission (thousand metric tons, 2007)	CO_2 emission per cap (metric tons, 1990)	CO_2 emission per cap (metric tons, 2007)
China	16.8	21.2	2460744	6538367	2.2	4.9
India	21.5	22.8	690577	1612362	0.8	1.4
Indonesia	64.3	48.8	149566	397143	0.8	1.8
Cambodia	73.3	59.2	451	4441	0.0	0.3
Malaysia	68.1	63.6	56593	194476	3.1	7.3
Philippines	35.5	24.0	44532	70916	0.7	0.8
Thailand	31.2	28.4	95833	277511	1.7	4.1
Vietnam	28.8	39.7	21408	111378	0.3	1.3

Source: ADB (2010).

TABLE 13.4b
Environment: Other Measures

Country	GDP/unit of energy use (1)	Deforestation rate (2)	NOX (3)	Methane (4)	Agri land (5)	Arable land (6)	Cropland (7)
China	3.4	−2.1	566.7	995.8	59.3	15.1	1.3
India	4.9	−0.0	300.7	712.3	60.5	53.4	3.6
Indonesia	4.1	2.0	69.9	224.3	26.8	12.1	8.6
Cambodia	4.8	0.5	3.8	14.9	30.9	21.5	0.9
Malaysia	4.7	2.0	9.9	25.5	24.0	5.5	17.6
Philippines	7.1	2.1	18.9	44.8	38.6	17.1	16.4
Thailand	4.7	0.4	28.0	78.8	38.7	29.8	7.3
Vietnam	3.7	−1.9	37.5	75.1	32.5	20.5	9.9

Notes: (1) 2005 PPP USD/kg oil equivalent, (2) Average percent change 2000–07, (3,4) Million metric tons C02 equivalent, 2005, (5,6,7) Percent of land area, 2007
Source: ADB (2010).

TABLE 13.5
CO_2 **Emission in 2005 (million tons)**

Province	Industry (Coal)	Industry (fuel)	Household (fuel)	Transport (fuel)	Electricity	TOTAL
Aceh	0.00	0.05	0.25	1.40	0.74	2.45
North Sumatra	0.02	1.34	1.31	4.08	3.93	10.68
West Sumatra	7.50	0.21	0.60	1.22	1.21	10.73
Riau	3.82	1.36	0.54	2.31	1.27	9.29
Jambi	0.00	1.71	0.39	1.12	0.47	3.68
South Sumatra	1.46	1.55	0.64	1.36	1.35	6.36
Bangka-Belitung	0.02	0.05	0.37	0.43	0.22	1.09
Bengkulu	0.00	0.02	0.29	0.33	0.25	0.89
Lampung	0.05	1.44	0.68	1.20	1.24	4.61
Jakarta	0.02	3.12	3.70	15.03	17.99	39.87
West Java	2.77	12.94	3.08	4.09	15.10	37.98
Banten	1.32	8.80	0.95	0.61	2.17	13.85
Central Java	5.69	1.79	1.97	10.08	8.01	27.54
Jogjakarta	0.01	0.09	0.55	2.00	1.16	3.81
East Java	12.28	3.54	2.57	10.35	13.21	41.94
West Kalimantan	0.05	0.45	0.63	1.20	0.78	3.12
Central Kalimantan	0.00	0.08	0.37	0.57	0.34	1.36
South Kalimantan	1.57	0.25	0.55	1.34	0.92	4.63
East Kalimantan	0.00	0.48	0.51	1.55	1.02	3.56
North Sulawesi	0.00	0.13	0.35	0.44	0.59	1.51
Gorontalo	0.00	0.02	0.19	0.12	0.14	0.46
Central Sulawesi	0.00	0.02	0.35	0.99	0.35	1.71
South Sulawesi	10.22	0.23	0.91	1.24	1.99	14.58
Southeast Sulawesi	0.30	0.03	0.42	0.22	0.25	1.22
Bali	0.00	0.03	0.72	2.80	1.79	5.35
West Nusa Tenggara	0.00	0.02	0.45	0.67	0.43	1.56
East Nusa Tenggara	0.31	0.02	0.30	0.31	0.32	1.27
Maluku	0.00	0.23	0.09	0.27	0.21	0.80
North Maluku	0.00	0.14	0.03	0.00	0.12	0.29
Papua	0.00	0.49	0.06	0.35	0.42	1.32
Total	47.41	40.62	23.82	67.67	78.01	257.52

Source: Yusuf (2010).

land also constrains agriculture — the capacity of land declines as agriculture activities increase. (Table 13.4b shows how agricultural land, arable land, and cropland in Indonesia are limited.)

It is also interesting to compare emission levels within the country, as shown in Table 13.5. In general, western Indonesia emits more CO_2 than eastern Indonesia. This might be due to at least two factors: the majority of Indonesia's population (and the majority of the poor) lives in western Indonesia. Second, western Indonesia has more fertile soil. This is good for agriculture (including livestock), but this sector consumes a lot of energy, and so emits more CO_2.

OPPORTUNITIES OF POVERTY REDUCTION THROUGH A GREEN ECONOMY

Most Indonesians work in agriculture and the informal sector. The two sectors have served as a shock absorber in times of crisis. Furthermore, agricultural multipliers are strong: growth in agricultural output stimulates general growth in rural economy, for example, through expenditure linkage (McCulloch, Wisbrod and Timmer 2007). However, it is also true that many current practices in agriculture are not environmentally friendly. As for the informal sector, there is obviously far less job security than in the formal sectors. These two reasons, among others, motivate workers to move out of agriculture and into the informal sector. As argued by McCulloch, Wisbrod and Timmer (2007), the pathways out of poverty in Indonesia include the following: agricultural productivity growth;[4] sectoral shift to rural, non-farm enterprises; and rural–urban migration. It is also important to note that the formal sector is preferable since it reduces workers' exposure to tax and corruption payments (McCulloch, Schultze and Voss 2010).

There is less doubt now that climate change is happening and that it will affect the economy via many channels. This will affect especially the poor, as they are the ones working and living in the less advantaged regions. Therefore, poverty reduction and environmental protection should not be seen as two independent policy activities. The poverty increase of 2006, for example, had much to do with the rice and fuel price increases, both of which were related to environmental conditions, directly or indirectly.

The politics of environmental protection in Indonesia is also complicated due to the many agencies involved. There are at least nine ministries at the national level directly involved in policies that affect natural resources and the environment, namely the ministries of forestry, mines and energy, agriculture, environment, marine affairs and fisheries, transmigration and manpower, human settlements and regional infrastructure, trade, and finance (Marifa 2005). This becomes even more complicated when it comes to planning and managing regional development.

In its Law 32/2009 on Protection and Management of the Environment (a revision to Law 23/1997 on Environmental Management), Indonesia commits itself to basing national economic development on principles of environmental sustainability. One of the main features of this law is its emphasis on good governance in dealing with sustainability (Santosa 2010). One year prior to the enactment of Law 32/2009, the government established the National Council for Environmental Change (Dewan Nasional Perubahan Iklim, or DNPI) with Presidential Regulation 46/2008 (Niode 2010). This Council is assigned to formulate national climate-change policy (including carbon trading), coordinate and monitor and evaluate policy implementation (including technology transfers and financing), and represent Indonesia in international climate-change forums.

Despite the laws and regulation, it seems that existing policies addressing poverty and the environment are disconnected. It is true that in the government's stated intention to revitalize agriculture, one can easily see the connection with poverty reduction since most of the poor work in agriculture. But the environmental aspect of agriculture has been overlooked. Furthermore, the growth of total factor productivity has been very low in the agriculture sector. Since this is largely caused by low productivity which is in turn caused by poor infrastructure, it will be necessary to make a considerable investment in infrastructure (roads, irrigation) and land reform (land titling). Such investments should take the environment into account.

Many have proposed tackling poverty and environment at the same time, such as through green jobs programmes. The government of Indonesia raised such an idea in the early years of President Yudhoyono's first term. It established a policy that was designed to encourage biofuel production. The objective was to convert 6 million hectares of land to oil palm production that would generate 22.5 million kilolitres of biofuel and create 3–5 million jobs (Barichello and Patunru 2009). Other biofuel initiatives proposed included a ban on crude palm oil exports and sugarcane molasses exports so these things could be used instead for biofuel production. Estimates of the 2007 budget cost for these initiatives ranged from US$100 million to US$1,300 million. This programme has attracted more than its share of criticism. In addition to the questionable economic viability of the investments, and even their energy viability, they have been criticized for not doing much to reduce unemployment (Basri and Patunru 2006).

SOME PROPOSALS

In the absence of a policy that integrates poverty and environment, we propose the following measures. The first, modest step should be to publicly disseminate green GDP estimates. The conventional ("brown") GDP excludes estimates of environmental degradation and natural-resource depletion. Measuring the green GDP is long overdue.[5] However, until now there has been no political will to officially announce it along with the conventional GDP. By regularly issuing the green GDP estimates, it is expected that public awareness will rise and a demand for more environmentally friendly economic activities will emerge. The public will be interested to see who has caused the divergence between green GDP and brown GDP. And businesses will not want to be seen as environmentally unfriendly or responsible for the gap between the two GDP measures. Figure 13.2 illustrates the estimate of green GDP, plotted together with brown GDP (estimated and actual). The values are based on a study done by LPEM-FEUI (2004). The diminishing gap between green GDP and brown GDP lines indicates increasing effort to preserve and conserve the environment.[6]

A similar approach can be implemented at the sub-national levels. Yusuf (2010) has recently estimated the green GDP (or "eco-regional GDP", or ERDP) for provinces in Indonesia and contrasted them with the usual brown GDP (i.e., gross regional domestic production, or GRDP). Table 13.6 shows the results. The third column provides the percentage ratio of ERDP over GRDP. The smaller the ratio, the less green the province is. It is interesting that in general, provinces in eastern Indonesia or remote areas are less green than those elsewhere.

FIGURE 13.2
Green and Brown GDP Growth, 2001–09 (%)

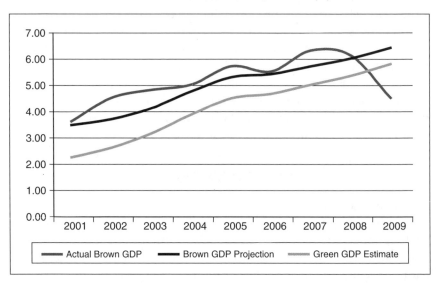

Papua, for example, has a ratio of 56 per cent, while Jakarta has 91 per cent. This is again consistent with the view that those who suffer most from environmental problems usually live in poor areas.

The second measure calculated to integrate the environmental protection and poverty reduction is green budgeting. This simply means reducing the subsidy for energy consumption, and in the later stage, even taxing it. It might be very difficult to impose tax for environmental purposes (called "green tax") in Indonesia at the moment as the government is still struggling to reduce the budget burden that comes from heavy subsidies, especially on fuel.

As shown in Table 13.7, the subsidy allocation is very high, between 2 per cent to 3 per cent of GDP (as a comparison, our budget deficit is around 1.5 per cent to 2.2 per cent of GDP). The table shows that the energy subsidy takes up a huge portion of the total subsidy. Further the fuel subsidy dominates the total energy subsidy. Subsidies for non-energy items include those for food, fertilizers and seeds for agriculture, public service obligation, credit, and taxes. It is obvious that this subsidy regime is not sustainable, as a big portion of budget

TABLE 13.6
GRDP and Eco-Regional GDP 2005

	GRDP	ERDP	ERDP/GRDP (%)
Aceh	56,952	47,481	83.37
North Sumatra	139,618	125,938	90.20
West Sumatra	44,675	37,946	84.94
Riau	180,004	130,992	72.77
Jambi	22,487	17,864	79.44
South Sumatra	81,532	63,345	77.69
Bangka-Belitung	14,172	11,601	81.86
Bengkulu	10,134	8,921	88.03
Lampung	40,907	36,700	89.71
Jakarta	433,860	395,011	91.05
West Java	389,245	348,137	89.44
Banten	84,623	75,228	88.90
Central Java	234,435	207,283	88.42
Jogjakarta	25,338	22,019	86.90
East Java	403,392	353,319	87.59
West Kalimantan	33,869	29,997	88.57
Central Kalimantan	20,983	18,882	89.99
South Kalimantan	31,794	25,291	79.55
East Kalimantan	180,289	129,862	72.03
North Sulawesi	18,763	16,921	90.18
Gorontalo	3,481	3,052	87.69
Central Sulawesi	17,117	14,817	86.57
South Sulawesi	56,203	46,223	82.24
Southeast Sulawesi	12,981	10,987	84.64
Bali	33,946	28,804	84.85
West Nusa Tenggara	25,683	18,536	72.17
East Nusa Tenggara	14,810	13,629	92.02
Maluku	4,571	3,925	85.88
North Maluku	2,583	2,247	87.00
Papua	51,529	29,136	56.54
Total	2,669,976	2,274,093	85.17

Source: Yusuf (2010).

TABLE 13.7
Subsidy in National Budget

	2009	2010	2011
	(Actual)	(Revised)	(Proposed)
Total Subsidies (USD bn)	13.3	22.0	19.9
% of GDP	2.5	3.2	2.6
% of Expenditures	14.7	18.0	15.4
Energy (USD bn)	9.1	15.7	14.4
Fuel (USD bn)	4.3	9.7	10.0
Electricity (USD bn)	4.8	6.0	4.4
Non-energy	4.2	6.3	5.5
Memo:			
Exchange Rate (IDR/USD)	10408	9200	9300
Budget Deficit (% of GDP)	1.6	2.2	1.7

Source: GOI (various years).

is allocated for non-productive uses. In the approved state budget for 2011, the environment takes up only US$1.2 billion out of total US$88 billion of central government expenditures. This is in stark contrast to the amounts allocated to general service (US$56.5 billion), economic development[7] (US$10.3 billion), and education (US$8.8 billion). Of this US$1.2 billion, 43 per cent goes to natural resource conservation, 27 per cent to waste management, and 23 per cent to land and spatial management.

Table 13.8 compares the rates of subsidization of energy in Iran, Russia, China, India, and Indonesia. These are countries that provide large subsidies for energy consumption. Again, the table implies the dependence of energy consumption on subsidies. It is important to note that in addition to these two measures (green GDP and green budgeting), there are many other possible ones. At the micro-level one could adjust prices for electricity, fuel, etc. Finally, Indonesia needs to comply with international agreements on environmental protection. In the 2009 G20 meeting in Pittsburgh, USA, President Susilo Bambang Yudhoyono said that Indonesia was committed to cutting 26 per cent of its CO_2 emissions by 2020. This target would increase to 41 per

TABLE 13.8
Rate of Subsidization (per cent of Market Price)

	2008				2009			
	Coal	Oil	Gas	Electricity	Coal	Oil	Gas	Electricity
Iran	n/a	90	94	84	n/a	88	95	82
Russia	n/a	n/a	54	32	n/a	n/a	50	27
China	6	9	26	6	7	3	2	4
India	n/a	31	80	11	n/a	18	77	12
Indonesia	n/a	28	n/a	35	n/a	28	n/a	31

Source: International Energy Agency (2010).

cent if Indonesia received assistance from other countries or donors. But this commitment is not sufficient, especially if other countries do not provide support. Therefore, multilateral and regional dialogue is still important as a way of achieving a socially optimal common understanding. The skyrocketing price of food, commodities, and oil in 2006 was the result of a lack of such coordination.

CONCLUSION

With regards to macro-level (national) policy, the central government strategy needs to increase awareness and bring environmental concerns into mainstream public discussion, so that policy perspectives are ultimately affected. Two areas of possible implementation in the short run are Green GDP and Green Budgeting.[8] The green GDP numbers would have to be appended to and published together with the conventional measure of GDP. The point of issuing green GDP is to increase public awareness. As far as the green budgeting is concerned, the national budget is expected to reflect the government's intention to respond to climate change. In Indonesia, there has been a clear plan to cut the subsidies on gasoline and kerosene (expenditure side) and at a later stage to tax energy consumption (revenue side). Another application is to embed payment for environmental services[9] into the formula of the central government's transfers to regions. Such greener budgets will provide direction to fiscal policy that also addresses environment issues. For example, fuel subsidy cuts will bring the price closer to its economic price and therefore create incentive for investment in renewable resources.[10] At the same time, the money could be allocated to infrastructure development.

At the micro-level, policies need to be directed to influencing the behaviour of households and firms. Such policies would include electricity tariff adjustment, fuel price adjustment, etc. However, the government should see all this in a development perspective. For example, raising the price of electricity should be paired with policies to increase electrification, especially in rural areas, while adjustments in fuel prices should consider alternative modes of transportation. Finally, given the nature of climate change (and almost all environmental problems), namely external and extraterritorial, it is crucial to have good coordination between countries. Therefore, all the policies should be in line with any agreements Indonesia has signed.

Notes

1. The national poverty line is measured with an anchor to daily calorie consumption that is equivalent to US$1.55 per day. Using the more common threshold of US$1 per day and US$2 per day (at purchasing power parity), the poverty incidences were 5.9 per cent and 42.6 per cent, respectively in 2008, while it was 15.4 per cent with the national poverty line.
2. These dynamics are not very clear from Figure 13.1. In fact, there was rising unemployment in 2003–05 (shown on the figure that happened to be in what the World Bank report calls "job recovery" period). The figure simply plots the unemployment data issued by the Statistics Office. The World Bank report, however, makes its case using not only unemployment rate as the measure, but also employment rate, share on non-agricultural employment, share of formal sector employment, and median hourly wages for employees (World Bank 2010). This might explain such apparent contradiction.
3. According to a report by the World Bank (2006).
4. That is, agricultural productivity growth that is also environmentally sound (not environmentally degrading).
5. Repetto et al. (1989) have started the accounting for Indonesian economy.
6. The graph is based on LPEM-FEUI (Institute for Economic and Social Research, University of Indonesia) study conducted in 2004 in which the

motivation was to compare the green- or environmentally-adjusted estimates and President Yudhoyono's targets (in his first presidential term, 2004–2009) — hence 2009 being the end year of the series. Note also that the 2007–08 global crisis was completely unforeseen in 2004.

7. This part covers functions such as trade, agriculture/forestry/fishery/marine, irrigation, fuel/energy, transportation, etc.

8. It is important to note that indicators such as green GDP and green budgeting involve complex calculation and estimation with many proxies. Environmental benefits are non-market goods and hence valuing them poses a great challenge. Further research in this line would therefore include refinement of methodology as well as valuation techniques.

9. "Payment for environmental service" (PES) is an incentive given to an economic actor for managing his resources so as to provide ecological services.

10. Before the price increase, alternative renewable energy resources could not compete with fuel because their prices are much higher than the subsidized price of the fossil fuel.

References

ADB. *Key Indicators for Asia and the Pacific 2010*. Manila: Asian Development Bank, 2010.

Barichello, Richard, and Arianto A. Patunru. "Agriculture in Indonesia: Lagging Performance and Difficult Choices". *Choices: The Magazine of Food, Farm, and Resource Issues* 24, no. 2 (2009): 37–41.

Basri, M. Chatib, and Arianto A. Patunru. "Survey of Recent Developments". *Bulletin of Indonesian Economic Studies* 42, no. 3 (2006): 295–319.

International Energy Agency. *World Energy Outlook 2010*. Paris: IEA, 2010.

LPEM-FEUI. "Green GDP Measurements for Indonesia". Report in collaboration with and submitted to the Ministry of Planning, Republic of Indonesia, 2004.

Marifa, Isna. "Institutional Transformation for Better Policy Implementation and Enforcement". In *The Politics and Economics of Indonesia's Natural Resources*, edited by Budy P. Resosudarmo, pp. 248–58. Singapore: Institute of Southeast Asian Studies, 2005.

McCulloch, Neil A., Julien Wisbrod, and C. Peter Timmer. "Pathways Out of Poverty During Economic Crisis: An Empirical Assessment of Rural Indonesia". *World Bank Policy Research Working Paper* No. 4173, 1 March 2007 <SSRN: http://ssrn.com/abstract=975844>.

McCulloch, Neil, Günther G. Schulze, and Janina Voss. "What Determines Firms' Decision to Formalize? Evidence from Rural Indonesia". *University of Freiburg Department of International Economic Policy Discussion Paper Series* Nr. 13, 15 November 2010.

Niode, Amanda Katili. "Negosiasi, Kebijakan, dan Komunikasi Perubahan Iklim". In *Pembangunan Berkelanjutan: Peran dan Kontribusi Emil Salim*, edited by Iwan J. Azis, Lydia M. Napitupulu, Arianto A. Patunru, and Budy P. Resosudarmo, pp. 174–94. Jakarta: Kepustakaan Populer Gramedia, 2010.

Repetto, Robert, William Magrath, Michael Wells, Christine Beer, and Fabrizio Rozzini. *Wasting Assets: National Resources in the National Income Account.* Washington, D.C.: World Resources Institute, 1989.

Resosudarmo, Budy P. and Arief A. Yusuf. "Survey of Recent Developments", *Bulletin of Indonesian Economic Studies* 45, no. 3 (2009): 287–315.

Santosa, Mas Achmad. "Greener Constitution: Solusi Pengarusutamaan Pembangunan Berkelanjutan". In *Pembangunan Berkelanjutan: Peran dan Kontribusi Emil Salim*, edited by Iwan J. Azis, Lydia M. Napitupulu, Arianto A. Patunru, and Budy P. Resosudarmo. Jakarta: Kepustakaan Populer Gramedia, 2010.

Suryahadi, Asep, Umbu Reko Raya, Deswanto Marbun, and Athia Yumma. "Accelerating Poverty and Vulnerability Reduction: Trends, Opportunities, and Constraints". Working Paper. SMERU Research Institute, Jakarta, November 2010.

World Bank. *Making the New Indonesia Work for the Poor.* Jakarta: The World Bank Office Jakarta/Washington, D.C.: The World Bank, 2006a.

———. *Sustaining Economic Growth, Rural Livelihoods, and Environmental Benefits: Strategic Options for Forest Assistance in Indonesia.* Washington, D.C.: The World Bank/Jakarta: The World Bank Office, 2006b.

———. *Indonesia Jobs Report: Towards Better Jobs and Security for All.* Jakarta: The World Bank Office Jakarta/Washington, D.C.: The World Bank, 2010.

Yusuf, Arief Anshory. "Estimates of the 'Green' or 'Eco' Regional Domestic Product of Indonesian Provinces for the Year 2005". *Economics and Finance in Indonesia* 58, no. 2 (2010): 131–48.

14

PROSPERING IN ENVIRONMENTAL DEGRADATION
An Illustration from an Upland Area, South Kalimantan, Indonesia

Aris Ananta, Haris Fadillah, Ahmad Yunani,
Gusti Fahmi Adliansyah, and
Danang Adhinata

Poverty reduction and environmental conservation are the twin goals in economic development.[1] However, the two goals can be in conflict. Since the poor are typically engaged in primary production and therefore highly dependent upon natural resources, environmental degradation undermines their means of subsistence much more than that of other people. Therefore, environmental conservation can reduce poverty. But the long-term interests of the poor can be at odds with their short-term interest. Since survival is the most important short-term interest, it is not a trivial conflict for them.[2] The poor have limited choices and control over their future. Improvements in the environment may not even be seen positively, as they do not have better alternatives for income. They resist environment rehabilitation programmes because they often benefit from environmentally harmful livelihoods. This is a classic conflict between the collectively rational and the individually rational behaviour.

In China, farmers, livestock grazers, and forest workers are disadvantaged by the Natural Forest Conservation Programme (NFCP) in the dryland areas of Northern Shaanxi Province (Cao et al. 2010). The programme had successfully banned logging and grazing in the forest, causing the people around the forest to lose their source of income. Cao et al. (2010) also showed that the poorer the people are, the more they suffer from the forest conservation programme. The youngest and oldest, as well as the female, suffered most from the conservation programme. They recommended that the government provide economic assistance to compensate for the loss of income. Salafsky and Wollenberg (2000) made a similar recommendation for people living near areas rich in natural resources, that is, to create alternative employment opportunities so that the people do not work in environmentally harmful activities.

An even better option would be to create employment opportunities that depend on the sustainability of the environment. This would make the micro view of the locals compatible with the macro view of the environmentalists. In this essay, we illustrate conflicts between the macro perspective on maintaining sustainable environment and the micro perspective on individual's short-term welfare in the Meratus Mountains of the province of South Kalimantan, Indonesia. We also make some recommendations on how to resolve the conflict.

RESEARCH GEOGRAPHY AND METHODOLOY

The province of South Kalimantan is the second largest producer of coal in Indonesia, after the province of East Kalimantan. Most of the coal is exported. Only the remainder is available for use in Indonesia, including in South Kalimantan. The soon-to-be-finished construction of a special road for transporting coal and the rise of China and India are expected to boost the demand for coal in Indonesia in general and in South Kalimantan in particular. Some of the companies doing coal mining have licences, while others are doing it illegally (Bank Indonesia 2007).

In 2010 mining and quarrying contributed 21.9 per cent to the province's GDP, the largest source, followed by agriculture (21.33 per cent). Agriculture absorbed a disproportionate percentage of total employment in South Kalimantan (43.10 per cent compared to mining's 4.90 per cent). This pattern implies that mining contributes much to the regional GDP, but very little to employment. Most of the natural resources, forests, plantations, and mining can be found in the Meratus Mountains and at the foot of the mountains. The mining industry has contributed much to the income of the province, and but this has led to environmental degradation. For example, surface mining is the preferred method because coal is usually found on the surface of the soil. However, this method often led to soil degradation and forest cover destruction (Fatah 2008). The soil may eventually become infertile (Ghose 2004).

The communities selected for the field study for the province of South Kalimantan are those living in upland area and on the foot of the Meratus Mountain Range. More specifically, the field study was concentrated in three villages in the regency (*kabupaten*)[3] of Banjar: (1) the village of Dekat Tambang (very close to the mining activities), (2) the village of Jauh Tambang (relatively far from the mining activities), and (3) the village of Dekat Hutan (which is very far from the mining activities, but close to the forest).[4] The regency of Banjar, with a poverty rate at 3.34 per cent in 2010, is not a poor region. Indeed, in terms of per capita regional GDP, this is the richest regency in South Kalimantan. The three villages were selected simply for an exploratory illustration on the relationship between environment degradation and livelihoods of the people. We examined how distance to mining activities affected the choice of livelihood and the quality of the environment.[5]

We interviewed about twenty people, mostly aged between thirty and forty years old, including community leaders and heads of villages, to find out their perceptions on environmental degradation, improvement in livelihood, and their quality of life. The field observation was conducted in July 2010. Almost two-thirds of the respondents have primary school education, and more than two-thirds work as farmers. We also gained insights from local knowledgeable persons (including scholars, bureaucrats, and NGOs) on this subject.

ENVIRONMENTAL INFLUENCES ON THE RURAL POOR: FINDINGS FROM THREE CASE STUDIES

Dekat Tambang Village: "Benefiting" from the Mining Activities

This village is located in the sub-district (*kecamatan*) of Sungai Cipinang, about 6 kilometres from the capital of the sub-district.[6] Most part of the 15-kilometre road in the village is made of soil and gravel, with only about 3 kilometres paved. This village is very close to the mining activities, about 2 kilometres away. It is relatively better off, but its environment has been polluted, and its soil fertility has degraded. However, the respondents perceived that the environmental degradation had been over-compensated with the improvement in their livelihoods — through new employment opportunities and monetary compensation from the mining companies.

The villagers used to work primarily in subsistence agriculture, which meant that they seldom sold their products. Instead, the agricultural products were for their own consumption. The arrival of coal mining activities changed their livelihood and economic condition. The local people worked mainly in the mining activities, and some even sold their land to the mining companies. They worked mostly as day workers. They could not work as contract workers because of their low educational levels. The contract workers were mostly people from outside the areas. Yet, their salaries were relatively high. At about 1.7 million rupiah (about US$200) a month, it was comparatively high for someone living in the mountains. As a comparison, a new graduate from a third-tier university in Indonesia, working at a call centre in a bank in Jakarta earned only 1.6 million rupiah a month, with the cost of living in Jakarta being much higher than in the mountains.

The younger generation, with their higher education level, prefer to work in the mining industry, while the older people are more likely to continue working in agriculture. The younger people aspire to reach the level of prosperity achieved by the wealthier migrants working in the mining industry. The village headman even helped mining companies to recruit and train local people. The mining companies helped raise the standards of living of the local people, for example, by funding the building of a sports facility, a mosque, and roads.

The local people experienced economic progress, judged by the appearance of their houses (mostly made of concrete), satellite TV dishes, motorcycles, and cars. The village also has schools (from primary to senior high school), a mosque, and a community health centre. Nevertheless, the local people were aware of the negative effects of mining on their environment and livelihood. As the mining method used in this village is surface mining, large areas of land and hills have been destroyed.

Coal mining is a noisy process. Dynamite is used to destroy the hills. The thunderous blasts from this process could be heard in a village 10 kilometres away. It rattled the houses in the village. The process also polluted the environment with ashes, dirtying fruits and cooked food sold in some eating stalls near the roads. Trucks shipping coal from the mining areas aggravated the situation by dispersing the ashes throughout the village.

The local people depend heavily on the river for their daily water needs and for fishing. However, the river became polluted and this led to a decline in the fish population. The respondents were also aware of the declining quality of the soil, and it might even become infertile as a result of the mining. The surface mining method usually eroded the soil, polluted the water, and produced dust and noise. It also disturbed the livelihood of the people, who depended heavily on the river.

In another village bordering with Dekat Tambang Village, we found the underground mining method being used instead of surface mining. Underground mining causes less environmental degradation as it does not require eliminating a large surface area or a hill. The trees on the surface are not disturbed. However the mining was carried out by a foreign company that brought in many workers from its own country. The village headman of Dekat Tambang was worried of the negative social influence of these foreign workers. He said that their foreign customs and behaviour irritated the local people.

However, the people in Dekat Tambang village did not seem to care much about the environmental degradation because they perceived that they were better off than before the arrival of mining. The effects of environmental degradation would affect the local people in the long term, but they can only be concerned about the present and near future. The absence of alternative employment and their low education may have resulted in their inability to maintain their environment.

Jauh Tambang Village: Subsistence Farming in a Non-Mining Village

Like Dekat Tambang village, Jauh Tambang village is located at the sub-district of Sungai Pinang. However, it is 16 kilometres further from the capital of the sub-district. The distance from the capital makes this village less economically fortunate than Dekat Tambang village. Its roads condition is generally very poor. There are no paved roads. Buses and cars ply the roads only once a week, mainly on market (*pasar*) day.

Despite its poverty, the village had a nice and green environment. The villagers were not as well off as the people in Dekat Tambang village. This village is located about 8 kilometres further from the mining areas, but closer to the forest. Some respondents participated in the mining activities, but these were small-scale traditional gold-mining activities which did not affect the environment significantly.

The villagers had not received much foreign influence. Electricity usage was minimal. The river was the main source of water (for drinking, bathing, and laundry purposes). There exist a primary school, a *pesantren* (Muslim school run by religious leaders), and a community health centre, but the houses in the village were mostly in a poor condition.

On the positive side, the environment had not been polluted. The local people continued working as farmers, hunters, and gatherers of forest products. They worked using the traditional rotational cultivation system, with a regular cycle of clearing land. They used the forest products for their own consumption only. Therefore, their activities did not disturb the biodiversity of the forest.

The people did not feel disturbed by the mining activities as they were relatively further away. The dynamite blasts were audible, but the people were not affected. The mining companies did not compensate the local people. An exception was a respondent who lived closest to the mining activities. The mining companies were obliged to restore the soil fertility of his farm after it was used for mining, so that the land can be used for agriculture again. He complained that the company did not do a good job in the restoration work. The company only sowed acacia seeds.[7] As a result, he could not plant other trees including rubber trees.

However, not everybody remained farmers. The rising traffic passing through the village by migrants working in the mines in Dekat Tambang village had created a business opportunity for a family near Jauh Tambang village. There was a *warung*, something like a convenient store, selling all kinds of daily supplies, including snacks. Its opening hours were from early morning until late in the evening. Other than the migrant workers, the *warung* was also patronized by the villagers. The owners opened the *warung* for business as soon as they woke up in the morning and closed shop only when it was near their bedtime. It was an entrepreneurial activity that tapped into the market opportunity arising from the arrival of mine workers.

Forest Incomes from Dekat Hutan Village

Unlike Dekat Tambang and Jauh Tambang villages, Dekat Hutan village is located at the sub-district of Paramasan, 3 kilometres from the capital of the sub-district. A 19-kilometre road has been paved, and it is the provincial road connecting one regency to other regencies. This road is busy with buses and cars every day. However, another 30-kilometre road is still in an unpaved condition. This village has a lush green environment but pollution is becoming more evident with "modern" waste, such as plastic.

The village is far from the mining activities, but very close to the forest. The local people used to engage in subsistence farming. Additional income was earned from rotational plantations. While waiting for the harvest, small-scale timber logging and traditional gold mining were carried out.

Changes in the village began to take place between 1980 to 1993 with the existence of the logging industry. The logging industry has now ceased operations. The logging companies brought outsiders to work in the village. The villagers were very open and friendly to the migrants who were from other parts of Indonesia, thus allowing the migrants to quickly integrate with the village life. The migrants also changed the way of life of the villagers. There were a lot of inter-marriages. The local people also learned that employment opportunities were not limited to farming.

The respondents said that the economic condition of the villagers had improved in the last decade. The local government helped with the improvement in the villagers' welfare. It provided electricity generated from diesel fuel and solar energy and built a community health centre, schools, a mosque, a weekly market, and a traditional community hall (*rumah adat*). The houses belonging to the more wealthy villagers were equipped with satellite TV dishes. In short, the people in this village became relatively better off with the existence of the logging industry.

Nevertheless, the migrants seemed to be richer than the locals. The migrants were more likely to engage in trade, work in motorcycle workshops, or were makers of window and door frames. The locals were still concentrated in the traditional employment of farming, plantations, and small-scale gold mining. With the arrival of logging, they also learned how to collect forest products for sale. Though the formal logging industries have ceased operations, the local people continued collecting forest products. Some products were used to build their own houses and some were sold. Such activities were actually banned by the local government, but the local people managed to bribe the officers.

The respondents did not say that the logging was carried out excessively. They even said that they took care of the biodiversity of the forest when logging. Nevertheless, from the way they answered, we guessed that they were not revealing the whole truth. We guessed that they knew the logging activities were excessive, but the activities were lucrative and they knew how to elude the rules and regulations. The paved road in the village, which connected the village to other villages and the capital of the regency, facilitated the transportation of the products of illegal logging.

Furthermore, as the village is far from the mining area, its environment did not suffer pollution. Dekat Hutan village is an example of a village living harmoniously with environment (here forest) and prospering with the help of the government. However, the current trend indicates that the forest has been much exploited.

CONCLUSION

The locals seemed to have their "local wisdom" (*kearifan lokal*) — that they understand the environmentally harmful activities conducted in their areas and the need to sustain their environment. However, the local people are often too weak, politically and economically, to resist the activities of the big businesses. Not surprisingly, macro (environmental) views often contradicted the micro (short-term) views. We cannot expect the people to protect their environment for the benefit of future generations without providing them with alternative livelihoods. Their immediate concern is their day-to-day livelihood. They are still struggling for their daily necessities. They also want to improve themselves economically and to follow the consumption pattern of those seen on television.

In addition to a strict enforcement of rules against environmentally harmful activities and other environment-related policies, we need to simultaneously implement two supply-side policies and one demand-side policy. The first supply-side policy is to provide alternative employment opportunities for the local people. The challenge is that the alternative employment opportunity must provide earnings larger than their current earnings. Therefore, this policy should include training and capacity building to make the poor able to grasp higher earning through environmentally friendly opportunities.

Nevertheless, this policy alone will not guarantee an end to the destruction of the environment. People from outside the area may still be recruited to work in the companies. Therefore, we need the second supply-side policy, namely, the creation of employment opportunities that depend heavily on the biodiversity of the environment. In this way, the local people will not have incentives to destroy the biodiversity. Furthermore, they will work hard to protect the biodiversity of their environment as it will allow them to climb the economic ladder faster. The local people will block any attempt to have activities that destroy the biodiversity. They will not allow migrants to work in environmentally harmful activities.

However, a large amount of compensation to the local community may still work to placate them from protesting the destruction of the environment. Therefore, we also need the demand-side policy of reducing the profit of the business by a worldwide campaign against consuming goods produced by environmentally harmful activities, including mining. The consumers have the right to know whether the goods and services they consume are harmful to the environment or are produced using environmentally harmful activities. Specifically, we need to educate people worldwide about the environmental danger of using coal. If the demand for coal declines, the demand for the environmentally harmful activities will also decline. The businesspeople will shift to more environmentally friendly activities.

The success of these policies will help match the macro and micro views on environment, reconciling the classic conflict between the provision of public and private goods.

Notes

This chapter has benefitted from the comments made by Evi Nurvidya Arifin (Institute of Southeast Asian Studies, Singapore), Eka Radiah (Lambung Mangkurat University, Indonesia), and the assistance of Chua Cheng Siew (National University of Singapore), as well as comments from participants of both the conference "The environment of the poor in the context of climate change and the green economy, making sustainable development inclusive", conducted by ADB in New Delhi, 24–26 November, 2010 and the informal meeting discussing the draft of this chapter conducted by the Faculty of Economics, Lambung Mangkurat University, South Kalimantan, on 25 January 2011.

1. Comim, Kumar, and Sirven (2009).
2. According to the United Nations Environment Programme (1995), poor people's educational, informational, health, and income constraints make them unable to engage in long-term planning.
3. A regency (*kabupaten*) is one of two types of districts, an administrative unit below the level of the province. Another one is the city (*kota*).
4. The real names of the villages are not revealed.
5. This is not supposed to be a rigorous statistical examination on the causal relationship between mining activities on one hand and livelihood and environment on the other hand. Further studies should be conducted if the statistics are available.
6. One regency (*kabupaten*) has several sub-districts (*kecamatan*).
7. Acacia (*acacia manggum*) wood is used mainly for making furniture.

References

Bank Indonesia. "Boks 1.1. Peran Sektor Pertambangan dalam Perekonomian Kalimantan Selatan". In *Kajian Ekonomi Regional Kalimantan Selatan* Triwulan II-2007.

Cao, Shixiong, Xiuqing Wang, Yuezhen Song, Li Chen, and Qi Feng. "Impacts of the Natural Forest Conservation Program on the Livelihoods of Residents of Northwestern China". *Ecological Economics* 69, no. 7 (15 May 2010): 1454–62.

Comim, Favio, Pushpam Kumar, and Nicolas Sirven. *"Poverty and Environment Links: An Illustration from Africa"*. *Journal of International Development* 21 (2009): 447–69.

Fatah, Luthfi. "The Impact of Coal Mining on the Economy and Environment of South Kalimantan Province, Indonesia". *ASEAN Economic Bulletin* 25, no. 1 (April 2008): 85–98.

Ghose, Mrinal K. 2004. "Effect of Opencast Mining on Soil Fertility." Journal of Scientific and Industrial Research 63 (December): 1006–1009.

Salafsky, Nich and Eva Wollenberg. 2000. "Linking Livelihoods and Conservation: A Conceptual Framework and Scale for Assessing the Integration of Human Needs and Biodiversity." World Development 28 (8): 1421–38.

United Nations Environment Programme. *Poverty and the Environment*. Nairobi, Kenya: UNEP, 1995.

15

MAKING A LIVING IN THE FACE OF ENVIRONMENTAL CHANGE
A Case in an Indigenous Community in Sarawak, Malaysia

Wong Swee Kiong and Ling How Kee

Malaysia is divided into thirteen states and three federal territories. Sarawak, located on the island of Borneo, is the largest state in Malaysia. It covers 124,450 square kilometres. Sarawak is richly endowed with natural resources, especially liquefied natural gas, petroleum, and rainforest. Its economy has historically been dominated by the primary sectors (agriculture, forestry, mining, and quarrying), mostly agriculture. But in line with the federal government's policy of economic growth through industrialization, the state government began promoting secondary and tertiary sectors in the 1970s (Kasim 1990). Sarawak was transformed from a poor backwater to a vibrant and industrializing state. By international standards, the level of poverty in Sarawak is now quite low. In 2009, 5.3 per cent (27,100 households) in Sarawak were found living in poverty and 1.0 per cent in extreme poverty. The national overall incidence of poverty and extreme poverty were 3.8 per cent and 0.7 per cent, respectively (EPU 2013). The incidence of poverty is higher in the rural areas.[1]

Parts of the transformative process, such as the Bakun hydroelectric dam, commercial agriculture, and logging, have required clearing parts of the rainforest (Ichikawa 2007). Development projects not only caused a dwindling of the rainforest,[2] but also the degrading of what remains. The primary economic value of Sarawak's rainforest has been as a source of income for the state through the exports of timber and its timber-based products. Timber industries have brought substantial earnings to Sarawak. In 2008, timber products constituted 9 per cent (RM7.9 billion) of the total export earnings of the major commodities in Sarawak though there was a slight drop in the total export earnings of timber products to RM6,698,067 in 2009, followed by a marginal increase to RM7,354,341 in 2010 (Sarawak Timber Industry Development Corporation 2011). The rainforest is a source of raw material for the residents of many of the rural communities of the interior (for rattan baskets and mats, and wooden furniture), and a source of wild boar and wild vegetables for food. Nomadic hunter-gatherers and indigenous swidden cultivators gradually became settled cash-crop peasants, plantation labourers, and urban workers (Wong 1992 cited in King 1993). But the introduction of wood-based and petrochemical industries and large-scale plantation cultivation, such as oil-palm, replaced the small-holding cultivation of cash crops such as rubber, cocoa, and pepper.

In this chapter, we look at how changes to the rainforest have affected the lives of people who have a close relationship with the natural environment, particularly the indigenous communities. This chapter is based on fieldwork we carried out in an effort to understand how an indigenous community experienced the changes in their environment as a result of development. We were particularly interested in how the changes affected their ways of making a living. In this essay we present the views of the affected people, adding to the body of knowledge that aims to let the voices of the local people be heard (Narayan et al. 2000a; Narayan et al. 2000b). By interviewing many of them, we were able to gain insights into the way the community experienced the changes. We chose two villages[3] near the forest in the district of Lundu (one of three administrative districts within the boundary of the division of Kuching). Logging had been going on in the vicinity of the two villages since the early 1970s. The Gunung Gading National Park, which bordered the logging concession area then, is famous for the world's largest flowering plant, the Rafflesia, which was once under threat from logging. Further, oil palm plantations were introduced into the region in 1990 and 2003. The villages are accessible by roads in the Lundu/Sematan area in the Kuching division. Access to the Lundu Bazaar from the city of Kuching (the administrative capital of Sarawak) was made easier with the construction of the bridge across *Batang Kayan* (Kayan River) in July 2005. The road from Kuching city to the Lundu district has also been straightened and sealed. What used to be a four-hour trip now takes slightly over an hour. Our villages, as well as others in the areas, are home to the Dayak-Selako or Bidayuh-Selako community, a sub-group of Sarawak's Bidayuh ethnic group. According to anthropologist Awang Hasmadi (1992), the ancestors of the Selako once lived along the Salakau River in West Kalimantan, before migrating to Lundu, which was then part of the Brunei Sultanate. The Selako people used to traverse the mountain range that divides Kalimantan (Indonesian Borneo) and Sarawak (Malaysian Borneo) to farm both sides of the border until 1875, when the Brooke administration persuaded them to settle at their present location.

At the time of our fieldwork, the two villages have 274 households and 1,687 people between them (Lundu District Office 2011). All households live in individual houses, except for 20, which are grouped in a traditional longhouse in one of the villages. Prior to the 1970s, the villagers were subsistence farmers who also collected forest products, either to eat, to use to make rattan mats and baskets and build houses. Although in recent years many of the villagers, particularly the younger ones, are engaged in wage employment, the latest employment statistics show that 40.51 per cent from one village and 46.17 per cent from the other are self-employed farmers (Lundu District Office 2011). This condition indicates that land and forest resources are still important sources of livelihood for the villages.

Fifty-eight respondents were selected from the two villages using purposive sampling, which selected respondents from both sexes and various ages, educational levels, and occupations. However, there was also some convenience sampling, as the researchers were dependent on who was available and willing to be interviewed. Twenty-seven males and thirty-one females from different demographic backgrounds were selected for face-to-face interviews. Most of the respondents older than twenty were able to confirm that the forests in the surrounding areas of the two villages have become gradually smaller. The data obtained may not be a good representation of the whole community, but it provided a valuable understanding of the subjective experiences of the community undergoing change. Besides interviewing the villagers, key informants, namely the headmen of the two villages, were interviewed. A semi-structured interview schedule was used. It consisted of questions about livelihood and the use of forest resources before and after the development project.[4] Respondents were asked to list the food sources (wild animals, fish, plants, nuts, and fruits) and jungle products (rattan, building material) and the monetary value for both consumption and sale. Respondents were asked about how development projects have changed their environment, and how this in turn affected various aspects of their lives and that of the other villagers.

FINDINGS

Several logging companies were said to have been involved in felling the trees near the villages from the 1970s to 2007. However, the respondents reported that they were not informed by the authorities whether the companies had been issued licences. Several respondents said that villagers protested against these logging activities by putting up blockades. There were fights between the villagers and logging workers. A sixty-two-year-old man from one of the villages said that during a fight some of the villagers were detained in the police station for six days.

A list of forest resources was obtained from the respondents, who were then asked to compare the current availability of those resources with their earlier availability. A reduction of the natural resources was described, even though the Gunung Pueh Forest Reserve and Samunsam Wildlife Sanctuary are in one of the villages. One of the special species that is still available, but in reduced quantity, is the *Jering* tree,[5] which could be found in the forest reserve area.

In general, the respondents from both villages expressed the view that changes in the environment due to logging had changed their ways of making a living. For instance, a few years ago they would go to the jungle to get vegetables, herbs, fruit, wild boar, prawns, and crab as food and medicine. Some went to forest to collect building materials to make their houses. Several respondents indicated that they used to collect rattan to make baskets, mats, and decorative items, for either use or sale. However, due to the logging, the forest and fishery products are harder to find. Some of the respondents claimed that they had lost their source of food and monetary income. This is because some of them used to sell the forest products or handicrafts made from them. Some respondents also indicated that they used to hunt boar for their own consumption. But they have a hard time finding even one to bring back home these days, although they still see the footprints of wild animals.

Billy (not his real name), a sixty-year-old married man with a family of six, said that logging had disturbed the habitat, reducing the amount of food it provides for the village.

> The source of food has gradually been reduced due to the logging near the village. Animals such as wild boars have decreased as they had run away to other places after the loggers disturbed their habitat. The piped water became muddy and could not be used for drinking, taking baths, or cooking. Other forest plants, such as forest *pandan*[6] and rattan, have also become fewer and fewer.

Billy's experience was similar to that of most respondents, who felt that logging had caused serious water pollution, particularly during the rainy season. After logging damaged their water catchment area, sediment and sand washed away by heavy rain caused the river to become muddy. As a result, they could no longer use the river water for washing, bathing, and drinking.

Hamdan, a forty six year-old man working as a farm worker from one of the villages, said:

> The most obvious effect of logging is water pollution. Water pollution has caused water channelled to every household to become so muddy each time after the rain. Because of this the water cannot be used for drinking or cooking.

Another male respondent, Michael, also said:

> Nearby logging has caused serious erosion, and the mixture of sediment and sand that flows into the river after it rains has caused the river in the village to become shallower. Soil erosion has made the soil

less fertile and the land unsuitable for planting vegetables or other edible crops.

Most of the respondents are very concerned about the way development has affected their water source. Knowing well that water is a basic necessity for everyone, Kollisa, a married woman of age forty, stated:

Water pollution is the most serious logging problem. The trees that were felled have not been replenished with replanted trees. Consequently, water at the catchment area on the mountain was polluted with mud and sand each time it rained. This made the water not safe for consumption anymore.

In addition to environment changes caused by logging, some agricultural development projects, such as oil palm plantations, were carried out in the vicinity of the two villages. Although a majority of the respondents in this study were favourable to the agricultural development, some thought the planting of oil palm had negatively affected the community. Gerry, a farmer lamented:

Pesticides, herbicides, and insecticides used in oil palm estates polluted the river near the estates. A lot of fish in the river have vanished due to water pollution.

This indicates that the villagers, who depended on fishing, could no longer get their food from the river. Those who sold the fish they caught lost a source of income.

However, there were a few respondents who supported agricultural development projects, particularly the oil palm plantation, either in or near their villages. Matthew, a twenty four-year-old married man with lower secondary-school education, said:

Oil palm plantation has less environmental effect on the villagers since the plantation is rather far from the village. In fact, oil palm plantation is very profitable as the developer, SALCRA [Sarawak Land Consolidation and Rehabilitation Authority], used abandoned land and the villagers were given dividends.

The same argument was made up by Lade, a fifty-year-old man who said that "the unused land was able to provide revenues to the villagers and indirectly improve the village's economy". A sixty-year-old man from the same village (Simon) supported this, citing himself as an example of someone who is now working on the oil palm estate and saying that

> the development of the oil palm plantation near the village improved the economic status of the villagers as the developer indeed paid dividends to the villagers who gave up their land for development purpose. This oil palm project has actually provided employment opportunities to the villagers."

The changes in the environment caused by logging, and oil palm plantation and a rubber plantation venture, had indeed changed the livelihood of the respondents in those two villages — from self-sufficient to market-based. Mobility had been facilitated by the construction, in tandem with the plantation, of tarred roads to connect the villages with the town of Lundu and the city of Kuching. As a result, more villagers obtained employment in Lundu or Kuching. Schooling opportunities in the last three decades have also enabled the younger generation to secure non-farm-related employment outside the villages. It seems that the cash income contented those who found work on the projects or outside the villages. But those who continued to depend on jungle produce and farming became increasingly worried about how they made their living.

DISCUSSION

Due to logging and development projects, a lot of previously forested area in interior areas of Sarawak can no longer provide food, medicine, materials for shelter and clothes, and goods for sales by the local community. Changes to the environment and the pattern of land use that resulted either from the development projects or logging have affected the livelihood of the local community. Villagers generally shifted from their dependence on forestry products as their source of livelihood strategies to other economic activities. Some were involved in construction work, others had their own farms to produce food themselves, besides selling those produce to the people in or outside the villages. The views of the villagers on this change were divided. A number of villagers preferred the new livelihood as they were able to draw a stable income in contrast with the uncertainty of hunting and harvesting forest products in the past. Many of them did not like the forests to be disturbed and to be forced to find other ways of living when logging activities and oil palm development projects first started in their villages. The same group also felt that their new standard of living was higher than that when they relied on forest products. Others, particularly those who are in the forties and above, lamented not only the loss of food sources (both animals and wild vegetable), but also jungle produce, which had provided a livelihood for their parents and grandparents when they were growing up in the villages. Many among them were also acutely aware of the effect of logging. They were aware of how soil erosion affected the water supply and soil fertility. They knew that changes to soil fertility seriously affected the crops they plant. The negative effect of the use of pesticides, herbicides, and insecticides in oil palm estates had also been felt by the villagers. Some observed that they are no longer able to get fish from the river. Yet some villagers felt the government should not have given licences to the logging companies as this has now left the present and future generations with dwindled natural resources and forest products.

POLICY IMPLICATIONS

As discussed above, the government should have been more judicious in introducing and implementing development projects with the livelihood and the well-being of the community as the prime consideration. Logging, in the absence of a social cost-benefit evaluation and consultation with the local community, has resulted in irreversible damage to the environment. In the future such evaluations and consultation should be carried out to avoid further loss of the rich natural resources of Malaysia, including the loss of biodiversity of the flora and fauna of the tropical forest of Sarawak.

In Sarawak, some of the laws governing the management of natural resources particularly on forestry to protect the environment from depleting include Forest Ordinance 1954, Wildlife Protection Ordinance 1998, Natural Resources and Environment (Amendment) Ordinances 1997, Environment Quality Act 1974, and Sarawak Forestry Corporation Ordinance by Sarawak Forestry Corporation. As natural resources such as forestry is a state matter, Sarawak state government plays a greater role in the implementation and monitoring of these laws. The ultimate goal should be to provide conducive livelihood strategies, particularly to the rural poor. It is crucial not only to narrow the income gaps between the rich and the poor, but also to ensure that future generations are able to enjoy the fruits of development. Development policies should be devised so as to not limit the livelihood options of the poor, especially when there is a change in environment due to government-initiated development projects.

Every development project has a cost. Sustainable development should be the foremost consideration in any future development projects. This is crucial as we do not want changes of the environment resulting from certain development activities/projects to deprive any group from enjoying the fruits of development or even to harm their sources of livelihood. Livelihood matters should be at the forefront of all efforts to sustain environmental resources.

Notes

1. Poverty is here operationally defined in terms of income, monetary or in kind. In the Malaysian case, poverty is based on comparisons of household income with the Poverty Line Income (PLI). The PLI in Malaysia is defined as an income sufficient to purchase the minimum requirements of a household for food, clothing and footwear, and other non-food items such as rent, fuel and power. A household is defined as poor if the household's income is below the PLI. A household is defined as extremely poor when the income received is insufficient to meet their basic food requirement (which is based on the dietary. requirements of Malaysian, namely, a daily requirement of 9,910 calories for a family of five comprising an adult male, an adult female and three children of either sex within 1–3, 4–6, 7–9 years of age. The minimum requirements for clothing and footwear were based on standards set by the Department of Social Welfare for the requirements of residents in welfare homes. The other non-food items were based on the level of expenditure of the lower income households as reported in the HES (UNDP 2008). The incidence of poverty in urban and rural areas of Sarawak in 2009 is 2.3 per cent and 8.4 per cent respectively, whereas, it is 1.7 per cent and 8.4 per cent respectively in Malaysia in 2009 (EPU 2013).
2. The dwindling of the forest is evident from government statistics and from satellite and cartographic data (Taylor et al. 1994)
3. The names of the villages are withheld to observe anonymity.

4. Development project here refers to project that was first meant to improve the standard of livings of the local community which might later also bring negative effect to the livelihood of the local community such as felling of the trees in the forested area by logging companies to build roads to connect the people of the areas to Lundu town; clearing initially a forested area for building houses/school/clinic and/ or for agricultural activities such as rubber or oil palm plantations (the agricultural development projects).

5. Or *jengkol* or dogfruit: *Pithecolobium lobatum.*

6. *Pandan* is the local language name for umbrella tree, or screw pine (*Pandanus odorus, P. Latifolius*).

References

Awang Hasmadi, Awang Mois. "Selako Worldview and Rituals". Unpublished Ph.D. dissertation, Department of Anthropology, Cambridge University, 1992.

EPU (Economic Planning Unit). Socio-Economic Statistics: Incidence of Poverty and Hardcore Poverty by Ethnicity, Strata and State, Malaysia, EPU, Prime Minister's Department Malaysia, 2013 <http://www.epu.gov.my/household-income-poverty>.

Ichikawa, Masahiro. "Degradation and Loss of Forest Land and Land-Use Changes in Sarawak, East Malaysia: A Study of Native Land Use by the Iban". *Ecological Research* 22, no. 3 (2007): 403–13.

Kasim, Mohamad Yusof. "Development Policies and Strategies of Sarawak in Relation to Malaysia's Economic Development". In *Socio-Economic Development in Sarawak: Policies and Strategies for the 1990s,* edited by Abdul Majid Mat Salleh, Hatta Solhee, Mohd. Yusof Kasim. Kuching, Malaysia: Angkatan Zaman Mansang (AZAM), 1990.

King, Victor T. "*Politik Pembangunan*: The Political Economy of Rainforest Exploitation and Development in Sarawak, East Malaysia". *Global Ecology and Biogeography Letters* 3, no. 4/6 (1993): 235–44.

Lundu District Office. Village Profile. Lundu District Office, Kuching, Sarawak, Malaysia, 2011.

Narayan, Deepa (with Raj Patel, Kai Schafft, Anne Rademacher, and Sarah Koch-Schulte). *Voices of the Poor: Can Anyone Hear Us?* New York: Oxford University Press for the World Bank, 2000*a*.

Narayan, Deepa, Robert Chambers, Meera Kaul Shah, and Patti Petesch. *Voices of the Poor: Crying Out for Change.* New York: Oxford University Press for the World Bank, 2000*b*.

Sarawak Timber Industry Development Corporation. *Statistics of Timber and Timber Products Sarawak 2009.* Kuching, Malaysia: PUSAKA, 2011.

Taylor, D. M., D. Hortin, M. J. G. Parnwell, and T. K. Marsden. "The Degradation of Rain-forests in Sarawak, East Malaysia, and its Implications for Future Management Policies". *Geoforum* 25, no. 3 (1994): 351–69.

UNDP (United Nations Development Programme). "Malaysia: Measuring and Monitoring Poverty and Inequality". Kuala Lumpur, Malaysia, 2008.

16

THE RESPONSE OF RURAL COASTAL HOUSEHOLDS TO TYPHOON MILENYO IN THE PHILIPPINES

Jonna P. Estudillo

There has been a dramatic rise in the number of natural disasters in the world in the past decade (CRED 2009). There has been a tenfold increase in the number of climate-related events such as droughts, storms, and floods since the data were first collected in 1950.[1] In 2009, the Philippines occupied the topmost rank in terms of disaster occurrence with 25 events, followed by China with 24, and the United States with 16 (CRED 2009). Of the 25 events, 14 were classified as meteorological (typhoon), 9 were hydrological (flood and landslide), and 2 were geophysical (volcanic eruption and earthquake). The three strong typhoons in 2009 — Kiko (Morakot), Ondoy (Ketsana), and Pepeng (Parma) — were three of the most devastating in terms of number of victims and extent of damage to property. According to the Philippine Atmospheric Geophysical and Astronomical Services

Administration (PAGASA), there were, on average, 20 storms entering the Philippine Area of Responsibility every year from 1948 to 2004. Given that meteorological events occur frequently in this country, it is necessary to identify risk reduction strategies and coping mechanisms to alleviate the negative effects of a meteorological disaster.

In this chapter, I present a case study of disaster management strategies undertaken by households and local government in response to the storm Milenyo (international code name Xangsane) that hit the Philippines on 28 September 2006. According to CRED, Milenyo was the tenth most destructive disaster in the world in 2006. Evidence in this chapter comes from a dataset drawn from a household survey conducted in a village, East Laguna Village (Hayami and Kikuchi 2000), on February 2007, barely four months after the devastation by Milenyo. This study has four important findings from the experience of East Laguna Village. First, the damages caused by Milenyo varied widely from household to household even within the same village depending on the ownership of paddy fields and tree crops. Households that earn income from a wide range of non-farm economic activities and those that use small-scale irrigation pumps were affected much less or not at all. Farmers who used pumps were able to plant and harvest early before Milenyo struck. Second, income diversification in favour of non-farm sources had offered the best insurance against declining income in agriculture. Third, reduction in expenditure food (particularly on meat), securing emergency loans through community and personal networks, and receiving remittances were important for the landless poor. Fourth, and finally, targeting the badly affected households — by providing temporary shelter and food baskets — was undertaken effectively by local government through the office of the village chieftain. Poorer households identified gift food baskets as particularly important for helping them survive Milenyo.

This chapter is divided into three sections. The first section describes the economic environment and identifies aspects of household vulnerability and household adaptation behaviour. The second section assesses the damages wrought by Milenyo, identifies the ways households coped, and describes the relief operations conducted by local government and civil society. The third section makes some policy suggestions.

ECONOMY OF A COASTAL VILLAGE[2]

Village Environment and Adaptation

East Laguna Village is surrounded by wet rice fields and there is little difference in the elevation between rice fields and Laguna de Bay, so the rice fields are often flooded during the rainy season.[3] Water logging is one cause of income instability in the village as rice production is a major source of household income. Flooding in the residential areas is also common during typhoons and heavy monsoons. As a precautionary measure, houses were constructed on slightly higher ground with elevated floors to reduce the risk of rainwater sipping through the floors.

Households in the village consist of three major classes: (1) farmers, who operate their own farms, either as tenants or as owners; (2) the landless, who have no farms to operate, but rather eke out a living on casual farm work; and (3) non-agricultural people, who do salary work (as teachers, clerks, and factory workers) or are self-employed in commerce and transportation. Landless households are the poorest in this village community. It is noticeable that the number of landless households rose more rapidly from 1966 to 1995 than did the farmer households (Table 16.1). The sharp rise in the number of such households

TABLE 16.1
Number of Households, East Laguna Village, Philippines, 1966–2007

Year	Farmer	Landless	Non-agricultural	Total
1966	46	20	0	66
	(70)[a]	(30)	(0)	(100)
1976	54	55	0	109
	(50)	(50)	(0)	(100)
1987	53	98	7	158
	(34)	(62)	(4)	(100)
1995	51	150	41	242
	(21)	(62)	(17)	(100)
2007	36	138	254	428
	(9)	(32)	(59)	(100)

Notes: (a) Numbers in parentheses are percentages.
Source: Estudillo et al. (2010).

can be attributed to population pressure, land reform regulations on tenancy contracts, and increased demand for hired labour associated with the diffusion of modern variety of rice (MV) and the substitution of hired for family labour. A spectacular growth in the number of non-agricultural households is evident from 1995 to 2007, and this was due to the opening in 2000 of a relatively low-priced residential subdivision that attracted non-agricultural households from nearby areas. These non-agricultural households are engaged in a wide range of non-agricultural activities.

Modern Rice Technology Reduces Risks

Farmers in this village were the earliest to adopt MVs. They continued to upgrade their rice seeds by planting newly released MVs that are generally characterized by shorter growing period. Traditional rice takes from 160 to 180 days to grow while MVs take from 90 to 110 days. Farmers started to invest in individual water pumps when the national irrigation system, which supplies water to the village, started deteriorating. The deterioration resulted in wide variations in the timings of rice production activities in the village. The adoption of portable water pumps and MVs with shorter growing periods enabled some farmers to evade the destruction of Milenyo. They were able to plant and harvest early, before Milenyo hit the village. According to the PAGASA, a large number of tropical disturbances in the Philippines occur between October and November. The availability of portable water pumps and faster growing MVs were instrumental in reducing the risks of crop damages by enabling farmers to plant in early June and harvest in mid- to late August to avoid the October–November spell of tropical disturbances.

Changing Sources of Household Income

There has been a shift of occupational structure away from farms from 1974 to 1997. Among the males, the proportion of those engaged in agriculture declined from 81 per cent to 53 per cent, and among the females, from 21 per cent to 15 per cent, (Hayami and Kikuchi 2000, p. 59, Table 3.7). The shift of occupational choice away from farms is an *ex-ante* risk management strategy. Income from non-farm sources is generally not affected by the vagaries of weather. Non-farm work serves as a self-insurance scheme. Self-insurance is defined in the literature as insurance against income uncertainty through one's own saving and dissaving. Other forms of self-insurance reported in the literature are (1) financial and physical asset accumulation, (2) crop diversification, (3) share cropping, and (4) micro-credit schemes (Alderman and Paxon 1992; Skoufias 2003). These self-insurance schemes could be effective in small localized disasters, where shocks are largely idiosyncratic across households, as in the case of Milenyo. But the schemes could be made ineffective in the case of mega natural disasters, where shocks are largely covariate (Sawada 2007).

A shift in occupation choice is accompanied by changes in the sources of household income. In 1974/76 and 1980/83, a larger proportion of household income came from farm sources than non-farm sources. The farm sources included rice farming, raising livestock and poultry, propagating high-value tree crops, backyard vegetable farming, and farm wages (Table 16.2). Non-farm sources include formal salary work in the government and the private sector, as well as self-employed enterprises in commerce, manufacturing, and transportation. In 1995/96, income from non-farm activities had become the dominant source of income because of the increase in non-farm wage earnings and remittances from household members working outside the village, including overseas contract workers. The proportion of non-farm income became particularly large in 2006 because of the increase in the number of non-agricultural households.

TABLE 16.2
Sources of Household Income, East Laguna Village, Philippines, 1974–2006
(Hundred PHP)[a]

Year	Total	Farm origin	Non-farm origin
1974/76	58(100)[b]	50(87)	8(13)
1980/83	53(100)	33(62)	20(38)
1995/96	56(100)	20(36)	36(64)
2006/07	76(100)	24(32)	52(68)

Note: (a) Deflated by CPI (1995=100). (b) Numbers in parentheses are percentages.
Source: Estudillo et al. (2010).

In brief, it is clear that households in this village have diversified their economic activities away from farm work to non-farm work. Income diversification is an effective means of self-insurance that enabled the households in this village to deal with economic shocks wrought by Milenyo.

WAYS OF COPING AND GOVERNMENT PROGRAMMES[4]

Damage Caused by Milenyo

There was a wide degree of heterogeneity in damages caused by Milenyo, even within the same village. As to human losses, there were no reported dead or seriously injured persons, thanks to the extensive television and radio broadcast on the intensity of Milenyo that made households aware of its potential for damage. Twenty-four per cent of the farmers, 42 per cent of the landless households, and 51 per cent of the non-agricultural households reported no damages caused by Milenyo. The most commonly reported damages were serious damage to the house — typically either the roofing was completely or partially destroyed — and income decline. Fifty-four per cent of the farmers and 27 per cent of the landless households reported a decline in income, especially because of damage to the standing rice crop. Interestingly, damage to crops, which was severe among fruit crops, appears to be common, even among the non-agricultural households.

Paddy harvest in the village as a whole declined by about 72 tons (i.e., 32 per cent from the normal harvest), whereas paddy price declined from the expected 8.89 peso per kg to 7.44 peso per kg (i.e., a 16 per cent reduction from the normal price). The loss in paddy production was, on average, 260 peso per household, which is almost equivalent to the minimum wage rate of 277 peso per day (equivalent to US$5.29 at US$1 = 52.35 peso). In contrast, the total loss from standing mango trees was 680 peso per household, which is 2.72 times the minimum daily wage rate. Clearly, the extent of Milenyo damages depended on whether one owned fruit trees or paddy fields.

Ways of Coping

Households in the village were able to cope with Milenyo by adopting one or more of five strategies: (1) reducing food consumption and switching from purchased to self-grown food; (2) obtaining emergency loans from relatives and village moneylenders; (3) receiving remittances; (4) receiving aid from local government and private persons; and (5) engaging in non-farm employment. Households change the quality and composition of food expenditures in response to a natural or manmade disaster (Frankenberg, Smith, and Thomas, 2003; Kang and Sawada, 2008). A larger proportion (76 per cent) of the landless households compared with farmer (27 per cent) and non-agricultural households (47 per cent) reported having decreased their food purchases, while maintaining their total nutritional intake, by shifting to fish they caught themselves (or were given by relatives) (Table 16.3).

There was a decline in the expenditure on rice (7 per cent) and more expensive rice substitutes, such as pandesal bread, bread loaf, and native cakes. There was also decline in the expenditure for the more expensive protein sources, such as pork and milk, and an increase in money allocated for cheaper chicken and fish protein. Interestingly, there was an increase in expenditure for house repair, apparently made necessary by Milenyo. It is important to mention that the brunt of Milenyo was felt more severely by the landless poor, as the gap in food expenditure between farmers and the landless rose. One week before Milenyo, the expenditure of landless households was 34 per cent of that of the farmer households, while one week after Milenyo, the expenditure of the landless became only 20 per cent of that of the farmers. Expenditure on firewood went up substantially, while the expenditure on liquefied petroleum gas (LPG) and charcoal went down, indicating that many households shifted their fuel use away from LPG and charcoal to firewood. Borrowing from close relatives is one of the more important ways of coping with disasters (Glewwe and Hall 1998; Sawada and Shimizutani 2008). Rural households' lack of consumption insurance is compensated for by access to an informal credit market (Glewwe and Hall 1998). Also, rural households are constrained from borrowing from the formal credit market because of high information costs and a lack of collateral.

In this village, the moneylenders, who are community members, played an important role as sources of emergency funds. For the landless, the nearby village variety stores (*sari-sari*) provided the most basic needs (rice, canned goods, candles, kerosene) either on credit or for cash purchase. This is evidence that village stores do not hoard

TABLE 16.3
Description of Household Coping Mechanisms, East Laguna Village, Philippines, 2006

Coping mechanism	Farmer (%)	Landless (%)	Nonagricultural (%)
1. Reduce food consumption	27	76	47
1.1 Rice	0	15	8
1.2 Protein	5	27	13
1.3 Food taken outside	22	34	26
2. Switch consumption to own produce	12	34	22
3. Reduce child schooling	2	1	4
4. Reduce medical expenses	0	3	3
5. Sale of valuable items	0	4	6
6. Emergency borrowing	33	50	30
6.1 Bank	5	3	2
6.2 Relatives	12	13	10
6.3 Friends	3	7	3
6.4 Neighbours	0	6	0
6.5 Moneylender	10	6	5
6.6 Pawnshop	0	0	0
6.7 Sari-sari store	3	15	10
7. Emigration	0	0	0
8. Received remittances	25	16	21
9. Aid from local government and NGO	46	65	58
10. Non-farm employment	85	60	94

Source: Sawada et al. (2009), p. 120.

basic goods during calamities, perhaps because their close association with the village people discourages opportunism. As reported in earlier studies (Otsuka, Estudillo, and Sawada 2009), remittances have become an important source of income in rural Philippines because of the rise in the number of overseas Filipino workers (OFWs). There were thirty-one OFWs in this village, as of the 2007 survey. Twenty-five per cent of the farmer households, 16 per cent of the landless households, and 21 per cent of the non-agricultural households reported having received remittances after Milenyo. In brief, the availability of emergency borrowing and remittances indicate the importance of personal networks in surviving a crisis.

Public Transfers

Through village officials, local government played a crucial role during the disaster by (1) immediately making the village meeting hall available as a temporary shelter for people whose houses had lost their roofs or who were affected by flash floods, (2) distributing grocery bags of basic food items (valued at about US$2 per household), (3) providing galvanized iron sheets to sixteen households whose houses lost their roofs, and (4) giving cash gifts amounting to about US$50 to eight households. There was also strict food price and supply monitoring undertaken by the local government in the local public market. This obviated unnecessary price hikes or a disruption of local food supply by opportunistic businessmen. The national government declared the province of Laguna under a state of emergency. Overall, disaster management was effective because there was no substantial asymmetry of information between the donors and recipients. This was due to the village officials' many years of association with the community.

Non-farm Employment

Non-farm employment served an important role in consumption smoothing. This is consistent with past studies in India (Walker and Ryan 1990; Kochar 1999) and Indonesia (Frankenberg, Smith, and Thomas 2003). This is done by increasing the number of workers, extending labour hours, or migrating to places where there are jobs (Kochar 1999; Walker and Ryan 1990). Even child labour income, which requires dropping out of school, is used as a coping device against parental income shortfalls (Jacoby and Skoufias 1997; Sawada and Lokshin 2009). We were not able to identify major changes in primary occupation after Milenyo. This indicates that it was the long-term employment in the non-farm sector that enabled the households to insure against the disaster. The number of unemployed — those workers who reported "none" as their primary occupation — rose from 57 to 67, indicating an increase in unemployment rate by 18 per cent.

COPING WITH SMALLER TYPHOONS

Typhoons occur in this village almost regularly during monsoon months, but the extent of damage caused by Milenyo was exceptionally great. During the usual-sized typhoons that hit the village between 1994 and 2003, "own savings and income" and "help from relatives" were the main coping mechanisms. The sale of physical assets, such as land or animals, and consumption reallocation played minor roles, regardless of the type of shocks (e.g., floods, typhoons, death or illness of a household member).

Liquidation of physical assets, borrowing, and receipt of assistance and remittances from family members living outside the household were found in both the responses to Milenyo and to the smaller typhoons. A major difference, however, appears to be the importance of the reduction in food consumption and consumption reallocation in response to Milenyo. This reflected the sheer magnitude of the damages to the households. During typical typhoons, households were able to shield their consumption through various informal insurance schemes (e.g., own savings and incomes, borrowing, and remittances), but the extent of income shock brought by Milenyo forced them to reduce their food consumption. A much larger proportion of households reported government aid as a coping mechanism after Milenyo because the severity of the damage of Milenyo necessitated larger scale relief operations on the part of the local government.

POLICY SUGGESTIONS

This study explored adaptation behaviour of rural households in response to the super typhoon Milenyo. These households live in a coastal village — called East Laguna Village — located in the province of Laguna in the Philippines. Milenyo caused widely heterogeneous damages across households, even within the same village. The poor landless households were those who conspicuously decreased their food consumption as a way of surviving Milenyo. Particularly helpful for the landless poor were community networks for securing emergency loans, personal networks for receiving remittances, and active local government management of the disaster. Overall, it is clear that the differential traumas caused by Milenyo were met with by both private and public transfers.

What are the lessons from the Milenyo experience in East Laguna Village? First, assistance from relatives and friends served as an informal risk-sharing scheme. This indicates that the community can play the role of an effective mechanism of insurance against various forms and intensity of shock (Estudillo et al. 2010; Sawada 2007). Self-insurance was reported by the villagers as one of their most important *ex ante* risk management strategies in smaller, regularly occurring typhoons. Second, the local government must play a role complementary to the community mechanism. During relief operations in the aftermath of Milenyo, the local government made transfers to the right people. The office of the village chieftain took major responsibility in distributing aid, thereby minimizing imperfect information and uncertainty about beneficiaries. Yet it is important to mention that in the case of covariant shocks, the community mechanism may prove to be largely ineffective. Only the state may be able to effectively undertake a large-scale relief operation. Third, the development of the non-farm sectors offers the best hope of reducing the risk of an income shock in agriculture. It is by now well known that participation in the non-farm labour market is a pathway out of poverty (Otsuka, Estudillo, and Sawada 2009). It is a way to diversify rural household income and avoid a drastic reduction in consumption in response to disasters (Sawada 2007). Fourth, and finally, for frequently occurring natural disasters, such as typhoons, floods, and droughts, it is important to design *ex ante* risk management policies. Disaster preparedness strategies, such as infrastructure and building safety, drainage systems (to reduce flooding), and early-warning systems, could enable rural households to better protect themselves against climate-related disasters.

Notes

1. The Center for Research on the Epidemiology of Disasters has not shown solid scientific evidence that climate change is a causal factor.
2. Parts of this section are drawn from Estudillo et al. (2010).
3. Hiromitsu Umehara conducted the benchmark survey in 1966. Hayami and Kikuchi (2000) then conducted eleven survey rounds in East Laguna Village between 1976 and 1997. Follow-up surveys were conducted in 2003 by

the International Rice Research Institute and in 2007 by Yasuyuki Sawada (Sawada et al. 2009).
4. Parts of this section were drawn from Estudillo et al. (2010) and Sawada et al. (2009).

References

Alderman, H., and C. H Paxon. "Do the Poor Insure? A Synthesis of Literature on Risk and Consumption in developing Countries". *World Bank Policy Research Working Paper* 1008. World Bank, Washington, D.C., 1992.

Center for Research on Epidemiology of Disasters (CRED). *Annual Disaster Statistical Review*. Brussels, Belgium, 2009.

Estudillo, Jonna P., Yasuyuki Sawada, Kei Kajisa, Nobuhiko Fuwa, and Masao Kikuchi. "The Transformation of Hayami's Village". In *Community, Market, and State in Development*, edited by Keirjiro Otsuka and Kaliappa Kalirajan, pp. 224–44. New York: Palgrave Macmillan, 2010.

Frankenberg, E., J. P. Smith, and D. Thomas. "Economic Shocks, Wealth, and Welfare". *Journal of Human Resources* 38, no. 2 (2003): 280–321.

Glewwe, P., and G. Hall. "Are Some Groups More Vulnerable to Macroeconomic Shocks Than Others? Hypothesis Tests Based on Panel Data from Peru". *Journal of Development Economics* 56, no. 1 (1998): 181–206.

Hayami, Y. and M. Kikuchi. *A Rice Village Sage: Three Decades of Green Revolution in the Philippines*. London: Macmillan Press, 2000.

Jacoby, H. and E. Skoufias. "Risk, Financial Markets and Human Capital in Developing Countries". *Review of Economic Studies* 64 (1997): 311–35.

Kang, S. J and Y. Sawada. "A Credit Crunch and Household Welfare in Korea". *Japanese Economic Review* 59, no. (2008): 438–58.

Kochar, A. "Smoothing Consumption by Smoothing Income: Hours of Work Responses to Idiosyncratic Agricultural Shocks in Rural India". *Review of Economics and Statistics* 8, no. 1 (1999): 50–61.

Otsuka, K., Jonna P. Estudillo and Y. Sawada. *Rural Poverty and Income Dynamics in Asia and Africa*. London: Routledge, 2009.

Sawada, Y. "The Impact of Natural and Manmade Disasters on Household Welfare". *Agricultural Economics* 37, no. 7 (2007): 59–73.

Sawada, Y. and M. Lokshin. "Obstacles to School Progression in Rural Pakistan: An Analysis of Gender and Sibling Rivalry Using Field Survey Data". *Journal of Development Economics* 88 (2009): 335–47.

Sawada, Y., Jonna P. Estudillo, N. Fuwa, and K. Kajisa. "How Do People Cope With a Natural Disaster? The Case of Super-Typhoon Milenyo in the Philippines". In *Development, Natural Resources and the Environment*, edited by

G. P. Carnaje and L. S. Cabanilla, pp. 99–120. Los Banos, Laguna, Philippines: Department of Economics, University of the Philippines, 2009.

Sawada, Y. and S. Shimizutani. "How Do People Cope With Natural Disasters? Evidence from the Great Hanshin-Awaji (Kobe) Earthquake". *Journal of Money, Credit, and Banking* 40, no. 2–3 (2008): 463–88.

Skoufias, E. 2003. "Economic Crises and Natural Disasters: Coping Strategies and Policy Implications". *World Development* 31, no. 7 (2003): 1087–102.

Walker, T. S., and J. G. Ryan. *Village and Household Economics in India's Semi-Arid Tropics*. Baltimore: Johns Hopkins University Press, 1990.

17

LIFE ALONG MANILA'S FLOODING RIVERS

Emma Porio

Planning the development of a city with rivers that flood requires an initial study on how the floods affect the residents. Among the city's residents, the poor are often the most affected. In 2008 the World Bank estimated that the Philippines loses 15 billion pesos (US$333 million) a year to floods, monsoons, and typhoons,[1] which is about 0.7 per cent of the gross domestic product (GDP). In September and October 2009, typhoons Ondoy (Ketsana) and Pepeng (Parma) hit Manila and the northern Philippines in quick succession, causing 3.8 billion pesos in damages and 24.8 billion pesos in immediate losses to agriculture, fisheries, and forestry, or about 2.7 per cent of the GDP. They seriously affected 9.3 million people and resulted in a loss of almost 1,000 lives (World Bank 2009). Such figures are impressive, but the harm done to the poor is often underestimated.

Starting in the early morning of 26 September 2009, Ondoy brought 450 mm (18 inches) of rainfall in a span of twelve hours (almost equivalent to the average monthly rainfall of Manila). There was deep flooding and damage all over the metropolis. Many poor communities were under water for several days; some for two or three months. A few days later, Pepeng brought heavy winds and rains, with a cumulative rainfall exceeding 1,000 mm (39 inches) in some areas. The damages brought about by Ondoy and Pepeng needed about US$4.42 billion for rehabilitation and recovery in the ensuing three years. Ondoy and Pepeng made it clear that every household, community, city, and country must have a plan in place for coping with future disasters (World Bank 2009).

In this essay, I describe the socio-economic conditions of the people who live along the major rivers in the flood plains of Metro Manila.[2] The description is based on a survey of 300 urban poor households I conducted between February 2008 and May 2009 in fourteen communities situated by the river side in the Metro Manila flood basin. This was done before the big floods brought by storms Ondoy and Pepeng in September and October 2009.

Metropolitan Manila has a land area of 636 square kilometres (246 square miles), a semi-alluvial plain formed by the sediment flows from the Meycauayan and Malabon-Tullahan river basins in the north, the Pasig-Marikina river basin in the east (Bankoff 2003), and the West Mangahan river basin in the west. The city is open to Manila Bay in the west and to a large lake, Laguna de Bay, in the southeast. Thus, the metropolis is a vast drainage basin that experiences frequent inundations from overflowing rivers and storm waters. The existing system of *esteros* (modified natural channels) and canals constructed during the Spanish and American colonial periods are inadequate (Liongson 2000 cited in Bankoff 2003). Climate change has raised the sea level and increased monsoon rains, typhoons, and floods.

About a third (31 per cent) of Metro Manila's land area is flood prone (Magno-Ballesteros 2009). Particularly prone are the cities of Manila, Navotas, Kalookan, Marikina, Pasig, Pateros, and Taguig. They are low-lying, have structurally inferior soils (Cabanilla 1996, p. 4 cited in Ballesteros 2009), and suffer from subsidence and siltation. Parts of Pateros and Taguig can remain water-logged for months (Magno-Ballesteros 2009). A lack of sound and consistent land-use planning has led to complicated, inefficient, and expensive system of permits and licensing, making land for housing unaffordable for the majority in the metropolis. This blocks the flow of the river resulting in major floods

FIGURE 17.1
Map of the Flood Prone Areas of Metro Manila River Basins and the Research Communities
(white rectangle boxes)

Source: JICA Research Institute and Emma Porio (2009).

(Magno-Ballesteros 2009). Land-use practices, infrastructure development, building standards, and urban development programmes have resulted in a highly congested environment that poses a high risk to residents and infrastructure. And climate change has compounded that risk.

Urban areas such as Metro Manila are highly susceptible to the effects of climate change because of the high concentration of buildings and people in an already degraded environment. Although Metro Manila has a lower poverty incidence than the rest of the country, it accounts for half (52 per cent, about 726,908 households or 4.4 million people) of the country's informal settlers (Porio 2010). Most of them live in environmentally degraded areas along waterways, swampy areas, and rivers because these are the only areas available to them and because the government has been unable to impose building codes and standards.

VULNERABILITIES OF THE URBAN POOR

Environmental Vulnerability

The households surveyed live in low-lying wetlands near the rivers. In addition to having been historically prone to flooding and water surges during storms and high tides, these areas are now highly exposed to the combined effects of climate change, such as monsoons, typhoons, sea-level rise, and tidal surges (in Camanava and West Mangahan). These problems are the greatest during the June–November rainy season. Most of these households belong to squatter slum settlements. There is no security of tenure in their housing and a lack of services such as water, electricity, sewerage, and drainage. These people also suffer from relatively higher levels of sickness, drug use, and petty crimes such as theft. Camanava has always been susceptible to sea-level rise throughout the year. But lately, the residents have experienced typhoons and monsoon rains even outside the traditional rainy season. In 2009, the first typhoon occurred in the last week of April (during the April–May dry season), although the most damaging typhoons (Ondoy and Pepeng) came in September and October. The environmental problems of the poor urban households interact strongly with their economic and social problems (low income, low education, etc.). The negative effects of climate-related changes are therefore heightened. Floods, tide and storm surges, sea-level rise, typhoons, and monsoon rains harm the poor more than the non-poor.

Economic Vulnerability

The survey showed that economic problems (e.g., unemployment and underemployment) are still the overriding concern of those living along the river, followed by security-related risks, such as thefts, hold-ups, fire, and drug use. These problems are closely related to physical congestion and economic insecurity. These household level risks also increase with the expansion of residential, commercial, and industrial development in these flood-prone localities. This is clearly demonstrated in the rapid expansion of building projects in the Mangahan River Basin, which do not have the necessary infrastructure support, such as drainage, sewerage, and roads. Thus, flooding near the Napindan Channel and Laguna de Bay have increased because these areas are not really suitable for habitation (or industrial use) as they are mostly wetlands and marshy areas. In these flood-prone areas, the expansion of congested, informal settlements alongside formal residential subdivisions in danger zones and public domain areas continue. Substandard sewerage and roads of these residential subdivisions have also worsened the living conditions of the informal settlers nearby. Aside from the congestion and the seeming impermanence of these informal settlements, building standards are also compromised by slum lords who take advantage of the expanding rental market and the lack of regulation by local officials.

Heightening the risk exposure of households, there are inadequate services, such as water, electricity, health, roads, drainage, and sewerage. Their environmental problems correlate highly with the social problems of informal settlers, as the worst-off urban poor households also come from the urban poor in highly environmentally vulnerable places.

Social Vulnerability

Most respondents were female (86 per cent) because women were more available and more willing to be interviewed. Ages ranged from 18–92 years old, with a median age of 42. Most respondents

(61 per cent) were legally married, 20 per cent cohabited with someone, and the rest were widowed or separated (14 per cent) or single (4 per cent). Their median monthly household income was 8,000 peso. Most of the very poor households (old, widowed or separated, had no income, lived in dilapidated housing, dependent on food support given by their relatives) came from low-income communities located in environmentally vulnerable places along floodways. They have clogged waterways and no services. Most respondents had an average of 8.5 years in schooling. Their low education, in part, explains their low levels of formal employment, with most of them deriving a livelihood from the informal sector.

TYPHOONS, FLOODS, STORMS, AND TIDAL SURGES

Basic Services

More than one-fourth (27 per cent) of the households have substandard toilets (*antipolo* type, dug-out latrines) or none at all (i.e., use their neighbour's toilet, deposit wastes directly into the river or any waterway). Of those who have toilets, 27 per cent complained that during floods their toilets get clogged with waste and overflow onto their floor. They are forced to use the river or a neighbours' toilet located far from the flooded area. They also complained that floodwaters would carry garbage to where they lived and clog up the nearby drainage channels. Environmental pollution can be seen in the very dark, sometimes oily, water in the rivers or under their floors. This continuous flow of garbage discouraged them from disposing off their own trash because even doing that, their environment would still be littered with garbage from other communities.

Only 39 per cent of the households have their own electric meter, while 42 per cent buy their electricity from a neighbour at a higher price. Meanwhile, 10 per cent obtained electricity through illegal connections, and 9 per cent use oil or gas lamps and candles for light, heightening the risk of fires. Those who had electricity complained about energy fluctuations, brown-outs, and "grounded" electricity sources during typhoons and floods.

Almost one-third (32 per cent) of the households have piped water, while the remaining two-thirds buy water at higher cost (about

300 per cent more) from suppliers or neighbors (65 per cent) who have water connections or have dug artesian wells. Slightly less than one-fourth (23 per cent) of the respondents said that during floods and storm and tidal surges their water becomes dirty and their wells become inundated. Thus, they have to buy potable water from the water suppliers, who in turn, increase their prices by about 100–300 per cent (Porio and Lao 2010). This increases expenditures on water, food, and transportation to 50–100 per cent.

Health and Socio-economic Losses

A substantial number of respondents reported that they or members of their household became sick because of typhoons, monsoon rains, and floods. But only a few of the respondents (13) said that they obtained free medicine from the *barangay*[3] health centre. Most of them spent between P20 and P12,000 pesos for medicines and health care (P1,930 pesos on the average, but the median was P200 pesos, suggesting a wide socio-economic variability among the households). The respondents from Taguig City (West Mangahan river basin), who had lower income and education levels, also spent the least on medical expenses (average of P241–350 pesos) as they did not have money to spare for the treatment of their sick household members.

Those who were absent from work or school could not get out of their place and could not cross the river or streets to get transportation to school or work. Those who were unable to work reported that business slowed as it was impossible to pursue their livelihood during high monsoon rains, typhoons, or floods. Those polled lost from 1 to 15 days (average 4) and had a mean income loss of about 925 peso (but median income loss was P500 pesos) during floods or tidal surges. Whether they work inside their house or within or outside the barangay or city, they were still negatively affected by the typhoons and floods. Inside their houses, work gets disrupted by dirty water reaching above their floors.

Those not able to work reported lost earnings of P98 to P2,000 pesos (average P1,081 pesos; median P500 pesos) in the last rainy season. Respondents also reported damages to household appliances (refrigerator, television, washing machine, mattress, house furniture, radio, electric fan, water dispenser, etc.) or partial destruction of their house (e.g., roof blown away, stairs or other parts need repair). Total losses ranged from P2 to P50,000 pesos, but the average loss per households was P4,615 pesos in the last rainy season. Meanwhile, parents complained that their children suffered from the monsoon rains, typhoons, and floods. About a third of their children missed classes (5 days average in the last rainy season) and had their academic performance negatively affected.

THE MOST SUSCEPTIBLE TO CLIMATE CHANGE

All of the polled households that were confronting severe social and environmental problem shared the following characteristics:

- where they live is low-lying or swampy or wetlands and experiences heavy rains, floods, and storm or tidal surges; they have a monthly median income of 8,000 peso (less than US$1 per person per day) for a household of six members;
- they live in slums or squatter settlements with no security of tenure and inadequate water, electricity, health services, drainage, and sanitation;
- they have no drinkable water and either no toilets or not one they could use during typhoons, floods, and storm or tidal surges. They have to resort the "wrap and throw" method or use their neighbors' toilets;
- they regularly suffer losses of things such as income, health, household appliances, garments, housing repair, days at school.

Of the two-thirds who are regularly affected by climate change, only a small portion (10 per cent) received help. Informal sources of support were more common than formal sources.[4]

All respondents claimed to be highly exposed to climate change induced flooding. About two-thirds of them suffered more losses (e.g., income, work, health, household appliances, housing damage) from typhoons, floods, and tidal and storm surges. The households from the bottom three income deciles appeared most exposed and consistently incurred higher losses (e.g., income, workdays, housing) and major inconveniences (e.g., water source buried by floods, toilets blocked and overflowing with waste and large worms) compared to the other two-thirds of the households or "better-off" neighbours.

Socio-cultural factors compound their vulnerability: 20 per cent of the interviewed households had two "spouses" who were not legally married. In 24 per cent there was only a single former spouse (now widowed or separated), and 4.3 per cent of the "households" consisted of a one or more people who were not cohabiting (were single). Children born in live-in arrangements often do not obtain birth certificates because the mothers use their money to buy food rather than pay registration fees, not realizing that legal identity papers will eventually be necessary for accessing school or health services. Meanwhile, households headed by widows or widowers, separated or single individuals need subsistence support, but their networks are also thin and unable to help.

Furthermore, it costs more in terms of health, transportation, household appliances, basic services, etc. to live in environmentally exposed places, such as near rivers and in wetlands in flood basins. There is little potential for moving up economically over time because of the social and economic (non-monetary) losses. Poverty reproduces itself from generation to generation. The intensification of poverty due to the environmental exposure is illustrated by the bottom 30 per cent of the respondents who come from the wetland areas of Mangahan Floodway and along the Napindan Channel (or River). Relocation would mean losing jobs and networks in nearby factories and workplaces. Those who suffered more losses of property, work days, and life were those whose homes and neighbourhoods were the most flooded. They belonged to the bottom three income deciles of the sample urban poor population.

The aftermath of floods and typhoons also consume more time, energy, and money of women than of men. Because of floods, women spend more time and energy than usual doing laundry, cleaning the house, and taking care of sick family members. Furthermore, the extra time women spend doing these things is less than the extra time men spent time repairing their houses and household appliances. Women bear the effects of climate change more because they have to attend to the demands of hygiene, household management, and monitoring the children who want to play in the rain and might drown in the floods. For the women respondents, floods make family and household management tasks more time-consuming and worrisome. Only a small portion (5 per cent) of the very poor interviewed obtained help from formal institutions (e.g., local government units, or charitable agencies) or informal support networks (relatives, neighbours, and friends).

WAYS OF SURVIVING

The urban poor have little choice but to adapt to the environmental degradation of their communities and to their social circumstances. Because they are repeatedly flooded and live in water-logged places, the urban poor crafted a "water-based lifestyle." To protect their houses from floods, or rising waters in the case of tidal surges, they raise and strengthen the posts and floors of their houses. If their finances allow it, they add floors, so that when floods come, they just move their things and activities to the second or third floor. In some parts of Camanava, residents have permanently abandoned the ground floor because of frequent floods or rising waters.

The informal settlers of the swampy areas near the Napindan Channel and in the Camanava area have built makeshift bridges, plastic and styrofoam boats, and higher body and wheels for their pedicabs and tricycles for transportation during floods and tidal surges. Some residents tie string lines with a pulley system from one house to the other to send foodstuff from the retail stores to houses nearby. For those who can afford it, rubber boots (protective in floods below knee-deep but useless in floods that are waist-deep) have become part and parcel of their apparel. They also have devised platforms for their appliances that can be raised when a flood or a storm surge occurs. They store clothes and other household belongings in boxes or baskets that can be pulled up by string pulleys tied to their house posts or walls.

In terms of livelihood, the urban poor have taken advantage of their environment by planting watercress along the flood lines (water prone areas) or by working in watercress farms along the Mangahan floodway, a channel provided as an emergency course to divert floodwaters from more populous regions. Men gather water hyacinth stems for sale to flower shops while the women dry them for sale to handicraft makers. During the flooding season along the Napindan Channel near Laguna Lake, men gather fish from the water that has overflowed from fishponds and sell them in the makeshift open market under the C-6 bridge in Mangahan. Floods also offer opportunities to earn more as pedicab drivers. Tricycles increase their prices by 200–300 per cent (from 10 to 50 peso depending on depth and distance). Labourers charge more than their regular rates when they offer to transport people or heavy household appliances across floodwaters. In preparing for typhoons and floods, residents along the rivers have a repertoire: storing food, water, and other necessities; making sure they have flashlights, batteries, and candles for the eventual brown-outs; having belongings ready-packed for evacuation; and reinforcing their homes.

Although a third of the respondents said that they have garments ready-packed in case they have to leave, only 10 per cent said they were willing to move when the flood waters came. They are afraid of losing their belongings, including planks from their houses, to theft. When asked about relocation as an option for avoiding these losses, most of them rejected it as most relocation sites were far from their place of work, have no basic services, and have high mortgage payments compared to their current residence which cost almost nothing. They said they have gotten used to the flooding and water surges. They are used to their "water-based lifestyle". Before Ondoy in 2009, they reasoned that *Hindi ka naman namamatay dahil sa baha* (You do not die from floods or the rising waters here). After the many death during Ondoy, they take more precautions, but in general, the crafting of water-based lifestyles in response to floods seems to have been "naturalized" by the urban poor. As one respondent quipped, "we are forever in an evacuation mode!".

When asked what kind of support they received from a network of relatives, neighbours, friends, and community officials, the respondents exhibited a high level of self-reliance. About a third consistently said that they try to solve their problems themselves. Only a small portion (range of 3–24 per cent) reported receiving support from their networks. This highlights the vulnerability of the urban poor households as they do not seem to have institutional sources of support. More importantly, interviews with the key informants revealed that poor and vulnerable households do not have much of a network of relatives, neighbours, and friends who are financially able to provide support. These households are also not able to get support from formal institutions, such as health clinics of the local governments.

The self-reliant attitude of the poor reflects the limits of their social capital, or networks that can help during calamities.

GOVERNMENT PROGRAMMES

To minimize the devastation caused by floods, typhoons, and sea-level rise to people, resources, and infrastructure, both the national government and the local governments of the three flood plains of Metro Manila have formulated mitigation and adaptation plans that include flood control programmes, the construction and repair of drainage systems, and water-diversion pumps. The flood control programme of the Metro Manila Development Authority has constructed flood walls, dikes, and pumping stations along certain portions of the floodways and rivers of the Pasig-Marikina River, Napindan Channel, and Tullahan River in the Camanava area (Kalookan, Malabon, and Navotas).

Meanwhile, the local governments of Taguig (West Mangahan), Navotas, Malabon, and Caloocan (Camanava area) have installed water pumps or water-diversion techniques, known locally as "bombastic", which have minimized flooding in some areas. Drainage and roads continue to be built by the national government and local governments (e.g., Marikina, Taguig). These have helped in diminishing the flooding in some areas. Recently, the National Disaster Coordinating Council lodged under the Department of National Defense was reorganized as the National Disaster Risk Reduction Management Council with the Department of Interior and Local Governments at its helm. This change was intended to increase the resources of both the national agencies and local government units, under a decentralized regime. Most government agencies usually provide relief and rehabilitation by distributing food, water, and other basic needs after floods. They also have community-based disaster warning systems implemented at the municipal and *barangay* levels. Local governments also increased their capacity to respond to disasters through capacity-building programmes.

Marikina City initiated a flood mitigation programme of putting concrete on dirt roads to reduce sand, pebbles, and mud entering the drainage system. It also constructed and rehabilitated major outfalls,[5] allowing flooded areas to recede faster. It engaged in massive dredging operations in the rivers in order to achieve a faster discharge of floodwaters from residential subdivisions. Obstructions produced by informal settlements along waterways were demolished or removed. Existing diversion channels and interceptors are being continuously improved. Marikina is the only local government in Metro Manila that has successfully cleared its waterways of major obstructions and resettled their informal settlers within the city. In September 2009, these programmes however proved insufficient for the Ondoy floods because the city is located at the bottom of the flood basin.

The Metro Manila Development Authority established "Flood Control Bayanihan Zones" in flood-prone areas in partnership with local governments and civil society organizations. Focused on clearing and dredging rivers, creeks, and other waterways, this programme hopes to restore old floodways and divert flood inflow from the mountains to Mangahan Floodway and Laguna Lake. Unlike the "bombastic" initiative of local governments, flood mitigation programmes have mostly been financed by loans or grants for multilateral or bilateral agencies such as the World Bank and the Japan Bank for International Cooperation.

RECOMMENDATIONS

This study has documented how urban poor households regularly incur economic and social losses from, and are increasingly threatened by, climate change hazards such as floods, heavy monsoon rains, typhoons, and tidal surges and storms. While the urban poor have adapted to a "water-based lifestyle" in response to their living in flood-prone living circumstances, their income losses from floods and the social and health costs of living in water-logged areas has put them in a spiral of poverty. Furthermore, because they are poor, they have less means to adapt to climate change, and hence are getting poorer when floods occur.

The effects of climate change hazards on the urban poor have been compounded not only by the ecological and socio-economic problems mentioned earlier, but also by larger forces, such as rapid urbanization, population congestion, ill-calibrated investments in infrastructure development, and inconsistent policies, programmes, land use, and building practices.

The poor would benefit if the government were to integrate environmental goals with political goals in urban planning. They would also benefit if political-administrative territories were reconciled with ecological boundaries in the allocation of resources and investments. A water-sensitive urban design must inform the revision of land-use and building practices when developing green spaces, infrastructure, technologies, and architecture in an effort to reduce flood-related risks.

Notes

1. World Bank (2009), p. 77.
2. Metro Manila covers the 17 cities and municipalities while Manila or City of Manila is one of the 17 cities as well as the capital of the Philippines.
3. A *barangay* is the lowest political administrative unit of the Philippine government.
4. The percentages are averages in the three studied flood basins. Among the three, those who receive help constitute between 3 per cent to 23 per cent; from formal sources, between 3 per cent to 6 per cent; and from informal sources, between 15 per cent to 24 per cent. On average only 10 per cent of them received help, with 4 per cent getting from formal sources and 19 per cent from informal sources.
5. An outfall can be a pipe, channel, or opening where water "falls out" and then into another body of water, typically a drainage channel.

References

Asian Development Bank (ADB). *Poverty in the Philippines: Causes, Constraints and Opportunities*. Manila: ADB, 2010.

Balisacan, A. *Poverty, Urbanization, and Development Policy: A Philippine Perspective*. Quezon City: University of the Philippines Press, 1994.

Bankoff, G. "Constructing Vulnerability: The Historical, Natural and Social Generation of Flooding in Metropolitan Manila". *Disasters* 27, no. 3 (2003): 95–109.

Bauer, Armin. "The Environments of the Poor: New Perspectives on Development Programs". Powerpoint presentation at the 13th Poverty and Environment Meeting, Manila, Philippines, June 2008.

Manda, E. "The case of Laguna de Bay Basin in the Philipines". PowerPoint presentation at Water and Climate Change Adaptation in Asian River Basins, Selangor, Malaysia, 1–5 December 2008.

Magno-Ballesteros, M. "Land Use Planning in Metro Manila and the Urban Fringe: Implications on the Land and Real Estate Market". *Discussion Paper Series* No. 2000–20, 2000.

Muto, M., et al. "Impacts of Climate Change Upon Asian Coastal Areas: The Case of Metro Manila". Research report of the Japan International Cooperation Agency, 2009.

Porio, Emma. "Climate Change, Governance and Sustainability of Cities". Paper presented in the ISA World Congress of Sociology, Gothenburg, Sweden, 12–17 July 2010.

————. "Social and Ecological Vulnerability of Urban Poor Communities in Metro Manila: Information Needs, Opportunities and Constraints". Paper presented at Cities at Risk Conference, Bangkok, 26–28 February 2009.

————. "Vulnerability, Adaptation and Resilience to Climate Change-Related Effects Among the Riverine Urban Poor Communities in Metro Manila". Research report submitted to JICA Research Institute, 2008.

Porio, Emma and Ma. Elisa Jayme Lao. "A Social and Political-Economic Assessment of an Urban Community in Metro Manila: The Case of Welfareville." A research report submitted to the World Bank (Manila), 2010.

Webster, Douglas, Arturo Corpuz, and Christopher Pablo. "Towards a National Urban Development Framework for the Philippines: Strategic Considerations". A report prepared for the National Economic and Development Authority (NEDA), Government of the Philippines, 2002.

World Bank. "Typhoons Ondoy and Pepeng: Post-Disaster Needs Assessment". Main Report, 2009.

————. *Climate Risks and Adaptation in Asian Coastal Cities: A Synthesis Report.* Washington, D.C.: World Bank, 2010.

18

QUANTIFYING THE HEALTH RISKS FROM PATHOGENS IN THE FLOOD WATER IN METRO MANILA

Tran Thi Viet Nga and Kensuke Fukushi

Waterborne diseases are caused by pathogenic micro-organisms that are directly transmitted when contaminated water is consumed or contacted. As a result of swimming in contaminated water, people often contract acute, but relatively benign, gastroenteritis with a short incubation period and duration (Cabelli 1982). In the flood season, there is a higher risk of infection due to more frequent direct contact with severely polluted water over a longer period. Infectious disease is a major health problem in many flood-prone areas, especially where infectious disease is already endemic (Few 2004). Infectious disease outbreaks of varying magnitude and rates of mortality have been reported following major floods in developing countries. There is some evidence from India and Bangladesh that diarrhoeal disease increases after flooding.

In this essay, we aim to characterize and quantify the human health risks associated with varying levels of exposure to pathogens present in flood water. In our analysis, exposure scenarios according to inundation levels are developed in which direct and indirect contact with polluted water is assumed to occur. We estimated the probabilities of gastrointestinal infection based on established dose-response relationships for the key pathogen present in the flood water (E. coli) (Haas 1989) (See Appendix for dose-relationship details.) The more water one swallows, the more one is exposed to the pathogens, and so the more likely one is to get sick. Since there are no studies estimating the amount of water swallowed by people in flood zones, we adopted the United States Environmental Protection Authority's estimates of the exposure levels of different age groups while swimming or wading. We also assumed that residents are not able to leave the area during floods. As these assumptions are untested, our results may be over- or underestimated.

STUDY SITE

Metro Manila (population 11 million) is the social, economic, and political centre of the Philippines. See Figure 18.1. It is also at the heart of the tropical monsoon climatic zone. Frequent flooding associated with typhoons and other climatic factors is a perennial problem, intensified by the city's being located at sea-level. Furthermore, rapid urbanization, inadequate river channel and drainage capacity, poor maintenance, the growing number of informal settlers, institutional challenges, and financial restraints exacerbate the flood situation (JICA 2001).

In our study, data provided by the Japan International Cooperation Agency was used to calculate risk and to create maps of population density and inundation status-quo (JICA 2010). The data include *barangay*[1] boundaries of Metro Manila as of 2003, grouped together by district, population (National Statistics Office 2000 census), and the grid data of inundation scenarios. We used ArcGIS 9.2[2] to match population with boundaries districts. The newly created shapefile[3] contains the district boundaries of Metro Manila (as of 2000) and matched population of 2000. Based on this shapefile, we created a population density (people per hectare) map. Inundation grid data[4] was used to create the inundation map using the minimum level (in metres) of status quo 2003. We then calculated levels of risk associated with different exposure scenarios according to inundation levels. We then matched these results with

FIGURE 18.1
Map of Manila Metropolitan Administration

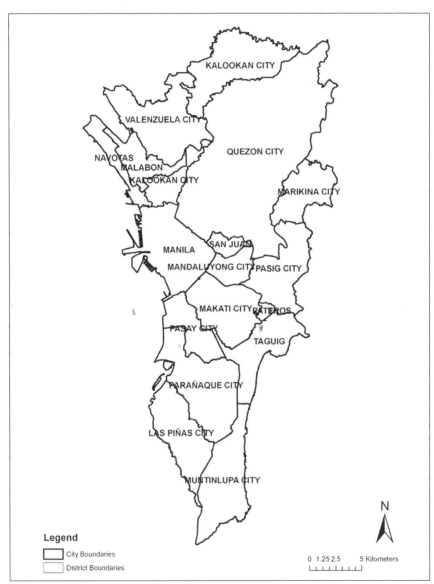

Note: The highest political division are the sixteen cities and the Municipality of Pateros which have
     political power independent from each other.
Source: JICA (2010).

the inundation map to create a new map of potential risks in relevant locations.

EXPOSURE SCENARIOS

We conducted a human health risk assessment. To this end, the following equation was used to calculate the single-exposure illness rate (Haas 1989) for E. coli:

Risk = 1 − [1 + (D/N50)(21/α − 1)] −α
With   Risk = probability of infection;
N50 = medium infectious dose
α: slope parameter

We evaluated the risks associated with exposure to polluted flood water (E. coli) using (i) inundation depth of less than one metre; (ii) inundation depth of a half to one meter, (iii) inundation depth of one to two metres, and (iv) inundation depth of above two meters. These scenarios were derived from effects set out in the Flood Fighting Act of Japan, 2001 (see Table 18.1). Peoples' vulnerabilities, experiences, coping behaviour, and other responses to flooding vary due to factors such as gender, age, occupation, lifestyle, and living standard. Because of data limitations, this analysis focuses on differences due to age. The population of Manila was divided into four age groups, (i) under 5 years, (ii) from 5 to 14 years, (iii) from 15 to 59 years and (iv) above 60 years old (National Statistics Office 2000 census). See Figure 18.2. We examined the daily activities and behaviour of each age group (via secondary

TABLE 18.1
Classification of Inundation Depth

Level	Inundation depth	Impacts
I	0–50 cm	most houses will stay dry and it is still possible to walk through water
II	50–100 cm	there will be at least 50 cm of water on the ground floor
III	100–200 cm	the ground floor of the houses will be flooded

Note: Classification based on Flood Fighting Act, Japan, 2001.

FIGURE 18.2
Distribution of Age in Metro Manila

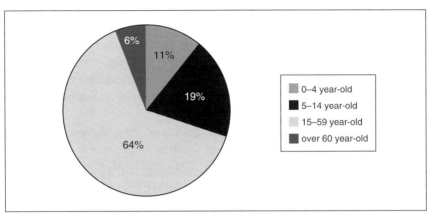

Source: NSO, 2000 Census of Population and Housing

sources) in order to confirm the amount of time people would spend in water during floods.

In our analysis, we used water to evaluate the risk of E. coli concentration in flood water, while assuming the exposure route to ingestion. We derived default ingestion intake values from the US-EPA Risk Assessment Guidance of Superfund (RAGS). We had four exposure scenarios, varying by inundation depth. We first calculated the risk for a single exposure.

The first scenario is a water depth of half a metre and less. At this inundation depth, it is likely that water contact would only occur while moving around in flooded streets. For the purposes of this assessment, we assumed that in one day the total amount of time spent outdoors for the age group of 4 years and under was two hours, from 5 to 14 and 15 to 59 years, four hours and over 60 years old one hour, assuming half of the total outdoor time to be spent in water.

A major route of pathogen exposure is the accidental swallowing of flood water. Hand-to-mouth transfer is viewed as most likely for those 4 years old and under who spent time playing with water. In this analysis, we assumed that, on average, children four years old and under would accidentally swallow around 50 ml per hour and those aged five years and over, 10 ml per hour. These values were derived from the US-EPS Risk Assessment Guidance for Individuals Exposed to Surface Water during Wading.

The second scenario is that of water depth of a half a metre to one metre. At this inundation depth, it is likely that people would be in water whenever they left the house. Exposure to waterborne pathogens would be through accidental ingestion while moving around in flood water or using flood water for bathing or washing personal belongings.

In the third scenario the depth is one to two metres. Here we assumed the water contact time to be the same as for scenario 2. However, at this inundation depth, it is likely that people would have to swim or do swimming-like actions while travelling around. Because children would have the opportunity to play or swim in the water and subject to repeated exposure within the one day, it was assumed that accidental ingestion of flood water could be considerably higher than for other age groups. Studies have indicated that non-adults ingest about twice as much water as adults during swimming activities (Dufour 2006). In this assessment, the incidental ingestion rate was assumed to be 100 ml per hour for children, and half that for adults.

The last scenario is a depth of two metres and above. At this depth, the first floor and often also the roof will be covered by water. Given the high frequency of water contact by inhabitants of flooded houses, it was assumed that incidental ingestion of flood water could be considerably higher than that occasioned by swimming. For the purpose of this assessment, we assumed the ingestion rate to be 200 ml children for children and half that rate for adults.

FLOOD IDENTIFICATION

Figure 18.3 shows that among 17 cities and municipalities of Metro Manila, the costal western district of Manila City has the highest population density, more than 500 person per ha. The areas in the south and northeast have lowest population density of less than 110 person per ha. See also Table 18.2.

We then used the grid data of inundation to create the inundation map. We used the minimum level (in metres) of status quo 2003 to

FIGURE 18.3
Population Densities Map of Metro Manila

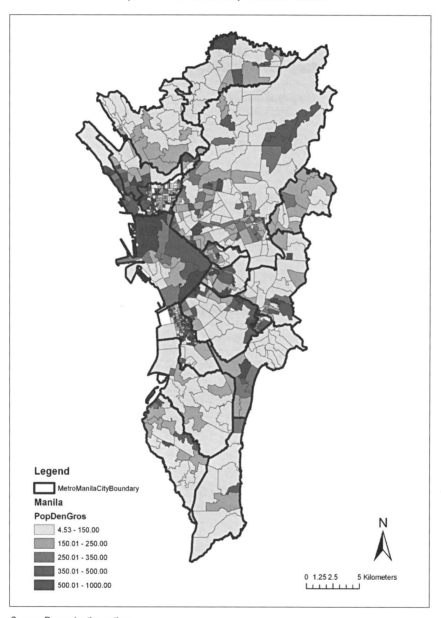

Legend

MetroManilaCityBoundary

Manila

PopDenGros

4.53 - 150.00

150.01 - 250.00

250.01 - 350.00

350.01 - 500.00

500.01 - 1000.00

N

0 1.25 2.5   5 Kilometers

Source: Drawn by the authors.

present the map (Figure 18.4). The serious flood areas, which have high inundation levels and high population density, are districts 1, 6, 12, and 14 (Table 18.3).

TABLE 18.2
Population Densities on City of Manila

District	Area (ha)	Population density (persons/ha)	District	Area (ha)	Population density (persons/ha)
1	865.13	682	8	158.91	38
2	66.11	176	9	67.26	111
3	84.69	291	10	259.58	298
4	163.85	253	11	278.69	230
5	309.01	347	12	166.00	476
6	774.71	455	13	315.28	80
7	91.37	184	14	337.45	526

Source: JICA (2010).

TABLE 18.3
Flooded Area by Districts, Manila City

District	Area (m^2)	Flooded-area (m^2) according to inundation depth of			
		0–50 cm	50–100 cm	100–200 cm	>200 cm
1	8,651,257	3,133,920	2,418,052	97,081	
2	661,052	97,532	433,096	107,356	
3	846,864	221,356	331,086	283,055	
4	1,638,521	374,456	224,576	40,318	
5	3,090,140	1,436,061	621,836	57,987	
6	7,747,139	2,694,595	1,716,456	469,742	13,187
7	913,711	20,703	204,298	535,774	
8	1,589,072	666,652	230,610	14,628	
9	672,642	87,122			
10	2,595,763	1,394,040	31,988		
11	2,786,865	664,108	1,326,063	172,772	
12	1,660,035	354,012	304,645	723,402	
13	3,152,817	923,386	14,442	9,459	4,634
14	3,374,456	1,184,077	508,537	702,738	

Source: JICA (2010).

FIGURE 18.4
Inundation Map of Metro Manila

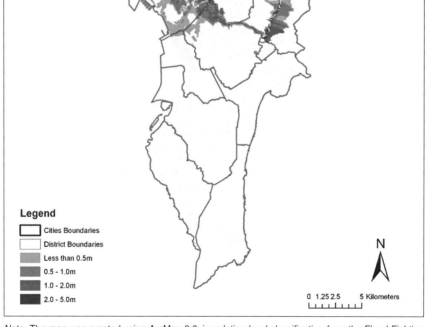

Note: The map was created using ArcMap 9.2; inundation level classification from the Flood Fighting
   Act, Japan, 2001, inundation data of year 2003.
Source: Drawn by the authors.

FIGURE 18.5
Quantifying the Health Risks o18.f Floods — Daily Risks

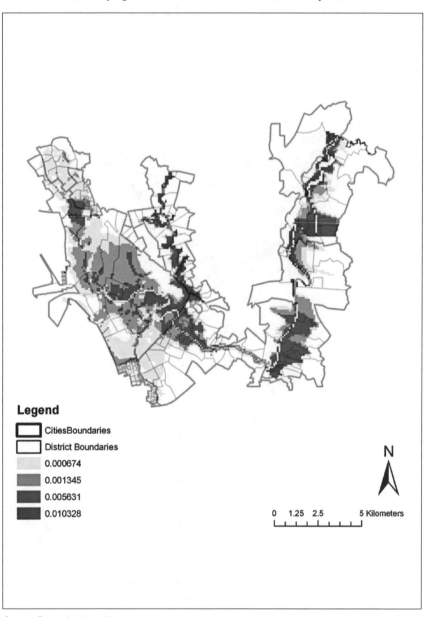

Source: Drawn by the authors.

FIGURE 18.6
Estimated Daily Risk of Infection via Incidental Ingestion of Flood Water in Metro of Manila

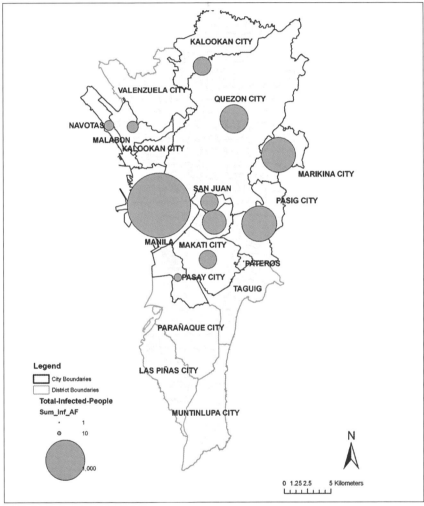

Note: The infected risk was calculated using the mean E.coli exposure level of 30,000 MPN/100 ml from the contaminated surface water data (Nga 1999) and daily risks of gastrointestinal illness via incidental ingestion were 0.000674, 0.001345, 0.005631 and 0.010328 for the inundation scenarios of 0–50 cm, 50–100 cm, 100–200 cm, and above 200 cm, respectively. The map was created in ArcMap 9.2 by overlaying polygons of districts boundaries on the classified risk levels
Source: Drawn by the authors.

According to Zoleta-Nantes (2000), eighteen to twenty floods occur in Metro Manila each year. A survey by the Japan International Cooperation Agency in 2000 reported that the duration of flooding ranged from ten to twenty hours. In our analysis, one flood is considered one exposure to inundation water, and, assuming that the time length for one exposure is one day, the annual risk based on a single exposure can be calculated. See Figures 18.5 and 18.6 and Tables 18.4 and 18.5.

TABLE 18.4
Number of Infected People per day Due to Gastrointestinal Illness via Incidental Ingestion of Flood Water in Metro Manila
(based on inundation data of year 2003)

District	Population	Infected people (person) according to inundation depth of				Total (person)
		0–50 cm	50–100 cm	100–200 cm	>200 cm	
1	590,307	142	223	37	0	402
2	11,619	1	10	10	0	21
3	24,615	4	13	46	0	63
4	41,517	6	7	6	0	19
5	107,154	33	29	12	0	74
6	352,329	83	105	119	6	313
7	16,798	0	5	55	0	60
8	5,969	2	1	0	0	3
9	7,466	1	0	0	0	1
10	77,398	28	1	0	0	29
11	64,184	9	42	22	0	73
12	79,003	11	19	193	0	223
13	25,243	5	0	0	0	5
14	177,480	41	34	208	0	283

Source: Authors' calculation.

TABLE 18.5
Single Risk and Annual Risk Associated with Pathogen Exposure During Flooding Period, for Different Group of people

Group of Age	Risk	Inundation depth (cm)			
		< 50	50–100	100–200	>200
0–4	daily risk	0.001491	0.002968	0.005879	0.005879
	total risk	0.029407	0.057715	0.111231	0.111231
5 to 14	daily risk	0.000598	0.001194	0.005879	0.011536
	total risk	0.011898	0.023615	0.111231	0.207095
15 to 59	daily risk	0.000598	0.001194	0.005879	0.011536
	total risk	0.011898	0.023615	0.111231	0.207095
>60	daily risk	0.000150	0.000299	0.001491	0.001491
	total risk	0.002992	0.005972	0.029407	0.029407
Total	daily risk	0.000674	0.001345	0.005631	0.010328
	total risk	0.013398	0.026556	0.106796	0.187491

Source: Authors' calculation.

SUMMARY

In our analysis, the risk of gastrointestinal illness due to E. coli via incidental ingestion of flood water in City of Manila over the course of a year varies according to inundation level and age. The risk level ranges from 1 per cent to nearly 20 per cent in flood levels of a metre or less to over two metres. The highest level of risk is to the five-to-fourteen-year-old age group. However, if flood heights of more than two metres become the norm due to climate change, and these foods occur more frequently and last longer, then the vulnerability baseline for all groups will shift accordingly.

As with any risk assessment, there are many sources of uncertainty in this analysis. While the health risks associated with E. coli in this assessment are considerable, the level of risk for gastrointestinal illness, in fact, may be significantly higher, because other pathogenic microorganisms may be present in the flood water. They could affect those who are exposed frequently. The most susceptible may also include women. As women are generally more involved than men in supervising the outdoor activities of young children, they may also incur a higher risk of accidentally ingesting polluted water. Urban poor women are also more involved in street trading, food preparation, washing, and other water-related activities.

The data presented here are suggestive. To verify the health risk estimation, data needs to be collected for group behaviour during floods and for the quality of the inundation water. However, our purpose was to quantify climate-change–related risks. In the case of illnesses caused by flooding, this quantification can be employed to make a rapid assessment of threatened areas where data, time, and resources are lacking. A useful contribution can thus be made to strategic health planning, and in particular pre-positioning health resources to manage areas under threat. When field-tested and validated, predictive quantitative assessments of climate change flood-related risks may also promote the development of financial instruments such as insurance.

APPENDIX

Dose-Response Relationship

The following equation was used to calculate the single-exposure illness rate (Haas, 1989) for E. coli:

$$Risk = 1 - [1 + (D/N_{50})(2^{1/\alpha} - 1)]^{-\alpha}$$

With   Risk = probability of infection;

N_{50} = medium infectious dose

α: slope parameter

Notes

1. Barangay is Philippines' lowest unit of administration. Filipino for village, district, or ward.
2. ArcGIS 9.2 is a geographic information system software named ArcGIS version 9.2 developed by Environment Research Institute—US (ESRI)
3. Shapefile is a file that contains geospatial vector data that used for geographic information system software. The data describe geometries with associated attributes. For example a shapefile of a lake spatially describes its geometry as a polygon and attributes such as the lake's name.

4. Grid is an ESRI data format for storing raster data that defines geographic space as an array of equally sized square cells arranged in rows and columns. In this case, inundation grid data are information of inundation level, which is associated in each cell.

References

Cabelli V. J., A. P. Dufour, L. J. McCabe, and M. A. Levin. "Swimming-associated Gastroenterist and Water Quality". *American Journal of Epidemiology* 115, no. 4 (1982).

Dufour, A. P, O. Evans, T.D. Behymer, and R. Cantu. "Water Ingestion during swimming activities in a pool: A pilot study". *Journal of Water Health* 4 (2006): 425–30.

Few R., M. Ahern, F. Matthies, and A. Kovats. "Floods, Health and Climate Change: A Strategic Review". Tyndall Centre for Climate Change Research Working, 2004.

Haas, Charles N., Joan B. Rose, and Charles P. Gerba. *Quantitative Microbiological Risk Assessment*. New York: John Wiley and Sons, 1999.

JICA. "Metro Manila Flood Control Project". 2001.

JICA. "Main report: The JICA-WB-ADB Joint Study on Climate Risks and Adaptation in Asian Coastal Mega-Cities, the Case of Metro Manila". Japan International Cooperation Agency, 2010.

Nga T. T. V. "Water supply and its effect to public health in Ha Noi City". Master's thesis. Asian Institute of Technology, 1999.

US-EPA. "Risk Assessment Guidance for Superfund. V01.1. Human health evaluation manual (Part A)". EPA/540/1–89/002. US-EPA, Washington, D.C.

Zoleta-Nantes, D. "Differential Impacts of Flood Hazards among the Street children, the Urban Poor and Residents of Wealthy Neighborhood in Metro Manila, Philippines". *Journal of Mitigation and Adaptation Strategies for Global Change* 7, no. 3 (2002): 239–66.

19

SLUM POVERTY IN THE PHILIPPINES
Can the Environment Agenda Drive Public Action?

Marife Ballesteros

In 2010, the projected population of the Philippines was 94 million. Of this population, 18.8 per cent (5 million) live in slums. Of the slum population, 80 per cent (4 million) live in cities. Between 2000 and 2006, the urban slum population grew at an annual rate of 3.4 per cent overall, but 8 per cent in Metro Manila (Table 19.1). Metro Manila, which accounts for 37 per cent of the Philippines' GDP and 13 per cent of its employment, is home to about 2 million slum dwellers. That makes up 16 per cent of the city's population of 11.5 million (2010). Metro Manila is a rapidly growing megacity. It ranks fourteenth among the twenty megacities of the world. Its population is projected to reach almost 15 million by 2025 (UNCHS 2010).

The incidence of poverty in the cities is 19 per cent. This is much lower than rural poverty of over 50 per cent (the national average is 32 per cent). Still, shelter deprivation is high in urban areas. It is in cities that disparities in living standards and access to basic services and infrastructure are most evident. We observe rich, well-serviced neighbourhoods and dense slum settlements existing in proximity to each other.

Households in slums are not necessarily income poor. About 32 per cent of the urban slum population in Manila (or about 1.3 million people as of 2010) — high compared to the overall poverty incidence — is poor based on national poverty lines of 20,688 pesos per capita (about US$2 in PPP 2010) (Table 19.2).[2] More than 50 per cent live above the poverty line and can spend between US$2 and US$4 per day, but reside in poor environments. The slum-dwellers who live above the poverty line usually make minimum salaries or wages and work casually. They continue living in the slums because there is no alternative shelter in the city and "they cannot afford the cost of travelling from distant, less expensive, peri-urban regions for work and income earning opportunities in urban centers".[3]

TABLE 19.1
Slum Population, Urban Philippines

	Slum Population 2006	% Slum	Slum Annual Growth Rate (%) (2000–2006)	Projected Slum Population		
				2010	2020	2050
Urban Philippines	2,936,011	7.10	3.40	3,819,766	6,572,683	12,967,806
Large Towns/ Cities	978,422	5.57	3.49	1,122,335	1,736,317	10,108,036
Metro Manila	1,351,960	12.17	8.55	1,877,003	4,689,943	6,668,187
Metro Manila[1]	4,035,283	36.33	3.14	4,565,951	6,294,181	8,949,102

Notes: (1) NSO defines slums as households in illegal settlements (i.e. without consent of owner in the occupation of lot/house). (2) Large town and cities refer to administrative towns/cities with population as of 2007 above 100,000 to 2,000,000. (3) Slum Population Growth Rate estimated using exponential growth; $r = \ln(Pt/Po)/t$; for large towns/cities, period covers 2003–06. (4) Slum Population projected based on estimated slum population growth rate. (5) Estimate on Metro Manila using data from the Metro Manila Urban Services for the Poor Project (MMUSPP). The MMUSPP is a Project of the Housing and Urban Development Council and the ADB. A survey of informal settlers in Metro Manila was conducted in 2002 using broader definition of slums which include not only the illegal settlements but also the "homeless and marginalized."

Source: National Statistics Office (NSO), Family Income and Expenditure Survey, 2000 and 2006.

TABLE 19.2
Slum Poverty Incidence, Philippines, 2006

	National Poverty Line		Subsistence Poor (below US$1.25 PPP)		Between US$2.00 and US$4.00 PPP	
	% to Population	Number of Poor	% to Population	Number of Poor	% to Population	Number of Poor
Urban Philippines	32.48	953,728	11.88	348,872	41.66	1,223,124
Large Towns/Cities	35.25	344,860	13.83	135,313	37.66	368,436
Metro Manila	20.66	279,361	3.26	44,127	49.00	662,472

Source: National Statistics Office, Family Income and Expenditure Survey, 2006.

At the same time, not all the poor live in slums. Some are scattered around the city in areas with similar physical environments as the slums — a deficit of infrastructure and an insecurity of tenure. This chapter is mainly based on interviews in four slum areas in Metro Manila, and enriched with some secondary statistics. It provides new insights on how the slum-dwellers of Manila are affected by climate change. It argues that flooding, heat waves, and congestion worsen income poverty, and mainly the living quality of the poor and vulnerable population, i.e. the lower 30–40 per cent of the population pyramid.

THE ENVIRONMENT OF THE SLUMS

The slums are the least safe and least healthy part of the city. They are characterized by poor sanitation, overcrowded and crude habitation, inadequate water supply, hazardous location, and insecurity of tenure. Although slums have similar physical attributes, the degree of environmental problems may differ. Slums may be clustered on the basis of the major risks in the environment. In Metro Manila, we find four main types of slums. Those situated along a river and on the coastal areas are frequently afflicted by typhoons and sea surges along a coast or seashore. These are afflicted by seasonal rains, sea surges, and erosion around a dumpsite. Other slums are communities developed by an infill or open dumpsite, with most households surviving

FIGURE 19.1
Slum Communities in Metro Manila

Notes: (a) Dumpsite poverty at Pier 18, Manila; (b) Floodway poverty at Pasig-Cainta Floodway; (c) Coastal slums at Baseco, Manila; (d) Poverty seen along roads and highway at the National Government Center, Quezon City.
Source: Author's photos.

TABLE 19.3
Environmental Problems Affecting Metro Manila Slums

Types of City Slums	Major Environmental Problem			
	Congestion	Flooding/Mud	Poor Sanitation	Pollution
Dumpsite	✓	✓	✓	✓
Along Rivers/Creeks	✓	✓		✓
Coastal Slums	✓	✓	✓	
Along main roads/highways	✓			✓

Source: Focus Group Discussions by author in slum communities. The selected communities represent the different environments of slum in Metro Manila.

by scavenging; and along heavily travelled roads, or by road corners and intersections. Figure 19.1 shows samples of these types of slum communities in Metro Manila. Congestion is a common problem for all types, while flooding and muddy roads affects slums in low-lying areas (Table 19.3).

MAIN WAYS SLUM ENVIRONMENT CAUSES POVERTY

On a daily basis, slum dwellers are confronted with congestion, substandard housing, and a physically deteriorated environment that lacks public services (roads, drainage system, garbage disposal, electricity, water) altogether or has them only in a poorly maintained state. Some slums have been formed in hazardous places — fault lines, unstable slopes, rivers banks, etc. These locations are vulnerable to natural disasters and climate change. These environmental conditions lead to deepening poverty and rising inequalities through the following channels.

Higher Expenditure on Basic Services

The deficit infrastructure has slum dwellers paying more for basic services, such as clean water and electricity, than residents living in adjacent fully serviced neighbourhood. In Metro Manila and Cebu City, residents of neighbourhoods not served by the city's water system pay more for water than households in serviced communities. On the average, non-serviced households relying on vended water pay twice as much for clean water than households in serviced areas (Table 19.4).

Higher Health Risk from Urban Environment and Climate Change

Slum dwellers are confronted daily with environmental problems that threaten their health. Urbanization and economic growth have given rise to air pollution, water pollution, flooding, and congestion. Most people in the cities experience these problems, but the slums are the most affected because of their location and limited infrastructure. They also have limited ways to protect themselves from changes in the climate. For instance, in coastal areas and along rivers, modifications inside the house are limited to the use of wooden planks to create an

TABLE 19.4
**Average Cost of Water and Per Cent of Household Income Spent on Water, by
Source of Water, Metro Manila and Metro Cebu, 1995**

	Metro Manila		Metro Cebu	
Water Source	Average cost (P/cum)	% of water bill to monthly income	Average cost (P/cum)	% of water bill to monthly income
City water system	5.5	2.0	12.0	3.6
Private waterworks	7.9	1.9	12.6	2.0
Self supplied (Deepwell)	n.a.	n.a	56.5	4.1
Public faucets	22–44	n.a	14.1	1.0
Water vendors				
City water system				
Pick-up	30.4	4.2	76.3	7.3
Hose (container)	48.3	6.2	59.8	4.4
Hose (fixed charge)	21.8	2.7	53.2	5.6
Delivered	71.9	11.9	106.4	6.3
Ground water				
Pick-up	40.2	5.7	76.3	4.8
Hose (container)	44.0	4.8	n.a	n.a
Hose (fixed charge)	58.9	3.8	n.a	n.a
Delivered	62.3	4.3	132.9	3.8

Notes: (1) n.a. = not available; (2) The results are based on the 1995 survey of 500 households in Metro Manila and 500 households in Metro Cebu
Source: Table recast from David et al. (2000).

elevated, dry space for the children and household equipment when flood water rise above street level. During hot days, most people simply sleep outside the house to cool themselves.

The health effects of poor housing have been established in several epidemiological studies. They show that poor housing fosters disease. Overcrowding increases respiratory illness. Contaminated water supply and unsanitary human and household waste disposal causes gastro-intestinal problems, skin ailments, cholera, typhoid, and other infectious diseases. Long-term exposure to traffic-related air pollution causes problems in the cardiovascular and respiratory systems. Living near dumpsites exposes the poor to harmful bacteria and other parasites, as well as furans and dioxins, which bring a lot of diseases (including cancer).

Econometric analysis has found a strong relationship between the health status of household and the home environment (Solon 1989). Houses with human and animal waste and stagnant water present have a low health scorecard. As much as 40 per cent of children's health is explained by housing. Improvements to the house (e.g., roofing, interior space) and to neighbourhood services, such as sewerage and solid waste disposal, improve health, especially for children.

Climate change is expected to increase illness in slums through increasingly severe and frequent natural hazards. Flooding, which is primarily caused by heavy typhoon rains, is the main effect of climate change in the Philippine urban areas. (World Bank 2010). Much slum areas are coastal and low-lying, where floods are the most common and highest. A health-assessment study of Metro Manila estimated the level of risk associated with direct and indirect exposure to polluted floodwaters.[4] The study specifically measured the probabilities of gastroenteritis caused by E. coli in polluted waters for different inundation levels (from less than 50 cm to greater than 200 cm). Those aged 4 to 15 years are the most affected by accidental ingestion of polluted water through bathing, laundry, and swimming. They tend to ingest twice as much as the adults. On average, the risk of infection of the population is 0.0134 per cent for inundation depth of less than 50 cm (street level flooding) and 0.19 per cent for floods above 200 cm (first floor of the house is flooded). The health risks could be higher considering that polluted waters also carry vectors other than E. coli.

Focus group discussions I conducted in the four slum areas in Metro Manila revealed that the health of the residents suffers as a result of their environment. For instance, respiratory ailments, such as tuberculosis, bronchitis, and asthma, are common complaints of people living in dumpsite and roadside slums. Mental stress and sleepless nights affect the residents, especially children and the elderly. Diarrhoea and skin ailments are common to all slum communities, especially those residing near rivers. Table 19.5 shows that the top four morbidity cases in public health units that serve floodway slums are acute respiratory disease, skin disease, diarrhoea, and parasitism. The rate of cases per 100,000 people in floodway area (Rural Health Unit, or RHU1) in the past five

TABLE 19.5
Top Morbidity and Mortality Diseases, Municipality of Cainta (Rate per 100,000 Population)

	Cainta		RHU I		
	Ave. Past 5 Years (2004–2008)	2009	Ave. Past 5 Years (2004–2008)	2009	% to Total Cases in Cainta
Top 5 reasons of Morbidity					
Acute Respiratory Infection	5,649.35	9,913	6,726	9,606.85	27.72
Skin Diseases	249.74	1,097	206.58	1,074.55	28.01
Acute Watery Diarrhea	273.47	409	127.45	326.98	22.87
Parasitism	160.60	342	264.80	300.05	25.11
Hyper-Vascular Disease	133.43	394	151.85	210.09	14.88
Top 3 reasons of Mortality					
Coronary Artery Disease	44.54	67.84	–	75.65	31.89
Pneumonia	16.69	49.5	–	44.87	25.19
Cancer	17.78	27.14	–	24.36	25.68

	2008		2009	
Child Morbidity (below 5 years)	% to Child Population	% to Total Cases, Cainta	% to Child Population	% to Total Cases, Cainta
Diarrhea	1.10	31.32	1.57	20.90
Pneumonia	0.40	–	0.32	–

Note: RHU — Rural Health Unit is a facility level for primary healthcare managed by municipal government; RHU 1is the health unit that services communities within the vicinity of the Floodway.
Source: Cainta Municipal Planning and Development Coordination Office (2009).

years (2004 to 2008) is higher than the average for the municipality. In 2009, the main cause of child morbidity in the municipality was diarrhoea, with 20 per cent to 30 per cent of cases being from residents of *barangays* (districts) along the floodway or canals.

Of the five most common morbidity cases in the slums of Manila, four are respiratory ailments, such as bronchitis, pneumonia, and tuberculosis (Table 19.6). Diarrhoea is also among the top five causes of morbidity. The rate of occurrence in the slum areas (Districts 1 and 2) is higher than the average for the city as a whole. For instance, of the total cases of bronchitis in Manila city (a city in Metro Manila) about 50 per cent are residents of the slum areas.

TABLE 19.6
Top Morbidity and Mortality Diseases, in the City of Manila
(Rate per 100,000 population)

	Manila		District 1[a]				District 5[b]			
	2008	2009	2008		2009		2008		2009	
	Rate	% to Total Cases in Manila	Rate	% to Total Cases in Manila	Rate	% to Total Cases in Manila	Rate	% to Total Cases in Manila	Rate	% to Total Cases in Manila
Top reasons of Morbity6										
Acute Respiratory Infection	–	67.18	–	–	62.02	23.00	–	–	73.33	18.78
Bronchitis	27.48	8.74	39.60	38.43	17.22	49.10	12.83	4.81	3.04	5.98
Pneumonia	26.77	5.90	19.34	19.26	4.56	19.25	24.27	9.34	7.30	21.29
Diarrhea	18.60	7.06	–	–	6.89	24.29	–	–	7.91	19.25
B Respiratory	11.74	3.80	12.29	27.93	3.73	24.49	21.71	19.06	4.19	18.99
Dengue	3.84	0.95	3.96	27.46	0.87	22.83	3.70	9.92	0.55	9.93
Top 3 reasons of Mortality										
Pneumonia	21.31	18.90	25.37	28.80	20.97	27.43	24.06	15.57	19.31	15.25
Heart Disease	19.79	24.50	19.59	23.95	25.81	26.04	21.70	15.12	27.76	16.90
Cancer	10.97	11.37	11.12	24.51	16.44	35.75	13.36	16.80	11.38	14.93

Notes: (a) *Barangay* 105 (Pier 18) belong to district 1 of Manila, (b) *Barangay* 649 (Baseco) belong to district 5 of Manila; (c) no data
Source: Manila Health Department (2009).

Damage to Social Fabric and Mental Well-Being

Bad environments weaken family relations and lower mental well-being. Slums have high rates of theft, robbery, drugs, and child molestation. Many slum residents have difficulty sleeping because of noise and heat. Street flooding or muddy streets are brought about even by normal rains. These factors result in frequent absenteeism at school and work. Furthermore, women tend to marry early (e.g., at sixteen). Some young women related that mental stress due to the difficult environment suppresses their desire for schooling or professional development. Population growth of *barangays* with large slums is significantly higher than of the larger districts or cities the *barangays* are a part of (Table 19.7). This is possibly due to natural increase, not in-migration, for reasons cited above and also mentioned by *barangay* (or village) officials.

Damage to Lives and Property of Slum Poor

The adverse effects of climate change on the lives and property of slum dwellers has been demonstrated by the recent flooding caused

TABLE 19.7
Comparative Population Growth Rate Cities/Districts vs. Slum Barangays

City/District/Barangay	% Annual Growth Rate
Metro Manila (1990–2007)	2.21
Manila City (1990–2007)	0.21
Tondo, Manila	0.76
Brgy. 105 (Dumpsite Slums)	5.57
Port Area, Manila	10.06
Brgy. 649 (*CoastalSlums*)	10.77
Quezon City (1990–2007)	2.78
Brgy. Holy Spirit (Slums *Along Main Roads/Highways*)	4.58
Cainta (1995–2007)	3.44
Brgy. San Andres (Slums along the foodway)	6.47

Note: Slum growth rate estimated based on exponential growth.
Source: Socio-Economic Profiles of the Sites; LGU and Barangay Census.

by Typhoon Ondoy which hit the country in September 2009. Typhoon Ondoy, the equivalent of a Category I storm, was an extremely rare occurrence in the country. The storm brought an unusually high volume of rain, approximately 450 mm daily based on records of the Manila Observatory. The intense rain exceeded the Marikina River's (eastern part of Metro Manila) carrying capacity, resulting in high flooding. Typhoon Ondoy caused extensive flooding in the metropolitan area and in neighbouring Rizal province. In particular, inundation level above 200 cm was experienced by slums along the Pasig River and the Laguna Lake shore. The flood receded only after two months. Many households were displaced and moved to evacuation centres or to relatives and friends. People died from drowning and flood-related illnesses such as leptospirosis. Houses were washed away or damaged, and some households have not been able to rebuild their homes a year after the typhoon. An estimated 15,000 families, mostly from slums by the Pasig River and the Laguna Lake, have been relocated (GOP, ADB, UN and the WB 2010). From the point of view of the economy, the disaster mainly affected the productive and social sectors,[5] with damages and losses valued at about 150 million pesos. For housing alone, it is estimated that recovery and reconstruction support will amount to 75 million pesos.

CONCLUSIONS

A bad living environment deprives people of a good quality of life. It also makes it harder — especially for women — to have a good income and gainful employment. A bad environment lowers physical and mental health, which lowers productivity and school performance and increases vulnerability to crime and climate-induced risks. The slum environment requires people with low income to pay more for basic services. It also requires them to pay for services to defend themselves from the likely effects of climate change in their living environment.

Unfortunately, these problems do not motivate the government to act since the government does not look at shelter deprivation as part of urban poverty caused by the environment. Shelter deprivation is mainly perceived as income poverty. Thus, government programmes on shelter are mostly directed to improving affordability of individual households. Less attention is given to settlement planning and infrastructure development. The threat to settlements brought about by climate change are mainly translated into activities and strategies for disaster response rather than effective prevention.

Slum poverty cannot be simply addressed by traditional poverty programmes such as cash transfers. It has been argued that there are trade-offs between bad housing and medical care, and between bad housing and education. Moreover, slums are not merely the natural and temporary consequence of urban growth, one that will disappear in time with improvements in income. Slum formation and growth is not the simple result of rapid urbanization or income poverty, but also of a weak regulatory environment for urban planning, land development, and land markets. Insufficient government spending on infrastructure is also a major factor in slum formation (Arimah 2010).

The solution to slum poverty thus involves giving adequate attention to town planning to ensure appropriate land use planning and proper implementation of building codes and environmental laws. The provision of space for housing low-income families and the expansion of urban infrastructure to underserved, informal settlements should be an integral component of town planning. Unlike in rural areas and smaller towns, where space allows more opportunities for the poor to change their environment, in metropolitan cities and slums individual households' adaptation to climate change induced flooding and heat waves, and to congestion cannot substitute proper town planning. Here, adaptation requires government investment and regulatory actions, which is only effective through a strong presence of the national government, specifically for concerns that cut across boundaries of lower administrative or political units.

Notes

1. The proportions are low estimates of slum population in the country since the national survey captures only illegal settlements. The Family income and Expenditure Survey (FIES) conducted every three years defines informal settlements as those occupying land without consent from owners. This does not include other forms of marginalized housing such as homelessness and households living in danger areas, lands intended for infrastructure projects or public lands not intended for settlement. In 2005, the Urban

   Asset Reform Office of HUDCC using the broader definition of informal families recorded in Metro Manila alone some 726,908 informal households or about 3.6 million population.

2. The methodology for estimating poverty threshold was revised in 2011. The revised method is based on a "new" basket of goods, which effectively lowered the threshold. Using the revised method, the 2009 poverty threshold for Metro Manila is 19,802 pesos per capita and for Philippines is 16,841 pesos per capita.

3. Based on MMUSP study (2008)

4. JICA (2010). Intangible Risks Analysis from Flooding. *A Study on the Social Impacts of Flood Events in Metro Manila.* Japan International Cooperation Agency. This study is also summarized in Chapter 18 of this book.

5. The productive sector includes agriculture/fishery, industry, commerce, and tourism. The social sector includes housing, education, health, and transportation.

References

Arimah, Ben C. "The Face of Urban Poverty: Explaining the Prevalence of Slums in Developing Countries". *UNU-WIDER Working Paper* 2010/30. United Nations University, World Institute for Development Economics Research, 2010.

Ballesteros, M. "Linking Poverty and the Environment: Evidence from Slums in Philippine Cities". *PIDS Discussion Paper Series* 2010–33. Philippine Institute for Development Studies, Manila, 2010.

Cainta Municipal Planning and Development Coordination Office. "Annual Accomplishment Report". Municipality of Cainta, Rizal, 2009.

David et. al. "Urban Water Pricing: The Metro Manila and Metro Cebu Cases". PIDS Policy Notes 2000–09. Philippine Institute for Development Studies, Manila, 2000.

Government of the Philippines (GOP), United Nations, Asian Development Bank and the World Bank. "Typhoons Ondoy and Pepeng: Post Disaster Needs Assessment: Main and Sector Reports". The World Bank, Manila, 2010.

HUDCC and Local Government Units. Metro Manila Road Map for Urban Renewal and Basic Services for the Poor Metro Manila Urban Services for the Poor Projects". Asian Development Bank, Manila, 2008.

JICA. "Intangible Risks Analysis from Flooding: A Study on the Social Impacts of Flood Events in Metro Manila". Japan International Cooperation Agency, 2010.

Manila Health Department. "Notifiable Diseases Report. Annual Report". Manila City Hall, 2009.

Solon, Orville. "The Health Impact of Urban Poor Housing and Environmental Conditions". Philippine Institute for Development Studies Working Paper Series 89–14, 1989.

UNCHS (HABITAT). *The State of the WORLD's Cities 2008–2009: Harmonious Cities*. Kenya: United Nations Centre for Human Settlements, 2010.

World Bank. "Climate Risks and Adaptation in Asian Coastal Megacities: A Synthesis Report". Washington, D.C.: The World Bank, 2010.